Hope for Democracy

Hope for Democracy

How Citizens Can Bring Reason Back into Politics

JOHN GASTIL AND KATHERINE R. KNOBLOCH

OXFORD
UNIVERSITY PRESS

OXFORD
UNIVERSITY PRESS

Oxford University Press is a department of the University of Oxford. It furthers
the University's objective of excellence in research, scholarship, and education
by publishing worldwide. Oxford is a registered trade mark of Oxford University
Press in the UK and certain other countries.

Published in the United States of America by Oxford University Press
198 Madison Avenue, New York, NY 10016, United States of America.

© John Gastil and Katherine R. Knobloch 2020

Library of Congress Cataloging-in-Publication Data
Names: Gastil, John, author. | Knobloch, Katherine R., author.
Title: Hope for democracy : how citizens can bring reason back into politics /
John Gastil and Katherine R. Knobloch.
Description: New York : Oxford University Press, 2020. |
Includes bibliographical references and index. | Identifiers: LCCN 2019039697 (print) |
LCCN 2019039698 (ebook) | ISBN 9780190084523 (hardback) | ISBN 9780190084530 (paperback) |
ISBN 9780190084554 (epub) | ISBN 9780190084561 (online) | ISBN 9780190084547 (updf)
Subjects: LCSH: Deliberative democracy. | Deliberative democracy—United
States—States. | Political planning—Citizen participation. | Political
planning—United States—States—Citizenparticipation. | Referendum. |
Referendum—United States—States. | Political participation. |
Political participatin—United States—States. | Democracy—Social aspects.
Classification: LCC JC423 .G3547 2020 (print) | LCC JC423 (ebook) | DDC 328.2—dc23
LC record available at https://lccn.loc.gov/2019039697
LC ebook record available at https://lccn.loc.gov/2019039698

1 3 5 7 9 8 6 4 2

Paperback printed by Marquis, Canada
Hardback printed by Bridgeport National Bindery, Inc., United States of America

To Cindy, Aaron,
Colette, and Gibson,
hopeful skeptics all.

CONTENTS

Introduction

Seattle holds a special place in the public's imagination. Without irony, it carries the *Wizard of Oz* nickname "Emerald City." Its skyline includes the iconic Space Needle. Beside it now lies a psychedelic smashed-guitar edifice housing entrepreneur Paul Allen's music and sci-fi collection. Across town, a glass-and-steel city library designed by Rem Koolhaas shimmers aquamarine when sunlight pokes through the clouds.

Unlike its quirky southern neighbor celebrated in *Portlandia*, Seattle takes itself seriously as an economic engine. Beyond forward-looking recycling initiatives and artisan foods, the greater Seattle metropolitan area boasts Starbucks, the Port of Seattle, a dot-com hub anchored on Microsoft and Amazon.com, and a sprawling biotech hub.

As the twentieth century neared its close, Seattle struggled to manage its population growth. Among its chief problems was a transportation infrastructure over-reliant on Interstate 5. Even with seven miles of reversible express lanes, Seattle's portion of that key arterial ranks among the nation's most clogged freeways. The hodge-podge of streets, highways, and bridges running east and west through the city give Seattle workers some of the worst commutes outside Los Angeles or New York City. These difficulties upgraded to a crisis when Boeing in 2001 cited congestion as a primary reason for moving corporate headquarters to Chicago.

Enter the Seattle Monorail Project. The city already owned a monorail that had been gliding from the Space Needle to the heart of downtown since the 1962 World's Fair. That one-stop route paid for itself in its first year, and it remains a cost-effective system for moving over two million passengers annually. As the traveling salesman voiced by Phil Hartman sang in a 1993 episode of *The Simpsons*, "Well, sir, there's nothin' on Earth like a genuine bona-fide electrified six-car monorail!"

Seattle's residents had the opportunity to support monorail expansion in one election after another because their city is one of the many places in the United States where citizens vote directly on legislation. A 1997 measure directed the

Hope for Democracy. John Gastil and Katherine R. Knobloch, Oxford University Press (2020).
© John Gastil and Katherine R. Knobloch
DOI: 10.1093/acprof:oso/9780190084523.001.0001

city to seek private funding for a new rail system, but after its passage, no money materialized. Three years later, voters empowered the city to spend six million dollars to design both the rail system and a public financing plan. Intensive study yielded a proposal to be funded by an automobile sales tax.

A spirited campaign for the proposal asked voters to imagine an above-ground train that would "rise above it all." Building the monorail network would distinguish Seattle from its urban peers by solving traffic problems with the same space-age transportation system promised to generations of children in Disney's Tomorrowland. In reply, critics launched a spirited opposition campaign that questioned cost estimates, rail routes, and the efficacy of the sales tax.

When Seattle residents went to the polls on November 5, 2002, few knew the nuances of the city's transportation problems nor the intricacies of the proposed solution. Like millions of voters before them and millions since, the people of Seattle assessed Citizen Proposition 1 based on their partisan allegiances, gut instincts, abstract hopes and fears, and bits of information gleaned from paid campaign advertisements and media coverage. The net result was a virtual tie: 94,993 ballots came back marked "Yes;" another 94,116 said, "No."

By less than half a percent, Seattle authorized a monorail.

Two years and $125 million later, the same electorate cut its losses. By a two-to-one margin, Seattle voters made their regret official. The vehicle sales tax had been a bust, with buyers stepping outside the city limits to purchase new cars.

Poster produced for the Rise Above It All/Monorail Yes campaign. *Source*: Ian Webste, Monorail Yes campaign.

Meanwhile, cost estimates soared. By the time the Seattle Monorail Project shut its doors, it hadn't built an inch of track.

Hindsight welcomes laughter at Seattle's folly, but mistakes like these happen regularly in democracies around the world. On June 23, 2016, for example, 52 percent of voters in the United Kingdom opted to leave the European Union, a decision known as Brexit. A *Daily Mail* poll commissioned after the referendum, however, showed that more than a million people who voted to exit the union wished they could take it back. That amounts to 7 percent of the UK electorate. "Even though I voted to leave," said one regretful citizen, "this morning I woke up and the reality hit me. . . . If I had the opportunity to vote again, it would be to stay." Since then, politicians have failed to devise a suitable plan for leaving the European Union. When a Brexit deal finally came before the House of Commons in January 2019, it failed by the largest margin in modern British history.

Poor political judgments can come not only from the public at large but also from elected officials. To take one infamous example, the United States rewrote its constitution in 1919 to outlaw the manufacture, transportation, and sale of alcohol. Prohibition had a negligible effect on sobriety, but it cost the federal and state governments billions in lost tax revenue on top of hundreds of millions on a failed enforcement campaign. With the loss of liquor sales, many restaurants collapsed, while organized crime and police corruption reached new heights. Fourteen years later, the Twenty-First Amendment ended the fiasco.

To avoid such policymaking mistakes, legislatures rely on committee deliberation, research bureaus, and complex parliamentary processes that force bills down an arduous path before passage. When bad legislation emerges from such bodies, the blame more often traces back to nefarious or partisan purposes, rather than ignorance.

The people of Seattle, by contrast, simply erred in their judgment. They did not willfully waste more than a hundred million dollars to mollify a special interest, advance a political cause, or prove some abstract principle. They established the Seattle Monorail Project to make their city a better place to live. If something—or someone—had convinced a few hundred more voters the project would fail, the electorate would have rejected it.

Seattle voters in 2002 and UK voters in 2016 needed the same things: direct access to better information, the ability to recognize its quality, and a willingness to use it when deciding how to vote. Given what we know about the spread of misinformation, the prevalence of biased reasoning, and the superficial ways people make voting choices, one might fear that democracy will continue to churn out bad judgments.

This book tells a more hopeful story. An electoral process now exists that could have spared Seattle voters their monorail miscalculation. Travel four hours south on the same clogged interstate that runs through Seattle and you'll arrive at the state capitol building in Salem, Oregon. There, the state legislature established the Citizens' Initiative Review (CIR) in 2009. The first of its kind in the world, the CIR empowers a small body of randomly selected citizens to examine ballot measures and write a succinct one-page analysis that appears in the official *Voters' Pamphlet.*

Few outside Oregon have heard of this novel political institution, yet it has begun spreading to other states, counties, and cities. This new process offers citizens a more effective means of thinking through proposed legislation. In a word, the CIR helps voters *deliberate.*

The idea of deliberative election reform percolated in Seattle's coffee shops years before the monorail debacle. While an assistant professor at the University of Washington in 1999, the first author of this book wrote *By Popular Demand,* which advocated using citizen panels to better inform the judgment of the mass electorate. This conception of citizen panels came from work by previous scholars, such as Yale democratic theorist Robert Dahl. "One of the imperative needs of democratic countries," Dahl wrote in 1998, "is to improve citizens' capacities to engage intelligently in political life. . . . Older institutions will need to be enhanced by new means for civic education, political participation, information, and deliberation."

At the time, most political scientists questioned the logic of convening a body of ignorant citizens for any purpose, let alone for enlightening their peers. A critical review of the idea in the *American Political Science Review* foresaw no scenario in which such a scheme could come into existence. Even so, that reviewer added, "One cannot help wondering what deliberative elections can accomplish."

Sometimes, curiosity is enough. Most of the modern institutions we take for granted began as radical notions that initially won more skeptics than adherents. The ancient Athenian assembly offered a novel approach to governance, which involved choosing thousands of male citizens by lot to form its legislature. In spite of obvious hazards, that untested idea became a reality in the fourth century BCE. More than a millennium later, the English jury emerged as a substitute for the wisdom of priests and judges, who resisted its encroachment on their authority. Most recently, staunch opposition has met each campaign to enfranchise an ever-wider swath of the public, yet minorities, women, and eighteen-year-olds all have won the right to vote.

Each of these ideas took time to develop into the refined institutions now commonplace in modern democracies. The legislative assembly required millennia to become a permanent fixture. The jury needed centuries to establish itself. Struggles for voter rights in the United States took up most of the twentieth century and continue to this day.

By contrast, deliberative reforms like those in Oregon are developing more rapidly—some over the course of a few years. In that time frame, it's possible to follow the footprints of those people whose small actions brought about lasting change.

Four individuals stand at the center of the CIR story, and you will meet each of them in this book. The same year that Seattle launched its monorail project, idealistic graduate student Tyrone Reitman started his studies at the University of Oregon to earn a master's degree in public policy. Tyrone soon met up with Ned Crosby, a veteran civic reformer who had been spreading the gospel of citizen deliberation for decades. In Tyrone, Ned found a capable champion.

When Oregon made the CIR a reality, Marion Sharp and Ann Bakkensen belonged to the first group of twenty-four registered voters who would test its efficacy. Unsure what to expect, Marion and Ann saw first hand what Tyrone and Ned had wrought, and the experience changed their lives.

The advocates who testified before the CIR also helped to shape its course. These include Justin Martin, a Native American policy advocate who faced off against corporate lobbyists in 2012 to prevent the establishment of non-tribal casinos. You will also hear from progressive lobbyists who sought to derail the CIR convened to discuss their proposed tax reform during that same election.

Even more diverse voices enter this story because the CIR has been part of a larger wave of deliberative democratic reform. In the late 1980s, for example, Brazilians invented Participatory Budgeting, which gives local residents direct control over portions of the government's budget. In fewer than thirty years, this innovation spread to over one thousand five hundred jurisdictions and institutions across the globe.

Ideas like this travel more rapidly than ever when civic reformers and enlightened public officials team up to give citizens well-structured responsibilities for self-governance. As a result of these innovations, everyday people have crafted, critiqued, or reviewed budgets and laws through a variety of processes. Each of these new institutions challenges citizens to reflect on their core values and passions while weighing credible evidence and reasoned arguments.

If one doubts the need for bringing deliberation back into politics, consider the present context in the United States. The 2016 presidential election nearly disproved the belief that facts matter. President Donald Trump's Republican rivals, and then rival candidate Senator Hillary Clinton, all pointed to their opponent's relentless repetition of false claims about policy matters both foreign and domestic.

Facts were never the lifeblood of US politics, but a proper cynic insists that no problem is so grim that it can't get worse. *PolitiFact* believed they could debunk misinformation, one piece at a time. Even that modest presumption now sounds quaint. Years earlier, Stephen Colbert coined the term "truthiness" to put out the political fire with bucket loads of satire. A decade after Colbert's brutal roast of President George W. Bush, the White House Correspondents' Association Dinner couldn't even draw its guest of honor.

Nonstop protest provides the most visible alternative response to the erosion of fact-based policymaking. In 2017, the scientific community joined the parade of coordinated global protest marches. A Neil deGrasse Tyson quip made for one of the most popular posters: "Science is true whether or not you believe in it." Fair enough, but truth has no vote.

Adversarial mobilization and dissent play crucial roles in democracy, but other approaches speak to the plurality of Americans who no longer identify with a political party. Even partisans can grow weary of the endless campaigning that devalues the very idea of serious discussion of policy alternatives that cross ideological divides.

This is the point where the CIR, and other reforms like it, could change the way we govern ourselves in the twenty-first century. The chapters that follow explain why this is happening, how citizen deliberation works, and what role you can play in transforming your own political community.

A Political Life Transformed

Marion Sharp arrived at the Grand Phoenix Hotel in Salem, Oregon, a skeptic. The accommodations were nice enough. Cool air in the lobby brought respite from the muggy August heat of Portland. The front desk offered warm chocolate chip cookies to guests. Whatever else lay ahead, at least she'd be comfortable.

As she checked in, Marion contemplated her task. She would participate in the first iteration of a new governing structure designed to strengthen the public's grasp on statewide ballot issues. The Citizens' Initaitive Review promised to give voice to Oregon voters and improve the quality of public discussion. Good concept, but she had her doubts.

Up to that point, Marion had lived a rather conventional political life. She paid attention to the news, but she'd never written a letter to the editor. Nor had she ever stepped inside Oregon's state capital and looked up to see the thirty-three stars in the rotunda dome that marked its point of entry into the United States. Marion cared about politics enough to sit down with her *Voters' Pamphlet* at election time. But when colleagues brought up controversial topics, Marion would retreat. A petite woman with burgundy hair and an open smile, she had no interest in fighting over politics, or reading past the "urgent" headlines her friends posted on social media.

Outside the political realm, however, Marion found ways to get involved in her community. Before moving to Oregon, she worked as a social worker and therapist in Florida. There, she had hoped to find long-term solutions for teens stuck in foster programs—some who'd survived horrific experiences. That job convinced Marion that many of these private tragedies could have been prevented with public action to reverse policy decisions made before her clients were born.

After moving to Portland, Marion hoped to have a more direct social impact through her job as a university administrator. She ran a series of talks on how to create more sustainable communities, and she developed certificate programs that helped people envision socially responsible careers. Marion felt good about

Hope for Democracy. John Gastil and Katherine R. Knobloch, Oxford University Press (2020).
© John Gastil and Katherine R. Knobloch
DOI: 10.1093/acprof:oso/9780190084523.001.0001

her work, but she knew that this piecemeal approach wasn't enough. Something needed to change.

Seeking a Different Kind of Politics

In interviews, Marion expressed a sentiment familiar to many citizens in modern democracies. She said that she cared deeply about the challenges facing her community but felt shut out of politics. How could her small voice compete with large campaign organizations and wealthy donors? It saddened her to reflect on the lack of serious discussion both in the media and among her own friends.

Marion's experience fits a larger trend. Voters in the United States report decreasing levels of trust in government, politicians, and the media. Political campaigns and lobbying efforts rely ever more on monetary donations, transforming political participation into a financial endeavor. Even those organizations that aim—or claim—to represent the public often rely more on the policy advice of political professionals than the people they purport to represent.

Like so many others, Marion was looking for an alternative to politics as usual. A few months prior to arriving in Salem, she thought she might have found just that. Hoping to reenergize her political life, she attended an America*Speaks* forum. Part of a national process focusing on "Our Budget, Our Economy," organizers billed the event as a "national discussion to find common ground on tough choices about our federal budget."

At the time, the US government faced a debt of $13 trillion and unemployment hovered just under 10 percent, as the country struggled to pull itself out of the Great Recession. Meanwhile, many European nations imposed austerity measures and slashed social programs, with Greece even veering toward bankruptcy.

People from across the country were taking part in America*Speaks* forums to consider alternative approaches to this omnipresent financial crisis. Portland was one of six major cities hosting a "National Town Meeting" all linked via satellite and the Internet. In thirty-eight other communities across the United States, volunteers led similar conversations, using the same agenda as the larger forums.

At the meeting, people who were normally left out of the conversation were going to be given an opportunity to participate. They would learn about the budget crisis and provide input to political leaders about what should be done to solve the problem. A column on the *Oregonian* website emphatically supported the project: "We have the chance to make a difference. By taking part in the discussion, we can send a message to Congress about the kind of nation and community we want to be."

Arriving at the America*Speaks* forum, Marion had high hopes. Here was a place where she could tackle a complex problem—maybe even make a difference. She had witnessed the effects of the recent recession, but with politicians bickering over policy objectives, solutions seemed scarce. Marion had faith that everyday citizens could make good decisions together, but too often citizens were left out of the discussion. America*Speaks* presented an alternative.

Before the event, forum organizers had sent Marion a workbook containing background information about the national debt and several policy proposals for reducing it by $1.2 trillion by 2025. The proposals had been developed by America*Speaks* in conjunction with fiscal experts from a wide range of political organizations and affiliations, such as the Brookings Institution, the Heritage Foundation, the American Enterprise Institute, and La Raza. Familiar proposals included raising the age for Social Security eligibility, moving to a single-payer healthcare system, or reducing the budget for military spending.

Even before the event, however, some activists were concerned that the forum focused on the deficit when many Americans were struggling to meet basic needs. A progressive think tank—the Center for Economic Policy Research (CEPR)—released a detailed guide to show what the workbook omitted. They argued that the booklet had a bias toward cutting vital social welfare programs: it claimed that increasing taxes on the wealthy could hurt the economy but failed to acknowledge that slashing social programs could have the same effect. The Oregon Center for Public Policy issued a statement publicizing the CEPR's findings, in the hope that liberal Oregonians would attend the event and speak in defense of social programs.

Whatever its drawbacks, Marion hoped this forum would be an opportunity to move past partisan bickering. She tried to remain optimistic upon arriving at the Oregon Convention Center on a Saturday morning in June 2010. From 8:30 a.m. to 3:00 p.m., Marion and her tablemates listened to speakers and talked about some solutions for reducing the federal debt. They voted on proposals that had been presented in the workbook and submitted their own ideas to a central "theme team" that organized ideas as they came in from across the country. Each table came up with their own bundle of solutions for the economy, all aiming to reduce the federal debt by at least a trillion dollars.

Marion enjoyed the conversations and learned from the presenters and her fellow participants, but after leaving the forum, she felt deflated. The event promised to lift the voices of everyday citizens, but the organizers were the ones with the real power. Marion didn't understand how decisions, such as how to frame key questions, were made behind the scenes. Even more discouraging, she worried

The signature feature of the America*Speaks* discussions process is using digital technology and "theme teams" to synthesize the insights from multiple small discussions happening simultaneously. *Source*: America*Speaks*.

that the work they'd done that day wouldn't matter. Engaging in a civil and fact-based conversation about the federal debt was refreshing, but would it make a difference?

The Future of Democracy, Abridged

In this case, disappointment counts as a civic virtue. Civics courses teach that democracy means *self-government*. Instead of dictators, enlightened or otherwise, democracy claims to rely on *the people* for its wisdom. Yet Marion's sense of powerlessness resonates with citizens the world over. Most people who live in countries called "democracies" tell any interviewer who cares to ask that they feel distant from the decisions that govern their daily lives.

Many respond to this reality with complacency, rather than anger or despair. In this view, the status quo represents the best we can hope to achieve. The general public will never care enough to really take the reins, and so long as competent elites keep the wagon moving, we'll be fine. In fact, their bickering is a sign of good health. It gives the rest of us a few choices on which we can opine, with some policy consequences but no real stakes.

Realists take an almost cynical comfort in accepting an imperfect system, but others have fallen into a disquieting apathy. You may have seen the battle cry of this clan on a bumper sticker: "Don't blame me, I didn't vote." It's a good joke, until you remember how history might have changed had the election gone differently.

The election of Donald Trump provides a stark illustration. A confluence of circumstances led to a person taking the White House with a minority of the ballots cast and a national approval rating below 50 percent. In this case, the most industrious members of the disengaged find other things to do with their time and try not to think of what might have been. Today, this begins with staying off Facebook. Synonyms include going "off the grid," returning "back to the land," or "dropping out" of political society.

To experience the kind of disappointment Marion feels after a bad public forum or a failed election, one must believe that things should *and could* have been better. For those who want a reason for such hope, good news is coming. Across the globe, political reformers have been busy inventing new approaches to democracy that give average citizens more meaningful roles in making decisions, joining policy debates, or giving direct advice to the electorate. The core idea of this new movement is "deliberative democracy."

By 2011, college students could learn about the US government in a textbook framed by this notion that "democracy works best when people embrace the duties of citizenship and when informed citizens and public officials deliberate to identify and promote the common good." The point was not to discard traditional institutions so much as reimagine and reform them. Even while reviewing much the same course content as their rivals, the authors of that textbook drew different conclusions because of their focus on one key concept—*deliberation*.

The deliberative approach to democracy has its academic origins in highly abstract conceptions of justice, reason, and the "public sphere"—that space we enter when we take political action together. Over the past two decades, these philosophical ideas have grown into eminently practical ones. Picture rich social networks and local communities working together to diagnose and address their most serious local—and interconnected—social, political, and environmental problems. Deliberative democracy has roles for a more vigilant media system, more serious-minded legislative bodies, and more frank public exchanges among competing interest groups and think tanks.

The deliberative democratic vision distinguishes itself further from other models of democracy by building up informal and formal institutions that draw community members together to reflect on their common concerns. The least demanding of these new public spaces simply provide opportunities for adult civic education. Since the early 1980s, National Issues Forums have spread across the country to offer discussion guides that ask participants to consider key facts before weighing a minimum of not two but *three* choices for tackling any given problem. And yes, citizens who participate in these forums—even for two quick hours—learn a great deal and tend to move from raw opinions to more considered judgments on important issues.

Forums such as these make stronger citizens, but they do not make policy— at least not directly. For a novel process that can meet that higher bar for citizen empowerment, consider Participatory Budgeting. This process began in Porto Alegre, Brazil, in 1989, when a political party sought a way to mobilize the city's poorest residents, both to support its candidate list and to play a more direct role in setting fiscal priorities. The simple idea is that if everyday citizens get a chance to face budget dilemmas, many will seize that opportunity to put in motion long-overdue public works projects, such as improved sanitation and better local roads.

Porto Alegre achieved both practical and political success, and Participatory Budgeting has spread to every populated continent. Though their designs vary considerably, more than one thousand five hundred public engagement pro-cesses lay claim to that name. In the United States, the Participatory Budgeting Project successfully adapted the process, starting with small discretionary bud-gets in Chicago before tackling the wider city budget in Vallejo, California. After individual city councilors in New York City experimented with Participatory Budgeting for several years, two-thirds of voters approved taking the process citywide in November 2018.

The newest generation of democratic reforms, such as the America*Speaks* process Marion witnessed firsthand, have sought to merge the policymaking power of Participatory Budgeting with the civic educational punch of a National Issues Forum. Figure 1.1 arrays this wider set of innovations, which begins with the Planning Cells and Citizens' Juries launched in the 1970s. Those early models had features that subsequent deliberative forums often adopted: select-ing participants at random; reimbursing travel and lodging expenses; giving citizens direct payments for their time; offering participants a modest role in shaping public policy, or at least ensuring they receive a meaningful government response to the judgments the citizens reach.

We have more to say about Citizens' Juries, Deliberative Polls, Citizens' Assemblies, and their many cousins, but those details will have to wait. We left Marion standing in the lobby at the Grand Phoenix Hotel in Salem, where she anticipated the beginning of the Oregon CIR, which appears at the bottom of Figure 1.1. We return to Marion's story and what led her to the conference hotel where the first official CIR would soon begin.

Discussion of spending proposals during a Participatory Budgeting process in New York City Council District 3. *Source*: Participatory Budgeting Project.

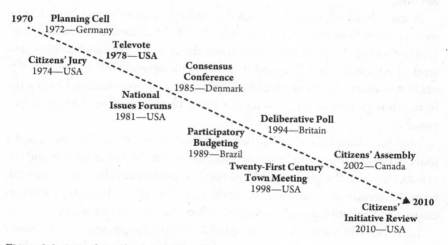

Figure 1.1 A timeline of recent deliberative reforms.

An Invitation to Improve Elections

Marion was unsure what to expect of this CIR. She was trying to find some way to get involved, so when she was selected at random as one of the invitees, she was willing to give it a try. It promised to improve initiative elections. Though a large majority of Oregonians, including Marion, treasured this part of their political process, most also thought it needed repair.

After unpacking her luggage, Marion took the elevator down to the ground floor for the welcome event. As she walked into a small ballroom off the main lobby, Marion thought about her experience at the debt forum. She had appreciated the intent of the America*Speaks* forum but wanted to provide more input and see more outcomes. On the brink of engaging in yet another attempt at citizen participation, Marion didn't think it could be done.

In the reception area, a handful of people milled about eating satay and egg rolls. Marion was curious about the forum and looking forward to meeting her fellow participants. She'd learned of the CIR a few months earlier from a mailed invitation to participate. The letter had briefly described a new process that was designed give everyday citizens a chance to provide input on upcoming ballot initiatives. The forum would gather twenty-four randomly selected (and demographically stratified) Oregon voters at a conference center in the state capitol for five days. Panelists would learn about and discuss a statewide initiative. At the end of the week, the panelists would write a statement for the Oregon *Voters' Pamphlet* that would help their fellow citizens make a better decision in the election.

Marion didn't expect to be selected or to have to take the five days off from work that would be required of her. Still, she filled out the accompanying postcard, provided the required information about her party identification and level of education, and dropped it in the mail. Several weeks later, she was contacted again. This time Healthy Democracy, the organization hosting the forum, was getting in touch to let her know that she had been selected as a panelist.

Like America*Speaks*, the CIR departed from everyday politics, but it had a more narrow purpose—to improve direct democracy. Ballot initiatives and referenda empower the general public to vote on laws or amendments to constitutions. Referenda are placed in front of the electorate by the legislature, whereas citizens and private organizations can develop and propose initiatives.

Initiatives and referenda were adopted during the Progressive Era to counter the corrupting influence of money on politics. The first initiative law was written into the state constitution of South Dakota in 1898. Oregonians followed suit in 1902. When Oregon voters approved direct primaries in 1904, they became the first US citizens to participate in an initiative election.

After their adoption by a handful of western states in the early 1900s, initiative and referenda elections slowly spread across the United States. Today, twenty-four states and Washington, DC, utilize initiatives and/or referenda, as do many Western European countries and former members of the Soviet Union. The process has been even more popular among smaller political units, with hundreds of towns and counties holding elections in which matters of public policy are put up for popular vote.

Over the years, though, the initiative process has become corroded by the same problems it was designed to avoid. Because states and other governing bodies require initiative proponents to gather a minimum number of signatures from registered voters, a signature gathering industry grew up to meet the need. Oregon requires petitioners to collect signatures from at least 6 percent of the population to place a measure on the ballot. Reaching that threshold often requires hiring idealistic, or opportunistic, individuals to gather those signatures, so only well-financed campaigns can expect to reach the general election, where they often spend millions of dollars on a single initiative.

Aside from the exorbitant costs required to win initiative elections, voters are often missing the information needed to reach a good decision. Because initiative elections exist outside of traditional party politics, voters lack the simple partisan cues that they use to make choices. Initiatives and referenda often deal with complex public policy questions, about which the voting public has limited knowledge. Recent initiatives have included both familiar ideas, such as raising the minimum wage, and more novel ones, such as labeling genetically modified foods. Making good decisions about each of these issues requires specialized scientific and economic knowledge, and campaigns interested in enacting or defeating these measures don't necessarily have an incentive to provide this information.

Laws implemented through ballot measures can have huge impacts on a community, its governing system, and its economy. They often deal with moral policies, such as bans on same-sex marriage or the legalization of marijuana. Voting directly on such matters allows the public to shape their community's future. Initiatives have been used to tie the hands of governing officials, with measures in both California and Colorado banning the state legislature from raising taxes without public approval.

Conversely, some measures require expanding government programs but provide insufficient revenue for that purpose. For example, if voters approve increased educational testing without providing the funds required to implement such exams, school districts face a dilemma. To fulfill this one mandate, they may end up cutting other programs the public would have preferred to keep, if given the choice. The net effect of such laws can be staggering. One estimate finds that half of Oregon's increase in state expenditures since 1990 has come as a direct result of initiatives, and states like California and Colorado have faced repeated budget shortfalls stemming from ballot measures that increased public expenditures but not the taxes needed to pay for them.

The CIR aimed to improve this process. Rather than simply trying to persuade voters for or against a measure, the CIR panelists would be tasked with finding out important information about an initiative and relaying their findings to voters. Because their statement would appear in the official *Voters' Pamphlet* for a vote-by-mail state, the CIR panelists' findings would reach a large swath of the voting public at the moment that most mattered—when they were filling out their ballots.

Whatever the ambitions of the CIR might have been, it got off to an unremarkable start that first evening in Salem. Marion met many of the people who had organized the event, as well as others who were there to study it. Saying hello to the other panelists who arrived that evening was pleasant enough, but the opening reception was no more inspiring than an awkward meet-and-greet on the eve of a spelling bee. She didn't quite know who to chat with, what to discuss, or what the ground rules would be for their upcoming conversations. The important work didn't begin until the next morning.

Taking the elevator back to her room, Marion couldn't help her skepticism. Before the America*Speaks* town hall, she'd let her hopes get the better of her, only to leave that event feeling as powerless as ever. The CIR would be different; she wouldn't let her guard down this time.

Pushing Citizens Aside

Anyone who has dipped a toe into the political pool has felt the mix of hope and fear that gave Marion goose bumps on the first day of the Oregon CIR. Many have dreamed of a world in which one can say, without irony, "I live in a *democracy.*"

The idea of self-government holds tremendous appeal to anyone who has taken personal responsibility for building a career, raising a family, or even just losing some weight. A healthy political system requires of its citizens the same judicious mix of freedom and self-control. Democratic citizens protest injustices but show forbearance. They enjoy their personal lives but also fulfill their periodic civic duties.

Reading the morning's headlines, however, dispels lofty democratic wishes. Just below the cheerful Facebook post from your old high-school friend, you will see one decrying the latest political scandal. Click on the headline and you'll read about a seemingly intractable problem that your government can't alleviate. The persistence of poverty, violence, environmental degradation, and corruption can make elected representatives appear feckless, capricious, or even cruel in the face of such tragedies. Individually, most of these public servants may be decent people, but the net result of democratic elections often disappoints the electorate.

In spite of such results, many people persist in hoping for a better political world. In our textbooks and our novels, we sometimes look backward to restore our faith in the prospect of a better future. Remembering the best moments in a nation's history can spark practical insights and remind us how we acquired our stubborn faith in democracy. Toward that end, we now turn to a singular moment in US history.

Democracy in the US Imagination

In the United States, democratic convictions have complex origins ranging from European philosophy to colonial and Native American methods

Hope for Democracy. John Gastil and Katherine R. Knobloch, Oxford University Press (2020).
© John Gastil and Katherine R. Knobloch
DOI: 10.1093/acprof:oso/9780190084523.001.0001

of local governance. This confluence of influences provided sufficient ideological propellant to launch a revolution. Breaking free from British rule
required more than a distaste for usurious taxation, or any number of griev-
ances. Instead, the colonists believed that a declaration of independence
would fulfill a dormant democratic destiny. They aimed to resume the pursuit of democratic self-government that humanity had largely abandoned
since antiquity.

Among the most poignant records of that moment in history, correspondence between colonists shows how it felt to challenge the English king. Two
such correspondents were Abigail Adams and her husband John Adams, whose
peaceful succession of George Washington as president of the United States gave
early proof of the new nation's political stability.

"I pitty you," Abigail wrote (in Colonial English) to John on June 17,
1776, "and feel for you under all the difficulties you have to encounter. My
daily petitions to Heaven . . . are that you may have Health, Wisdom and
fortitude sufficent to carry you through the great, and arduous Business in
which you are engaged; and that your endeavours may be crownd with success." Though the letter would digress to more earthly matters ("the corn
looks poor"), war and the Hand of God were on her mind. She offered John
encouragement.

> I feel no great anxiety at the large armyment designd against us. The
> remarkable interpositions of Heaven in our favour cannot be too grate-
> fully acknowledged. He who fed the Israelites in the wilderness, who
> clothes the lilies of the Field and feeds the young Ravens when they cry,
> will not forsake a people engaged in so righteous cause if we remember
> his Loving kindness.

John replied on the third day of July to tell his wife the deed was done.
"Yesterday," he wrote, "the greatest Question was decided, which ever was
debated in America, and a greater perhaps, never was or will be decided." The
King of England would soon see "a Declaration setting forth the Causes, which
have impell'd Us to this mighty Revolution, and the Reasons which will justify
it, in the Sight of God and Man."

The rest, as the cliché goes, is history. Even as the nation grew from colonies to confederation to constitution, Adams continued to write in defense of
his nation's revolution and the novel political institutions it spawned. A London
publisher released a collection of his letters in 1787, and these show that a touchstone for Adams's thought was ancient Athens, a prototype well-studied by US
intellectuals in his day.

Abigail Adams (1744–1818) and John Adams (1735–1826), as portrayed by Gilbert Stuart and an unidentified portrait artist. *Source:* National Portrait Gallery.

In one such letter, Adams wrote, "The republic of Athens, the school-mistress of the whole civilized world, for more than three thousand years . . . was, for a short period of her duration, the most democratical commonwealth of Greece." The problem, Adams concluded, was that the Athenians had relied too heavily on the Assembly, rather than balancing it with effective judicial and executive branches. Of necessity, Americans took a different course:

> Planted as they are over large dominions, [the] people in each of the United States . . . cannot meet in one assembly, and therefore are not exposed to those tumultuous commotions, like the raging waves of the sea, which always agitated the ecclesia at Athens. They have all elections, of governor and senators, as well as representatives, so prudently guarded, that there is scarce a possibility of intrigue . . . The legislature is so divided into three branches, that no law can be passed in a passion, nor inconsistent with the constitution. . . . This will be a fair trial, whether a government so popular can preserve itself. If it can, there is reason to hope for all the equality, all the liberty, and every other good fruit of an Athenian democracy, without any of its ingratitude, levity, convulsions, or factions.

Whereas the new US system constituted a "fair trial" of democratic principles in practice, its ancient forerunner was a more radical experiment in political chemistry. So posits the foremost modern scholar of Athenian politics, Stanford University professor Josiah Ober. Greece was, according to Ober, "just about as close as we can get to a laboratory." Its local governments tried to cope with foreign threats and domestic instability by "experimenting with a variety of constitutional forms, with more and less extensive participation by citizens."

Such participatory opportunities did not extend to women or slaves in ancient Athens, nor in the time of John Adams. But for the Greek males granted citizenship, each city-state counted as a "controlled political experiment."

The most promising results of this experimentation appeared in Athens. The key to that success, Ober argues, was a participatory spirit.

> Over 300 years of Athenian history, democratic participation is closely correlated with Athens' effectiveness at addressing economic, military, and social problems. Moreover, the Athenian democracy became more participatory over the course of its history, and we find that the increase in participation precedes the growth in effectiveness.

The lesson of Athens concerns not merely participation but free and forceful speech that could draw on the knowledge and values of a diverse citizenry. University of Michigan professor Arlene Saxonhouse dates the birth of ancient Athenian democracy to the day that it welcomed common citizens to speak in the Assembly. The aristocratic antecedent discouraged honest talk from such folk, such as when Odysseus told a soldier to "mind your tongue" and not to "quarrel with his betters." Athens flourished only after expanding its "deliberative circle" such that the full public could gather "for the sake of self-rule, criticism and counsel." The Athenian public's "affronts and demands find expression by those who are uninhibited by shame."

A contemporary voter might find it hard to imagine a governing system that calls on even the humblest of its citizens to fulfill such responsibilities. In the United States, voting itself is often too much to ask, with 40 percent of eligible citizens failing to vote in the 2016 presidential election; turnout rates are even lower for primary, local, and other non-presidential elections. Given that level of apathy, who could expect the public to show interest in day-to-day policy debates, let alone take part in them? Remarkably, the fulfillment of these more taxing political responsibilities built the foundations of contemporary US democracy.

Early US Experiments

John Adams and other alchemists of the US Constitution combined Athenian wisdom with many other ingredients. These included their own colonial experiences, a limited understanding of the Iroquois Confederacy, and contemporary ideas from European philosophers, such as Thomas Hobbes and John Locke.

Founders like Adams were quick to replace the random-selection method of the Athenian Assembly with an elected legislature, yet the New England colonies governed their local affairs through a Town Meeting system that welcomed all comers. In Massachusetts, Adams himself was the principal author of a state constitution that prohibited the local legislature from replacing such meetings with elected officials. That document read:

> No town of fewer than twelve thousand inhabitants shall adopt a city form of government, and no town of fewer than six thousand inhabitants shall adopt a form of government providing for a town meeting limited to such inhabitants of the town as may be elected to meet, deliberate, act and vote in the exercise of the corporate powers of the town.

In a Fourth of July speech given more than half a century later, Henry David Thoreau looked back on this system with fondness: "When, in some obscure country town, the farmers come together to a special town-meeting, to express their opinion on some subject which is vexing the land, that . . . is the true Congress, and the most respectable one that is ever assembled in the United States."

Word of these meetings spread around the globe thanks to a book by a French nobleman published in 1835. The success of *Democracy in America* transformed Alexis de Tocqueville's all-expenses-paid road trip across the New World into one of the best early arguments for establishing a science of politics. Forerunners to the Town Meeting already existed in Swiss cantons, but the US institution struck Tocqueville as a particularly effective way of creating the kind of citizens that new democratic governments would require. Such local public institutions, he wrote, "are to liberty what primary schools are to science; they put it within the people's reach" and teach us "how to use and . . . enjoy it." Political and civil associations show their members "how order is maintained among a large number" that they might "advance, harmoniously and methodically, to the same object." By undertaking small-scale civic endeavors, citizens

> learn to surrender their own will to that of all the rest and to make their own exertions subordinate to the common impulse, things which

it is not less necessary to know in civil than in political associations. Political associations may therefore be considered as large free schools, where all the members of the community go to learn the general theory of association.

The institutions and activities Tocqueville had in mind included not only town meetings, but also newspapers, various political and civil associations, and the "citizen-driven jury." Tocqueville came to believe that serving on a jury, in particular, could make even an apolitical citizen "feel the duties which they are bound to discharge towards society."

Tocqueville's conception of the jury proved a persistent idea in the American mind. As one example among many, the young Frenchman's words appeared in a 1991 US Supreme Court ruling on the right of all citizens to serve on juries:

> Over 150 years ago, Alexis De Tocqueville remarked: "The institution of the jury raises the people itself, or at least a class of citizens, to the bench of judicial authority and invests the people, or that class of citizens, with the direction of society. . . . [It] invests each citizen with a kind of magistracy; it makes them all feel the duties which they are bound to discharge towards society; and the part which they take in the Government. By obliging men to turn their attention to affairs which are not exclusively their own, it rubs off that individual egotism which is the rust of society." Jury service preserves the democratic element of the law, as it guards the rights of the parties and insures continued acceptance of the laws by all of the people. . . . Indeed, with the exception of voting, for most citizens the honor and privilege of jury duty is their most significant opportunity to participate in the democratic process.

It is a credit to US pragmatism that the nation could take such pride in an institution it *adapted*, rather than created. After all, the jury's roots trace back to the same country from which the colonists declared independence. In 1671, a full century before the American Revolution, English law established that a jury could render a verdict independent of a judge's opinion. (Before that, verdicts displeasing the crown were a dodgy business for the jurors involved.)

The US jury expanded its scope and developed in a way it never had in England. In 1735, a New York jury acquitted John Peter Zenger of libel after he published newspaper articles critical of his state's colonial governor. Once Congress ratified the Bill of Rights, both criminal and civil juries became enshrined in the US Constitution. From there, progressive jury reforms reshaped the institution through a more inclusive jury pool, standardized rules of evidence, and a clarification of the jury's role regarding indictment, verdicts, and sentencing. Some recent innovations, such as allowing jurors to take written notes, meet periodically during long trials, and ask questions (through the judge) have made the jury an ever-more reliable means of rendering reasoned verdicts.

Partisanship Trumps Deliberation

Centuries have passed since the jury system secured its place in the US government, and modern legal reforms have diminished the jury's role. Plea bargaining, civil settlements, and alternative dispute resolution have made jury trials the exception, rather than the norm, in the resolution of criminal—and especially civil—cases.

National surveys show that the average US citizen still trusts the judgment of juries, but that same public demonstrates its reluctance to serve by ignoring the majority of summonses sent out by county clerks. Getting out of jury duty rates as a special talent. Without a hint of irony, wikiHow lists eight ways to dodge this civic opportunity. One option: the invocation of the jury's right to ignore or "nullify" the law, a fact that, when spoken aloud, can result in a costly mistrial. Many prospective jurors sympathize with Liz Lemon, the character in *30 Rock* who attempts to avoid jury duty by arriving in court wearing the white gown and cinnamon bun hairdo of *Star Wars'* Princess Leia.

The Town Meeting has suffered a crueler fate. Though still celebrated by many New England residents, plus those who champion it as a model for decentralizing government, these meetings have faded into obscurity in US political consciousness. With local residents unwilling to show up to the meetings, some communities have lowered their quorum requirement to as little as one half of one percent of the electorate. Others are giving up altogether. Those jurisdictions have replaced traditional meetings with more professionalized forms of government that transfer responsibilities from citizens to elected officials, or even appointed city managers.

"Town halls" now held across the country bear little resemblance to their forerunners, as the idea of governing via fully inclusive meetings never took hold outside New England. Far from the noble meetings that caught Thoreau's eye, modern town halls evoke images closer to the healthcare forums witnessed in the summer of 2009. At one such event in Tampa, Florida, CNN reported that the gathering "dissolved into bouts of heckling and violent pushing and shoving" among the hundreds of people inside and outside the building:

> The meeting in Tampa, which featured Democratic Congresswoman Kathy Castor . . . , was another example of the tense battle lines that

have been created in the passionate healthcare debate. . . . As Castor first began to speak, scuffles broke out as people tried to get into the meeting room. Parts of the congresswoman's speech were drowned out by chants of "read the bill, read the bill" and "tyranny." . . . At one point, an event organizer told the crowd, "If pushing and shoving continues, we will have to clear the room. The police will make the decision if it is still safe."

One critic of such meetings is Sandy Hierbacher, a co-founder of the National Coalition for Dialogue and Deliberation, which she helped create to revitalize informed and respectful community engagement. From her vantage point, conventional forums often do more harm than good:

> They don't allow citizens to feel they've been truly heard, or to discuss issues in any depth. Like public hearings, town hall meetings tend to largely be gripe sessions, where the most passionate and bold attendees take turns giving three-minute speeches—usually after enduring long speeches from the front of the room.

Deliberative public gatherings no longer represent the touchstone of US politics, but just as far back in our memory lies the idea of an articulate political elite. There was a time when citizens expected their leaders to hold spirited and substantive debates. Rhetorical scholar Robert Kraig's study of Woodrow Wilson bemoaned the death of the "oratorical statesman," the same role that John Adams had recognized and sought. Kraig explains that Adams's political party, the Federalists, "feared that popular rhetoric operating on uneducated audiences would lead to a reign of demagogues." They "did not seek to banish political oratory but to restrict it," such that "its benefits would be maximized and its dangers controlled." Federalists hoped the Constitution would create an "institutional space for free deliberation by disinterested statesmen."

From the sincere arguments held at the Constitutional Convention to the famous debates between Stephen Douglas and Abraham Lincoln, and up through Woodrow Wilson's appeals for a League of Nations, the United States has a history of serious legislative discourse. In a deliberative democracy, floor speeches could serve as the most visible stage for crystallizing arguments and marshaling passions, evidence, and logic to persuade not only fellow legislators but also the larger public.

Instead, modern legislatures prefer to launch symbolic crusades to promote increasingly narrow partisan agendas. Now more than ever, the two major parties in the United States parade onto the floor of Congress a long lineup of speakers but no listeners. These well-disciplined orators ignore the opposition's speeches while waiting patiently to read a prepared text approved by the party leadership.

Even in statehouses, "legislative karaoke" has become the norm. One speaker after another gives an amateur performance of a prewritten script, occasionally glancing up from an iPad to make brief eye contact. As one speaker sings his or her talking points, the other legislators show scant interest while eating at their desks, reading their mail, or answering cell phones. The next person in the queue rehearses lyrics in anticipation of taking the microphone when signaled to do so by the chamber's presiding DJ.

Floor speeches carry so little weight that their broadcast on C-SPAN commands virtually no public attention unless rebroadcast for laughs on late night television. A quieter kind of deliberation happens now and again, particularly in committees discussing matters outside their parties' core agendas. Modern legislatures, however, conjure few deliberative visions in the public imagination. Instead, partisan conflicts have become so unhinged from any sense of the common good that shutting down the federal government has become a negotiating tactic.

US politics has always been a gladiatorial spectacle. The advent of televised presidential debates transformed what had been amateur battles into professional warfare. This ritual became most gruesome in the 2016 presidential election. Democratic nominee Hillary Clinton punched and parried her way through the debates, with a reserved style typical of the modern era. At the opposite podium, Republican nominee Donald Trump demonstrated the irrelevance of poise and substance in a hyper-partisan environment.

True to his training in reality television, Trump reached an unprecedented level of mean-spirited vulgarity. He quipped memorable one liners ("such a nasty woman") and even physically stalked his opponent around the stage during the ironically titled "town meeting" format. Vice presidential nominee Sarah Palin had lowered the public's expectations for substantive debate in 2008, but Trump managed to go even lower. During and between the debates, Trump persisted relentlessly in repeating falsehoods, even after fact-checkers refuted them. When Pulitzer Prize winning *PolitiFact* used its Truth-o-Meter to score Trump's claims, two-thirds rated as "false" or as evidence of a liar-liar, with his "pants on fire." By this same metric, Clinton stood apart from all other presidential candidates. *PolitiFact* rated a majority of her claims as "true" or at least "mostly true." Her relative veracity mattered not a whit in opinion polls, nor for the ballot boxes in states where she needed votes the most.

Idiosyncrasies aside, this most recent US election cycle followed the same path blazed by candidates who came long before Trump or Clinton. Presidential and Congressional contenders from both major parties employed an army of consultants paid by increasingly untraceable financiers. Gone from the main stage are the likes of John Adams and the "disinterested statesmen." In their place have come the demagogues that the Federalists' feared, with their "popular rhetoric operating on uneducated audiences."

The Internet and social media reduced the cost of mass communication. Rather than lowering spending, however, these new modalities simply absorb a growing share of campaign budgets. Political campaigns and the quasi-independent organizations that encircle them spent more than six billion dollars in both the 2012 and 2016 US elections—more than double the total spent in the 2000 election cycle, when George W. Bush and Al Gore battled to a virtual tie. Roughly two out of every three campaign dollars goes toward radio, television, mail, and online advertising, with the mercenary class of consultants taking in tens of millions for their trouble in direct fees and percentages of their "media buys."

Independent media that report on such campaigns offer further cause for despair. Citizens can't burst with civic pride at the corporate consolidation of large networks, the contraction of local newspapers, and the return of partisan broadcasting via Fox News and its pale imitator MSNBC. Rather than offering hard-hitting stories on substantive campaign issues, corporate media prefer to offer "horse race" coverage on political parties, strategies, and personalities. Such coverage focuses on who's winning and losing in the polls, often at the expense of serious policy discussions.

Online entrepreneurs now complement these larger media with smaller operations. Some of these are nothing more than lone meme-creators posting salacious stories now known as "fake news." As an example, a recent college graduate created ChristianTimesNewspaper.com to feature his fictional article headlined, "BREAKING: 'Tens of thousands' of fraudulent Clinton votes found in Ohio warehouse." This side gig netted roughly a thousand dollars for every hour he put into it.

There was a time when elections featured candidates arguing over matters of substance. The most famous of these—the Lincoln-Douglas debates of 1858—featured two candidates facing off in seven different Illinois towns in pursuit of a US senate seat. In the Internet age, it is hard to conceive standing in the audience for the full duration of such an event. The first candidate held the stage for an hour, the opponent took the next ninety minutes, then the first speaker used the final half hour for rebuttal. The theory behind such contests is that over the course of several iterations, such clashes can winnow out a kind of truth. Though Lincoln and his party couldn't secure the senate seat, the debates did advance his cause and led to him defeating Douglas when it mattered most—in the presidential contest between them two years later.

Defenders of the US electoral system point to this tradition of frequent debates as an effective means of vetting candidates over several weeks or months.

The election of President Donald Trump suggests otherwise. Disfavored by a majority of Republicans and general election voters, he campaigned his way to an Electoral College victory after thirteen Republican primary and three general election debates.

Trump's unlikely ascent overshadowed a pattern set four years earlier in an equally crowded 2012 Republican Party primary. Through a death-march of *twenty* debates from May 2011 to February 2012, voters learned a great deal about the postures and slogans of the ten candidates, who ran toward the rightmost wing of their party to seek out primary and caucus voters. The media feasted on the drama, as one underqualified underdog after another took the polling lead for a week or more, only to coronate a candidate, Mitt Romney, who ranked as the least popular nominee in his party's history, with only 42 percent of Republicans supporting him as the primary season came to a close.

When they coined the phrase in 1997, University of Pennsylvania communication scholars Joseph Cappella and Kathleen Hall Jamieson seemed prescient in dubbing the modern media environment a "spiral of cynicism." Now, that phrase sounds quaint. The spiral has turned so many times that electoral news coverage only validates a cynicism that could hardly grow stronger.

Exporting the Revolution

There was a time, centuries ago, when Americans were anything *but* cynical about democracy. Cynics didn't pen the Declaration of Independence, launch a triumphant revolution against an imposing monarch, nor ratify the US Constitution. More than two centuries removed from such events, one can forget how much influence the American colonists had on the rest of the world. The publisher of John Adams's letters knew those ideas had a ready readership in England, and a half-century later, Tocqueville's *De la Démocratie en Amérique* rewarded its Parisian publisher, along with those who bought the rights to print his books in London.

Though American political elites argued over whether to embrace the French Revolution, French revolutionaries drew inspiration from US democracy. In his Pulitzer Prize-winning book, *The Radicalism of the American Revolution*, Brown University professor Gordon Wood emphasizes just how remarkable the American Revolution seemed in its day. "In destroying monarchy and establishing republics," he writes, Americans were "changing their society as well as their governments, and they knew it." The catch was that "they did not know—they could scarcely have imagined—how much of their society they would change." As an early twentieth-century historian surmised, "the stream of revolution, once started, could not be confined within narrow banks, but spread upon the land."

From 1776 to the present day, democracy has changed from a defiant notion to a default. By modern metrics of governance, democracy has become more common than any other system. Authoritarian rule surged after the colonial independence movements of the 1960s, but autocrats have become less common than regimes where rival warlords run—and ruin—their country.

To be precise, many scholars avoid the term democracy and refer instead to the rise of "polyarchies." Democracy, after all, denotes *rule by all*, but no such nation exists. Polyarchy substitutes the more accurate idea of *rule by many*, an apt term for even the most progressive modern societies. One can scale the polyarchy ladder to attain the status of "full" polyarchy only after hitting all the necessary rungs: fair elections, freedom of expression, inclusive suffrage, associational autonomy, and so on.

Such multisyllabic terminology squeezes the joy out of hailing one's nation as a "democracy," but this is one of their purposes. If democracy represents the highest form of government, its achievement would mark an historical endpoint. If the best of all existing governments remain imperfect polyarchies, each requires further experimentation to move further toward democratic self-government.

One example of a persistent problem in modern polyarchies traces back to the United States and France—those same nations that invented the modern revolution in the eighteenth century. In 1968, Paris hosted the first formal gathering of professional campaign aides, who formed the International Association of Political Consultants. Statecraft was already an old trade, famously described by Italian historian Niccolò Machiavelli in *The Prince*, but the advent of televised politics had created a new political class.

A popular book on the 1968 presidential campaign of Richard Nixon, *The Selling of the President*, brought consulting into the broader public's consciousness. Since then, the rise of professional political consultants has never slowed. The intensive data mining of the 2008 and 2012 Obama campaigns defined the modern state of the art, and their advanced techniques became standard practice by 2016. Thanks to the worldwide export of the modern political consultant, one cannot run a successful campaign for a high-stakes office without a professional campaign organization. Even the maverick Trump campaign, which generated an estimated five billion dollars in free media through a Twitter account, required experienced staff to manage the candidate's self-destructive tendencies.

Professional political campaigns have moved us further away from the best features of ancient Athens than were the colonists who wrote the Declaration of Independence. Modern political systems ask little more from their citizens than an occasional marked ballot. The days leading up to such balloting consist largely of crafted campaign advertising and passive (or prurient) media coverage of the cage fight between left and right. The Fourth of July may swell hearts with a proud memory of the original US experiment, but Election Day brings more anxiety than elation. This is the world we now inhabit.

But beneath the surface, one can find ongoing political experiments designed to address the problems that beset even the world's best polyarchies. The heart of this book focuses on one such venture, which aims to bolster the power of everyday citizens in the electoral process. Before turning to this and other efforts to make politics more deliberative, however, we need to better understand politics as it exists today. We will begin by viewing contemporary campaigns through the eyes of a single citizen who became a civic reformer only after a brief career as a partisan activist.

3

Losing Our Minds

Tyrone Reitman struggled with the same feelings of disillusionment that plague many who live in contemporary democracies. In an interview, Ty confessed that he paid cursory attention to politics as a young adult. He blended in by fitting the norm of a Pacific Northwestern white male: medium build, short dark hair, and a relaxed bearing in a T-shirt under an unbuttoned shirt.

His family didn't talk politics at the dinner table, and nobody encouraged getting involved in public affairs. The exception was Ty's grandfather. A boxer in the Navy, he'd lied about his age to sneak into World War II. Growing up, Ty saw that his grandfather wanted to impart a passion for politics to his grandson. Ty's grandfather distrusted politicians, but he spoke his mind and wrote trenchant letters to the president of the United States. In the early 1990s, Ty learned about the first Gulf War and the North American Free Trade Agreement (NAFTA) in conversations with the old veteran, but Ty didn't feel any impetus to get involved. At the age of twenty-one, when his first presidential election arrived, he followed his grandfather's advice and marked his ballot for Ross Perot, the independent candidate.

A middling student in high school, Ty floated through college. He switched from fine arts to religious studies without much sense of purpose. All that changed when he met his future wife, a sociology student at the University of Oregon in Eugene. Natalie was politically engaged. An activist at the university, she was passionate about fair trade and environmental issues. Hoping to spark her interest, Ty tagged along to protests, and he listened attentively as she enlightened him on environmental politics and labor rights.

When Natalie left to join the 1999 World Trade Organization (WTO) protests, Ty stayed home to write a paper on fair trade. As the violence in Seattle escalated, Ty stayed up late in his cabin behind campus listening to NPR for reassuring news. When the anarchists began breaking windows and diverting the aim of the march, Natalie realized the protestors had lost control of their message and returned to Eugene on a bus full of disgruntled activists.

Hope for Democracy. John Gastil and Katherine R. Knobloch, Oxford University Press (2020).
© John Gastil and Katherine R. Knobloch
DOI: 10.1093/acprof:oso/9780190084523.001.0001

After Natalie disembarked from the bus, Ty met her at New Max's Tavern, a dimly lit college bar. She reeked of tear gas and regaled him with protest stories. It was then that Ty understood the importance of the event and developed an appetite for political engagement.

Ty and Natalie started dating. Working alongside his new girlfriend, Ty volunteered for fair trade and anti-sweatshop campaigns. He met local activists and made connections within the Eugene community, a hotbed for social activism. Like his peers, Ty tried on many causes, from environmental campaigns to attempts to form third parties. Still distrustful of the two-party system and frustrated by the nearly identical stances on trade and labor issues taken by presidential candidates George W. Bush and Al Gore in 2000, Ty joined the Nader campaign and saw firsthand the problems endemic to electoral politics.

Once he graduated from college, Ty sought to find a way to put his newfound activism to use. He drove a recycling van around campus and was paid a quarter per signature to gather support for ballot initiatives on topics such as campaign finance reform. After a crushing defeat of an initiative to label genetically modified foods, Ty began to wonder if grassroots engagement could compete with heavily financed campaigns.

As he became more embedded in the activist community, he lost more of his naivety. Infighting within grassroots movements was chronic. Activists with

Tyrone Reitman. *Source*: Healthy Democracy.

broadly shared goals ate each other alive in three-hour consensus meetings as they bickered over slight differences. Newly wary of disorderly engagement, Ty sought to learn about possible alternatives by returning to the University of Oregon for a master's degree in public administration.

Few citizens can stop their lives and plunge into advanced studies on their own political system. A world in which we *all* followed Tyrone's calling would become a dystopia with a collapsing economy and an acute coffee shortage. To avert such a crisis, this chapter provides a crash-course in contemporary politics to reveal the institutional forces that marginalize us and dull our deliberative instincts, both in the US and across the globe. Understanding how the system works and the role we unwittingly play within it can help us see our way out—or at least the path that Tyrone would eventually follow.

Pushing Citizens to the Margins

The preponderance of social scientific evidence shows that most US voters have become polarized, disengaged, or both. A disdain for politics and a distrust of politicians leave most citizens with little appetite for new political information. Deep biases skew our responses to the news we do encounter. Even if we imagine ourselves as personal exceptions to these trends, we cannot deny the wider landscape we share with our less public-spirited peers.

To take one example, fewer than one-in-five Americans now report that they "trust the federal government to do what is right" at least "most of the time." A half-century ago, nearly three-quarters of Americans were willing to place such trust in their government. Though the tumultuous 1960s account for most of that decline, Figure 3.1 shows another steady downward slide since 2002. Tea Party Republicans seethe about the federal government's expanding powers and its subservience to special interests. Liberals distrust a government steered by corporate interests—the "one percent" who unduly influence even the Democratic Party. Left and right agree that a Congress built by the Founders now serves its funders.

What could transform a nation from the collection of civic-minded farmers and laborers who took up arms against a monarchy into the electorate we see today? In a word, *institutions*. To replace the institutional architecture of the British monarchy, the American founders built a political system designed to keep a newly empowered mass public from veering toward mob rule. Refinements of those novel institutions gave greater power to ever more citizens, yet bureaucratization and the entrenchment of policy elites has pushed citizens farther from the inner workings of government. During elections, the professional campaign system (noted at the end of chapter 2) treats voters as political commodities to an unprecedented degree.

Figure 3.1 Declining trust in the US federal government, 1958–2019.
Note: Data compiled by Pew Research Center from numerous sources.

In the modern context, the very idea of self-government can sound ludicrous. As one of the authors of this book wrote nearly twenty years ago, "There are two problems in American politics. The first problem is that the public doesn't believe that the government represents its interests. The second problem is that they are right." Years later, that quote became a minor meme on Facebook because it resonated with many people's sense of alienation from politics and government.

Alienation may sound too strong, but it is an apt word. For a time, Marxists popularized the idea that capitalism could alienate people from their labor. When the blacksmith devolved into the listless factory worker, he could no longer take pride in seeing horses walking on shoes he'd pounded by hand at the forge. Work became nothing more than a means of obtaining currency—with worker, seller, and buyer unknown to one another. This impersonal economic system thrives in spite of such alienation because it yields market efficiencies and offers workers extrinsic rewards in the form of salaries. Political alienation, by contrast, offers no recompense to the dispirited voter.

Hungarian philosopher István Mészáros explains that alienation converts "human beings into 'things' so that they could appear as commodities on the market." It fragments "the social body into isolated individuals" who pursue "their own limited, particularistic aims." The system of alienation "makes a virtue out of their selfishness."

A more analytic definition of the term plucked from the *American Sociological Review* distinguishes five facets of alienation one can see refracted in modern politics. Citizens have become *commodified* as targeted voters in a way that *isolates* them from one another, leeches out of politics much of its *meaning*, degrades prevailing *social norms*, and leaves citizens feeling *powerless*. As the following discussion shows, contemporary citizens experience each of these forms of political alienation.

Just as the local blacksmith guild devolved into anonymous laborers, so has the engaged community broken into discrete voters in an impersonal political marketplace. Even the public interest groups that might inspire people moved by common causes have become professionalized. They now operate more like ongoing campaigns than collections of engaged citizens. They cultivate new members at a distance, often through social media, and they call on members to contribute money and recirculate crafted messages. Organizations hope to mold their members' opinions on targeted issues to improve the electoral viability of a specific candidate or ballot measure. Relatively few now bother with organizing on-the-ground actions in which everyday citizens meet and discuss common concerns. For national issue advocacy organizations, building a stronger local community isn't the point.

Even when citizens see a political choice placed before them, on a ballot or in an online survey, they find only a false dilemma. Complex fiscal problems, such as managing the federal deficit, get framed as a crisis of the moment, be it raising the debt ceiling or extending unemployment benefits. Absent are deeper questions about federal spending priorities and the kind of labor market we want in our country. The narrower questions that appear on our screens each week ask even less of our intelligence. Stark symbolic choices between Democratic and Republican talking points obscure the nuanced alternatives within and beyond each party.

Just as Congress has strayed from a deliberative ideal, so do citizens live in a wider political system that discounts the value of serious discussion. Philosophers and political theorists have emphasized the need for a more vibrant public sphere, a realm in which private citizens come together to talk, reflect, and act in concert. This idea lies at the heart of deliberative theories of democracy, which call for a sincere pursuit of sensible solutions to our most challenging problems. Such deliberative norms, however, must compete with the more prevalent practice of strategic politics, whereby parties and candidates pursue pre-defined agendas and mobilize people to advance those causes, no matter the cost.

The final facet of alienation is a sense of powerlessness. The forces that influence government, particularly at the state and federal level, operate in a way that leaves citizens with little confidence that what they say and do will make any difference. Some of this comes of necessity because in large democracies citizens have greater collective power but must share it more widely. Professional politics compounds this problem by habituating citizens to impulsive responses to the specific demands made by campaigns and elections. Citizens may appear responsive in such a system, but they are not creative. They may answer the call, but they don't get to formulate the question behind it. In truth, one's ballot droppings have real heft, but those who leave them more likely feel a momentary sense of relief than a lasting political potency.

It might be hard to think of politics as anything but polarizing and alienating, but there is an alternative. Chapter 1 introduced the concept of deliberative democracy, and it can help to think of how that democratic ideal might operate in practice. A deliberative system would have roles for political parties, floor debates, opinion polling, and social media campaigns, but the character and function of these familiar practices would change.

UK public policy professor John Parkinson and Harvard political theorist Jane Mansbridge offer one account of such a process:

> A deliberative system is one that encompasses a talk-based approach to political conflict and problem-solving—through arguing, demonstrating, expressing and persuading. In a good deliberation, persuasion that raises relevant considerations should replace suppression, oppression, and thoughtless neglect.

In this view, institutions perform well when they serve deliberative functions, such as producing opinions and decisions "informed by facts and logic" as a result of "substantive and meaningful consideration" of relevant arguments. Deliberative institutions also cultivate listening to one another as an ethical imperative. When deliberating democratically, we show respect for one another by letting each person have a say and acknowledging, even in the midst of disagreement, our shared stake in common problems.

Every conception of deliberative politics stresses the importance of these two features—rigorous analysis and respectful relationships. In most modern polyarchies, however, neither rigor nor mutual respect would be the first terms used to describe politics and government.

Voting with Limited Information

Think about the last election in which you participated. On what basis did your fellow voters choose which candidates to support? Did they weigh the issues carefully, listen attentively to all sides in every debate, and make judicious selections? If there were local ballot measures or statewide initiatives, did voters support or oppose laws on their merits? Based on the research collected to date, the likely answers to these questions are "no." Or, to be kind, "not so much."

Consider the model of voter behavior constructed by political scientists Richard Lau, at the Whitman Center for the Study of Democracy at Rutgers University and David Redlawsk at the University of Iowa. These two scholars collaborated for years on a series of studies, determined to better understand how voters make use of the information they obtain from media, campaigns, and fellow voters. Following the experimental tradition, they manipulated the messages available to voters then measured whether their candidate choices meshed or clashed with voters' core values.

If you participated in one of these experiments, you would be asked to make a voting choice after studying rival hypothetical presidential candidates under significant time pressure. On your computer monitor, you see an ever-shifting menu of information categories. Want to learn the Republican nominee's view on abortion? Click fast on the "Abortion Views" button on your monitor before that tidbit of information disappears. Want to know where the Democratic nominee grew up? Hurry up and click "Hometown." Suddenly, the virtual campaign ends. Time to mark your ballot.

Before you get up to leave the lab, the experimenters give you a chance to reconsider your vote. They lay before you all the available candidate information and give you plenty of time to study the two candidates more carefully.

If this second vote deviates from the first, Lau and Redlawsk mark this as voting "incorrectly" the first time. In such cases, a hurried analysis of limited facts yielded a choice that, on reflection, didn't match a more considered judgment of who would best represent the voter's views.

By the time Lau and Redlawsk compiled their findings in *How Voters Decide*, they had brought through their lab larger student samples and more representative cross-sections of the United States. Overall, seven out of every ten experimental participants got their vote right on the first try.

Seventy percent accuracy sounds less impressive when one remembers that half the experimental subjects would have voted correctly in these hypothetical two-party contests by flipping a coin. The 30 percent who erred in their judgment represent a proportion larger than the margin of victory in every presidential election in the past two centuries. Even the 1984 Reagan landslide was roughly half that at 18 percent.

This finding was no quirky laboratory anomaly. Lau and Redlawsk found a similar result in a careful analysis of the historic 2000 presidential contest between Republican nominee George W. Bush and the Democratic Vice President Al Gore. That election came down to the hanging, dimpled, and "pregnant" chads on ballots across Florida. Had voters fully understood those two candidates' positions, like the experimental subjects who got a second chance, the final tally would not have been close. Lau and Redlawsk took stock of voters' policy preferences, their underlying value commitments, and the information about Bush and Gore readily available in the course of the campaign. Crunching those numbers showed that if voters had accessed all that data about the two candidates, Gore's share of the popular vote would have risen to somewhere between 52 and 57 percent, an easy victory that neither chads nor third-party challenger Ralph Nader could have spoiled.

Far from a case of partisan sour grapes, Lau and Redlawsk's analysis found voting errors all across the political spectrum. Vice President Gerald Ford's share of the vote in 1976 fell nearly 4 percent against Georgia governor Jimmy Carter, who benefitted from voters' limited deliberation in that post-Watergate election. By that analysis, a better-informed electorate would have given Ford the popular vote—and probably the election.

Ross Perot's independent candidacy in 1992 suffered more than any other. By Lau and Redlawsk's reckoning, the maverick candidate lost nearly 21 percent of the national vote to confusion or ignorance—Ty's grandfather likely being the exception. Put that lost vote share back in Perot's column, and it would have brought him close to 40 percent—perhaps enough to win the three-way contest.

The most striking result, however, comes from the 1984 electoral landslide noted earlier. In that contest, President Reagan won re-election with a commanding 58 percent of the vote. Walter Mondale badgered Reagan during one of their debates with a question swiped from a Wendy's hamburger ad: "Where's the beef?" Had voters found the answer to that question, by becoming more fully informed about both candidates' positions, a fourteen-point swing would have given Mondale a comfortable margin of victory.

Lau and Redlawsk juxtapose their findings with the more sanguine view popular in political science, which holds that party membership provides a ready shortcut to reaching voting decisions. It would seem to "allow voters to act as if they were fully informed" without applying "the cognitive effort" to become so. This particular shortcut, known as the "partisan heuristic" or the "partisan cue," tells busy voters what to say when phoned by survey interviewers and how to mark their ballots, just as cue cards guided candidates through their lines before the invention of the teleprompter.

In some states, voters can still cast their ballots by choosing a "straight party ticket." Different ballot designs and voting machines have encouraged this behavior over the years. The blanket ballot developed in South Australia in the 1850s listed all the candidates for all offices, each lined up in columns within their respective parties. A circle atop each column invited one to "vote the ticket" with a single mark. Mechanical gear-and-lever machines gave one the option of either flicking a dozen or more separate levers on the ballot or simply "pulling the party lever" to support one party's nominees in each election.

Voters can't so easily follow the lead of their party when they mark ballots during primaries, in nonpartisan contests, nor for ballot measures. Even in high-profile primary elections, voters have difficulty identifying the candidate who best matches their underlying policy preferences. Applying Lau and Redlawsk's experimental method to the 2008 presidential primaries showed that voters' naïve vote choices matched their fully informed candidate selections only slightly better than chance.

The partisan cue holds no meaning at all for many nonpartisan voters. In presidential and partisan general elections, a growing proportion of US voters identify themselves as independents. Figure 3.2 shows that in the late 1980s the public was split evenly between Democrats, Republicans, and nonpartisans. Since 2013, however, a plurality of Americans have rejected both party labels. Some of these independents lean left or right, but neither party can take their support for granted.

When the partisan heuristic becomes irrelevant, Lau and Redlawsk explain that voters turn to "more specifically defined cognitive heuristics"—an array of shortcuts that help them decide how to mark their ballots. Contrary to the beliefs of many political scientists, these alternative heuristics "are not the saving grace for the apathetic US voter. In fact, if anyone benefits from using heuristics, it is political experts."

What are these "more specifically defined" cognitive shortcuts that professional consultants exploit? Answering that question requires looking deeper into

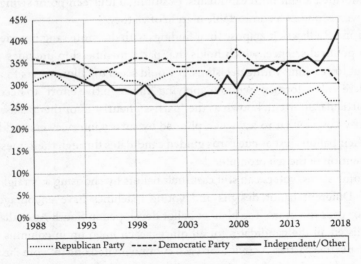

Figure 3.2 The rise of nonpartisan voters, 1988–2018.

the voter's mind. Beneath surface-level party and policy preferences lie the cultural foundations of our choices.

Commitment to Biased Judgments

Before we mark a ballot or tap a touchscreen in the voting booth, weeks or months of information has accumulated in the backwater of our brains. Our voting choices rise from the slurry of impressions we hold from TV and radio commercials, banner ads, yard signs, emails, idle conversations, and news stories about the political parties, candidates, and issues on our ballots. Far from an unbiased repository of salient information, the considerations that settle into our long-term memories reflect a history of selective attention, biased filtering, and impulsive reactions to new stimuli.

This cognitive and emotional processing begins with the particular cultural worlds we inhabit. There exist an infinite number of variables that define each of us—from how we dress ourselves to how we address each another. When it comes to political judgment, the relevant element is one's *cultural worldview*. Each of us holds a conception of how people and governments ought to behave.

A particularly stark contrast divides two groups in the United States. The first group believes that the world works best when economic and social forces sort individuals into different roles and statuses based on their talents and resources. The opposite worldview seeks to build strong communities that treat their members as equals.

Recent research suggests that these dueling cultural worldviews are more than a difference in philosophy. If you bring representatives from these two groups together, they might not only disagree about policy choices. They might prove unable to perceive identical objects the same way.

These insights flow from the work of Yale law professor Dan Kahan, who leads a multi-investigator effort called the Cultural Cognition Project. For more than a decade, he has gathered evidence on the strength of cultural biases. Like Lau and Redlawsk, he deploys multiple research methods but often employs experimental designs for their explanatory power.

Figure 3.3 shows a crude representation of how Kahan and his colleagues map people's cultural orientations in two-dimensional space. The key contrast in these studies, as in US politics, is between the top-left quadrant (the hierarchical individualists who approximate a "conservative" ideology) and the bottom-right quadrant (the egalitarian collectivists, who best fit the "progressive" or "liberal" labels).

To understand how these cultural orientations bias our perceptions, put yourself in the role of research subject for one such study. You sit down to watch a

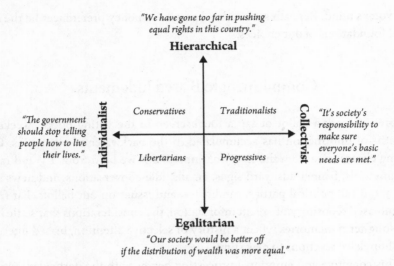

Figure 3.3 A cultural map with representative survey questions and ideological labels.

video and see these words on the screen: "Outside the campus recruitment center 15 minutes before it was scheduled to open." You see young people in royal blue sweatshirts hoisting hand-painted signs outside a white office building. Even with shaky camera footage, it's clear that a protest is underway. Police in black uniforms and silver helmets stand nearby. Another title slide appears: "Scene at the entrance of the recruitment center. Student approaches but does not enter." A pedestrian approaches the demonstrators then turns away. In the end, police order protestors to disperse.

What did you see? The answer depends largely on who you are. Seventy one percent of those who prefer egalitarian communities saw police abridging protestors' right to free speech. Only 17 percent of those who favor a society that sorts individuals hierarchically witnessed the violation of anyone's speech rights.

And so it goes. If experimenters change the title slide to call the white building an abortion clinic and show research participants the same video, perceptions shift. Hierarchs see a legitimate anti-abortion protest being dispersed, and egalitarians see police ensuring safe passage for women seeking medical services.

Study after study, the same basic pattern repeats. Researchers can replace the video footage with a news story about a vaccine. Or they can show study participants a fact sheet about gun violence. Or data about rival candidates. It doesn't matter. In each case, divergent cultural orientations steer people to different conclusions about the same information.

Our cultural worldviews tell us not just where we should stand on issues, but also who we should believe, where we should focus our attention, and how to react to new information. Most of all, these cultural cues are among the most powerful "specifically defined" cognitive heuristics that shape our voting behavior. Nevertheless, one shouldn't misconstrue worldviews as nothing more than heuristic aids to decision making. The Cultural Cognition Project's studies show that busy cultural partisans can also develop strident views when they stop to analyze data more carefully.

When Kahan surveyed the public's perceptions of climate change hazards, he found the same pattern of cultural divergence as with the protest video. The gap between the groups' attitudes widened the greater their comprehension of science. Those who idealized egalitarian communities perceived climate change as a serious risk, but the subgroup most literate in math expressed the gravest worries. Those favoring a more hierarchical and individualistic society doubted the gravity of climate fluctuations, but all the more so if well trained in math and science.

Whether one hailed from the Tea Party or supported the Occupy Wall Street protests, Kahan finds scant differences between such groups' ability to reason, think with an open mind, or understand scientific facts. Each social group has the same capacity for biased information processing, and each is determined to reimagine the world in ways that bolster their underlying cultural commitments. Whether politically liberal, conservative, or fiercely independent, we all use a cultural compass to navigate the political world, including those occasions when officials invite us to complete a ballot. This enables even those without a political party to make confident choices on Election Day. Likewise for the partisans among us, party leader cues serve less as a shortcut than as a stimulus for biased reasoning.

From Cynicism to Action

Returning to Lau and Redlawsk's voting experiments, the strength of our cultural biases calls into question what should count as a "correct" vote. The problem is not simply that most voters lack information. The problem is that few are motivated to process information in an unbiased manner. Cultural values don't just guide our decisions, they can control them.

Far from being a distinctly US problem, this pattern of unreflective response to elite opinion persists across the globe. Every modern polyarchy includes political contests among two or more major parties that use cultural symbols (along with genuine policy differences) to stake a claim on the electorate. Whether privately owned, state-sponsored, or a mix thereof, the mass media in these systems rely heavily on the political elite for the content and framing of their public affairs reporting. In the past decade, for instance, partisan elites, such as—candidates, elected officials, and party spokespersons—accounted for 51–66 percent of the sources in political news within the United States, Germany, Switzerland, Italy, and Great Britain. These systems also produce an increasing number of news stories that convey commentary or opinion, a feature found in 16 percent of US news stories compared to 27 percent in Great Britain.

Were elections simply a referendum on the nation's values, there would be no harm in the symbolic battles political elites wage through campaigns and news coverage. In reality, elections create binding laws and empower lawmakers to make (and unmake) more laws. Good laws and good lawmakers require more than evocative cultural symbols, so a collective failure to consider hard facts during elections should worry us. Worrying is a good start.

If it makes us reflect on our own voting choices, a bit of healthy fretting might push us past our habitual biases. The same researchers who sounded warnings about our political system have also found conditions under which change is possible. Lau and Redlawsk's experimental subjects could align vote choices and policy preferences when given more time and information. Later research by Redlawsk showed that even those individuals most motivated to protect their preexisting biases can become so overwhelmed by contrary evidence that they reach a tipping point, after which their opinion flips.

The Cultural Cognition Project also has found situations in which people can break free from their cultural moorings, such as when a prominent member of their cultural group challenges in-group orthodoxy. When Bill Clinton endorsed deficit reduction or when John McCain championed campaign finance reform, their actions had the potential to reshuffle the beliefs of their cultural camps.

After all, public opinion on major issues *does* shift over time—sometimes in ways that seem refreshingly rational. Political elites have shifted their stances to shape and reflect changing public attitudes toward women's rights, healthcare, defense spending, same-sex marriage, and numerous other issues. Periodic campaigns turn up the partisan and cultural heat, but the potential for a more cool-headed electoral politics exists.

Concern about the quality of our electoral system might inspire more than self-improvement. It can lead us to demand more not just from ourselves but from our government. Just as institutions have molded our political system, their transformation can save it.

A solution may draw once more from the lessons of earlier political systems, but it can learn only so much from systems of the past. Ancient Athens had no political parties, nor a media system in the modern sense of the term. The eighteenth-century British Parliament had proto-political parties, but the American colonists had little direct experience with them. In fact, they derided parties. As John Adams said in one of his letters, from 1789, "There is nothing which I dread so much as a division of the republic into two great parties, each arranged under its leader. . . . This, in my humble apprehension, is to be dreaded as the greatest political evil under our Constitution." George Washington, Thomas Jefferson, James Madison, and many of their contemporaries shared the same disgust for partisan conflict experienced by the plurality of Americans who refuse to identify with a political party.

The myriad problems posed by partisan and cultural biases are ubiquitous. They reach across the country and across the globe. Thus, if we scan the galaxy of governments large and small, we should find efforts to remedy these biases. There should be signs of intelligent life. Surely, a visionary public official or dogged activist has crafted a deliberative innovation to improve their political institutions.

That same desire to find a better way to govern ourselves propelled Tyrone Reitman into graduate school. In spite of his wariness about the inefficiency of activism, he retained enough hope to seek out a solution for electoral politics. He knew that there were other people who cared about democracy just as much as he did. He'd seen that same passion in Natalie. Close friends of theirs had faced down riot police during the WTO protests.

Change required more than bravery. While working for campaign finance reform, Ty met concerned citizens who yearned for a breakthrough—something that would clear the way for genuine public debate and more serious-minded elections.

Ty could feel the same mix of courage and hope that animated his grandfather. They'd both inherited the rebellious spirit of the American colonists, who believed they could do something no one before them had achieved. Dissatisfied with the status quo, Ty had taken on any job that could make a difference. During long hours driving the recycling van and gathering signatures, he felt a sense of purpose, even as others around him became disengaged, or disillusioned.

Growing up in the Pacific Northwest, Ty may have also absorbed that region's ethic of self-sufficiency. Entering graduate school, Ty knew he'd find a way to put both his passion for democracy and a desire for real social change to use. He also knew, however, that strength came in numbers. He'd need to find allies. Soon enough, they'd find him.

Progressive Politics in the Pacific Northwest

Ty didn't go to graduate school just to win over his girlfriend, Natalie. He was hoping to regain the inspiration he had experienced when he listened to coverage of the WTO protests in his cabin. He wanted to promote fair trade, find a way to regulate campaign finance, or do something, anything. Graduate students often enter their studies with a similar sense of purpose—wanting to make a change, but not sure where to start.

As his coursework got underway, Ty found the material exciting and tried to imagine putting his new knowledge to use. Studying public administration felt like an opportunity to hone his activist skills, but before long, he became disillusioned. His coursework kept digging into the day-to-day drudgery of government bureaucracy, not how one could develop and implement public policy. The point was to learn practical skills for public service, not to dwell on theoretical questions or imagine innovations.

When Ty had arrived at this conclusion, he connected with another student, Elliot Shuford, who had entered the same program for similar reasons. They had met before graduate school, moved in the same circles, and had run into each other at rallies and protests more than once—even their girlfriends were friends. When they reconnected as grad students, they became fast friends, sharing a passion not only for political reform but also for exploring the wilderness, savoring craft brews, and enjoying the hallmarks of the Oregon lifestyle.

One of their most memorable evenings occurred at Taylor's Bar & Grill, which Ty described as "a classic seedy frat house bar." As they debated on the upstairs deck, the patrons around them were "chain smoking and partying into the wee hours." Ty drank a Pabst Blue Ribbon, while Elliot had a Long Island Iced Tea. "Elliot's frugal," Ty explained, "so his drink selection was based on whatever was the deal of the day."

As closing time approached, their debate got into the relative influence of cultural versus structural forces on public policy and social change. Ty took a

Hope for Democracy. John Gastil and Katherine R. Knobloch, Oxford University Press (2020).
© John Gastil and Katherine R. Knobloch
DOI: 10.1093/acprof:oso/9780190084523.001.0001

Elliott Shuford, co-creator of the Oregon CIR. *Source:* Christine McCrehin, *Public Administration Times.*

structuralist stance, maintaining that norms and institutions were the most powerful social forces. "Elliot," Ty said, "took the position that a culture could change political structures" just as much as politics could change a culture, and they debated that proposition in depth.

At the time, Elliot was studying the Rogue Valley Wisdom Council, a deliberative process invented in the Pacific Northwest that placed tremendous faith in the political power of facilitation and honest dialogue. Elliot believed people could "change minds and open possibilities" through such processes. Their own conversation was a testament to the idea that debate could be productive—even fun.

A few weeks later, Elliot forwarded Ty an email with something like a "top ten list" of ideas for deliberative reform that he had received from another deliberative democracy advocate, Tom Atlee. The traveling preacher of "co-intelligence," Tom had helped found a co-op in which Elliot was living. Tom and the other co-op residents would invite guest speakers and share inspiration for political change. The email that caught Elliot's eye argued that randomly selected citizen councils could increase democracy's "potency." The Citizens Jury was one of the items on that list. It's founder, Ned Crosby, had visited the co-op and sparked Tom's imagination. Its inclusion in Tom's email would create an unlikely partnership, one that led Ty and Elliot's vision for democracy out of the dimly lit bar and all the way to the state capital.

A Lifetime of Democratic Reform

In an extended interview, Ned recounted the winding road that led him to Ty. A tall man with an easy smile and piercing eyes, Ned was the great-grandson of one of the founders of Washburn Crosby Co., which later became General Mills. Though Ned came from a wealthy family, he forged his own path in life. Beginning his undergraduate studies in 1954, Ned was continuing his family's tradition of graduating "Yalies." In the middle of his junior year, however, Ned dropped out of Yale, frustrated by its elitist environment. Instead, Ned enlisted in the Army. The only paycheck he ever received came from his two years' service as a private.

After his stint in the armed forces, Ned enrolled at the University of Minnesota. After receiving a BA in psychology, he pursued doctoral work in political science. Graduate studies were a deviation from the path that had been laid before him. Someone of his social class was more likely to be found at the Woodhill Country Club, which his grandfather and four other wealthy families had founded in Minneapolis. Had his wife not made plain her dislike for the club's social scene, Ned suspected he might have been "sucked into that life."

The balance of evidence suggests otherwise, as Ned's life is a story of intellectual curiosity and commitment to social change. When Ned delved more deeply into his studies, he became disheartened with the behaviorist theories prominent in social science at that time. Made famous by B. F. Skinner's theory of "operant conditioning" through rewards and punishments, behaviorists sought to understand human society through the observation and manipulation of behavior. In this view, what people feel and think matters little and cannot be measured reliably in any case.

Recognizing Ned's dissatisfaction with this approach, one of his psychology professors encouraged Ned to explore other fields. Alas, Ned encountered behaviorist orthodoxy even outside psychology. The turning point was the day a political science professor told Ned, "Your views on the Vietnam War are fine for you to hold on your own, but they have no more validity in political science than your preferences for chocolate over vanilla ice cream."

Ned realized that he would have to design his own program of study if he was going to learn how individuals make decisions. He wanted to get inside people's minds and understand what makes them think and feel. He wanted to know what leads us to form attitudes, such as his own views on Vietnam or the cultural beliefs that were so prominent at the country club he rejected.

As his studies progressed, Ned struggled with the slow pace of academia. He described himself as "very much a child of the 60s," though he was "ten years too old" to belong to that generation. Still, he shared its tastes and sensibilities. "I couldn't stand Elvis," he admitted, "and I loved the folk movement. I wanted to be part of the counterculture but felt it was failing. The dreams of the left-wing movement were dreams that were not well founded."

When the '60s finally arrived, Ned wanted to do more than just talk about a better future. He wanted to create one. Juggling his scholarship with activism, Ned worked with inner-city neighborhoods in Minneapolis and lobbied Congress on the issues of the day. These efforts sometimes made him anxious about his graduate research. Nonetheless, Ned stuck with his research. "The amount of time I was spending in graduate school," he explained, "was due to the fact that I was neurotic. Were I any less so, I wouldn't have been doing it. Were I any more so, I surely would have failed."

The creative tension between the scholar and the activist led to a breakthrough. Just as Ned had rejected the rigidity of behaviorism, he concluded that moral arguments do not resolve themselves simply through intellectual analysis. Ned concluded that democracy required a new institution that could bring together a microcosm of the public to think deeply about an issue. Such an institution could help people both weigh evidence and develop empathy.

In the broadest sense, that idea had a classical pedigree. Regardless of our superficial political attitudes, Aristotle insisted that deep down we are "political animals." Aristotle saw politics as a natural function of humanity; our ability to communicate with one another makes us political beings. He wrote, in *Politics*, "Why man is a political animal in a greater measure than any bee or any gregarious animal is clear. For nature . . . does nothing without purpose; and man alone of the animals possesses speech." The gift of speech lets us "indicate the advantageous and the harmful, and therefore also the right and the wrong." Thus, a person "has perception of good and bad and right and wrong and the other moral qualities, and it is partnership in these things that makes a household and a city-state."

This philosophy underpins the call for a more deliberative democracy. It suggests that we aren't realizing our democratic potential because we lack opportunities and incentives to engage in meaningful dialogue and debate. Deliberative democrats argue that we can rediscover our appetite for responsible self-government if given the chance to work together with fellow citizens to address shared problems.

Faith in that capacity has strong roots in modern democratic theory as well. Philosopher John Dewey, for example, placed his pragmatic hopes in the cultivation of a well-educated public. Citizens today have more formal education than ever, yet *civic* education receives relatively little emphasis in school. This leaves unanswered the question of how to turn over complex policy questions to a mass public that desires deliberation but lacks the requisite experience or knowledge.

Rather than lamenting such problems, Ned decided to address them. In 1971, while still working on his doctoral degree, Ned proposed a novel institution—the Citizens Jury. This new process reflected Ned's belief that ethics should be negotiated through reason—not by the philosopher or policy expert but by diverse individuals drawn from across a society. Convening a Citizens Jury would enable a microcosm of the public to sort through complex policy data, while reflecting on the lives and circumstances of their fellow citizens.

A year after receiving his degree, Ned founded a nonprofit organization devoted to democratic innovation that would later become the Jefferson Center and embarked on his own journey of democratic experimentation. Like idealists from centuries past, who had envisioned the assembly in Athens and juries in England, Ned believed he could develop new citizen-centered institutions to help governments make more just and prudent decisions. The idea was novel, but not inconceivable.

Gradually, the Citizens Jury came to life. Year after year, Ned and his colleagues at the Jefferson Center paid small groups of citizens to spend four-to-six days discussing local policy issues or candidates for public office. Participants would often hear from and pose questions to advocates or experts, with the assistance of trained moderators. Decades of fine-tuning permitted the testing of new procedures, forum durations, and mechanisms for connecting the recommendations of Citizens Juries with official policymaking.

When asked about the first Citizens Jury, which tackled health policy, Ned's recollections were vivid:

> I hired three graduate students. It took ten weeks from when I hired them 'till when it was done. Two were experts on healthcare, and they drew up info on healthcare and solutions, which we presented to randomly selected people we'd recruited by knocking on doors and paying them a modest sum. The six sessions we ran were held on the upstairs floor of a small house, rented for almost nothing. At one point, a mouse dropped down from the ceiling and ran across the foot of one of the citizen jurors. Not the most elegant quarters.

Among the citizens attending those first healthcare juries was a nurse, who channeled her inner political animal when she compared the discussions to popcorn. "The more you eat," she said, "the more you want." When Ned heard that, he said to himself, "Okay, we've got something here."

These jurors came to recognize the tradeoffs facing any healthcare system. Ned recalled that they arrived at a simple rule: "Everyone would have to pay *something* for every visit to the doctor." The plan they devised had a sliding scale, with taxes and subsidies that ensured care would be accessible to all people.

Though they knew their potential for influencing policymakers was slim, the jurors worked hard to pull together a cohesive plan.

This first jury was a raw experiment, but its results were encouraging to Ned and others who observed it. Since their inception, hundreds of Citizens Juries have been held in the United States, United Kingdom, Australia, Canada, Japan, Spain, and many other countries. Though they often deviate from the Jefferson Center model, these events have shown citizens capable of judging rival candidates for public office or tackling any issue, from energy security to education policy.

The same year that Ned founded the Jefferson Center, he met his proverbial Abigail Adams. Pat Benn shared Abigail's passion and directness, albeit with a more modern hairstyle. Before becoming Ned's second wife and co-pilot for his work on democracy, Pat taught French and German. Ned happened to speak both languages, and they bonded while traveling to countries where they could practice one or the other language.

While Ned worked on Citizens Juries, Pat became an activist within her teachers union. The democracy she found in the union inspired her, and she took on the role of meeting chair. In union meetings, she saw the necessity of facilitation, respect, and fairness—all of which translated well to the Citizens Jury. Eventually, Pat became president of the Robbinsdale Federation of Teachers. One of her first tasks was to preside over a debate about using secret ballots. The question came from a union member petition, which gave Pat her first experience with initiative elections.

Pat used insights from these union meetings to provide input into the evolving design of the Citizens Jury. First off, the juries would avoid using a formalized discussion procedure, such as Robert's Rules of Order. Instead, the process would find its own way of achieving clarity and fairness, with clear norms and a structure that wouldn't devolve into bureaucratic rules. Pat said she had to use Robert's Rules for the union, lest it fall apart. But the juries needed something else.

Working out the discussion procedure was relatively easy. What was harder was designing a process that would make for real political change. One approach Ned took was to link the Citizens Jury with a subsequent lobbying effort. A friend explained to him that one unresolved public policy problem in Minnesota was the impact of agriculture on water quality. "The legislature wouldn't touch it," Ned recalled, "because the major industries that were polluting didn't want to deal with it." Still, there was the hope that the legislature would act if a sound proposal came to them.

Ned and Pat got their first grant, from the Joyce Foundation in Chicago, to run a four-day Citizens Jury on the subject. Before then, a typical jury would run for two hours each evening, but this time, they recruited five twelve-person

Ned Crosby and Pat Benn (with Australian deliberation scholar Lyn Carson). *Source:* Tom Atlee or John Gastil.

juries across the state filled with members willing to put in full days in exchange for modest compensation for their time and the expenses of travel and lodging. After that, three representatives from each jury participated in a five-day wrap-up discussion.

Thanks to official sponsorship and support for the Citizens Jury, its recommendations went into a bill to give farmers $10 million for water source protection. The juries' five-person lobbying committee, however, failed, perhaps because of external challenges such as the snowstorm that kept the committee's chair from arriving for a key hearing. But the jurors had also reverted into more familiar roles. The farmers on the committee promoted the interests of farmers, and the committee's two women from Minneapolis ended up feeling out of place. The bill itself also changed substantially as it wended its way through the Minnesota legislature. In the end, neither the law nor the citizen lobbyists were recognizable.

Citizens Jury failures came in many forms, and they frustrated Ned tremendously. Time and again, citizens would arrive at thoughtful recommendations that would end up having negligible influence on policymakers. In 1976, Ned tried to empower the Citizens Jury process by connecting it to elections. A first test asked participants to evaluate Gerald Ford and Jimmy Carter in that year's presidential contest. Even this approach didn't garner much national attention until 1990, when David Broder of the *Washington Post* called a Citizens Jury on the Minnesota gubernatorial election "one of the two most interesting voter reform projects in the nation." More acclaim came for a 1993 Citizens Jury evaluating the Clinton healthcare plan against viable alternatives.

This newfound visibility came at a cost. In 1993 the Internal Revenue Service (IRS) revoked their tax-exempt status, charging that the juries had become a form of political advocacy. After a three-year fight, the Jefferson Center finally reached a deal with the IRS, which agreed not to prosecute as long as the center quit hosting candidate forums.

Ned recalled that this three-year rumble with the federal government "brought us to a grinding stop, because we couldn't solicit foundation grants when under investigation. Any foundation was liable if they took a misstep." He fought vigorously, though, because he "discovered that voters were the ones interested in the Citizens Jury process—much more so than legislatures."

Around the same time, Pat retired from the teachers union and began working more directly with Ned in their attempt to expand the reach of Citizens Juries. One collaborator who helped with the IRS negotiations suggested that state governments might be interested in funding evaluations of gubernatorial candidates. Ned and Pat had bought a home in Washington State to be closer to family, and they soon had an audience with the state's former governor Mike Lowry, who led them to Ralph Munro, who served five terms as secretary of state. Munro found the idea intriguing but said it had to remain outside state government.

At Ned's request, Lowry convened a day-long "design lab" with a group of political experts. Just before lunch, Lowry said, "Why don't you use the method to evaluate ballot initiatives? After all, that's what is driving politics in most western states." Ned and Pat recalled that they "had a thirty-five minute lunch break to decide whether to change what we had been working on for two years. But it seemed like a good fit, so we decided to go for it."

Thus, the CIR was born.

In this new model, citizens would evaluate ballot measures rather than candidates. The details of the proposal were worked out through—what else?—a Citizens Jury. In conjunction with the League of Women Voters, Ned and Pat convened a randomly selected body of citizens to meet for a week in the city of Bellevue, just minutes east of Seattle. In her interview, Pat recalled that participants in the jury "worked through all the basic concepts." Their ideas "were fairly detailed," and the jury concluded that the proposed reform "should be paid for through public funds." Pat hoped the idea would resonate with the wider public in the same way it had with the jury. Nonetheless, she sensed that the idea's support was broad, but shallow. "We became exhausted," she recalled. "We realized we would never get enough backing to put an initiative on the ballot. At the same time, we took what the Citizens Jury had wanted and started fine tuning it into a formal law."

Triumph North of the Border

In the succession of Citizens Juries since the 1970s, Ned and Pat had seen how citizens benefited from access to good information when participating in a deliberative process. While Ned searched for a way to leverage this information to reform US politics, Canadian officials established a helpful precedent for citizen deliberation.

The CIR would not be the first successful attempt to link small deliberative groups to the larger public. Instead, the 2004 British Columbia Citizens' Assembly claimed that status. The assembly concept began as a campaign promise from a conservative provincial political party called the British Columbia Liberal Party (BC Liberals). (Don't ask; it's a Canadian thing.) That party had experienced one too many elections in which it won a sizable share of the provincial vote, only to end up with precious few seats in the legislature owing to the allotment of seats by district. Knowing that voters wouldn't trust a political party to rewrite the rules, the BC Liberals promised that if elected, they would let a randomly selected assembly of citizens design a new electoral system.

Their pledge to enact such reforms helped the party win 57 percent of the popular vote in that election. Though the status quo system translated that into seventy-seven out of seventy-nine possible seats, the BC Liberals resisted the temptation to renege on their promise and instead formalized their assembly proposal in a 2002 report to the parliament of British Columbia. Two years later, the process was underway.

The BC Citizens' Assembly consisted of 160 randomly selected citizens— one man and one woman from each riding (electoral district), plus two at-large Aboriginal members. Over the course of that year, the assembly met several times to study different electoral systems and choose the one best suited to British Columbia. In October 2004, 146 out of 153 assembly members voted in favor of a single transferable vote model, which lets voters rank candidates within multimember districts.

What made the Citizens' Assembly powerful was its access to the ballot. The parliament put the assembly's recommendation to a ratification vote by the people of British Columbia. The chair of the assembly, the former president of Vancouver's Simon Fraser University, noted this fact in his letter, featured in the body's final report:

Deliberations on electoral reform at the BC Citizens' Assembly. *Source*: BC Citizens' Assembly.

> Never before in modern history has a democratic government given to unelected, "ordinary" citizens the power to review an important public policy, then seek from all citizens approval of any proposed changes to that policy. The British Columbia Citizens' Assembly on Electoral Reform has had this power and responsibility and, throughout its life, complete independence from government.

When election day arrived on May 17, 2005, a majority of voters in all but two of British Columbia's seventy-nine ridings approved the proposal, with 57 percent of all votes cast in favor. Alas, the legislature had set the bar for passage at 60 percent, so the proposal failed. Post-election polling showed that many British Columbians backed the assembly's recommendation precisely because it had come from a deliberative body. Though many voters didn't understand what, exactly, a single transferable voting system would entail, they trusted the judgment of their peers.

An earnest attempt to replicate the BC Citizens' Assembly came in 2007, when Ontario took the same basic approach to electoral reform. Organizers had more difficulty establishing the legitimacy of their process and had even less buy-in from political parties and key media, such as the *Toronto Star*, which warned that chaos would ensue if the province adopted multimember districts. The end result was a crushing election defeat for the Ontario Assembly's proposal, which earned less than 37 percent of the vote and passed in only 5 of the province's 107 ridings.

Electoral Reform in Washington

Ned had the chance to see the BC Citizens' Assembly in person, and he was struck by the fact that its organizers had created it almost out of thin air. Their inspiration had been the use of random selection in ancient Athens, which had come up in a classroom discussion of election reform led by a teacher who knew prominent members of the BC Liberals. Few of the assembly's organizers were aware of the growing movement for deliberative democracy, though at least one had attended a Deliberative Poll in the United States. Once the assembly got underway, organizers sought advice from other scholars and practitioners, including Ned.

If a Canadian province could come so close to a successful reform without even standing on a tradition of deliberative experimentation, surely something could be done in the United States. Thus, in 2005 Ned and Pat developed draft legislation that asked Washington State lawmakers to fund citizen panels that would review statewide initiatives.

They found allies who believed they could champion the House and Senate bills in Olympia. From 2005 to 2007, Ned, Pat, and their supporters met with legislators and lobbyists. After a productive "informational public hearing" with the legislature in 2006, they hired a lobbyist of their own and thought they could have viable legislation the very next year. They garnered bipartisan support, with over a dozen co-sponsors in the House and eight in the Senate. They also had pledges from the two chairs of the relevant committees in the House and the Senate to hold hearings on the bills.

After a 2006 victory by the Democrats, however, both committee chairs took new assignments. Their replacements showed little interest in reforming initiative elections.

The last straw was a failed endorsement, which would presage future troubles. To make his case for the Citizens Jury, Ned commissioned a survey and found that 60 percent of Washington voters supported the reform he and Pat were crafting. Among those supporters was the head of a union. Ned said he'd "seldom met anyone who got the idea so quickly." Hoping to build on that potential, Ned and Pat sought formal backing. "We really thought we were going to get an endorsement from the public employee union," Ned recalled. "Their lobbyists had helped us pro bono after we made a presentation in front of them."

When the time came to pledge their support, the union lobbyists decided it wouldn't be politically expedient. As Ned recalled, their response was, "I can see what you're doing, and, frankly, I'm agnostic." A lobbyist put it this way to Ned: "It seems like more work for me because it means I would have to add another campaign to lobby the citizen panel, on top of what we already do." There would be no promise that any given citizen panel would go the lobbyist's way, so why bother?

In the end, the union stayed neutral. With a scattering of opponents wary of the cost that an unproven institution may add to an already overburdened state budget, the bill languished and died before coming to a vote.

Chance Encounters

Despite this setback in Washington, news of Ned and Pat's proposal reached that state's southern neighbor. In 2003, Ned had pitched their idea for citizen panels to the Walnut Street Co-op in Eugene, Oregon. Still developing his plans to introduce Citizens Juries to the formal electoral process, but before the unsuccessful attempt in Washington, Ned laid out his idea for democratic experimentation to an audience of activists interested in similar prospects.

In the audience that day was Elliot Shuford, the same young civic reformer who shared a love of beer with Tyrone Reitman. Elliot shared the details of Ned's talk with Ty, and they saw the power of Ned's citizen panels to address the problems inherent in direct democracy. Like many scholars and political actors before them, Ty and Elliot believed that manipulative campaigning distorted the original intent of the initiative process. Like others, they worried about the impact of campaign spending on electoral decisions and feared that voters often lacked the information they needed to make good decisions. Ned's idea for reform was inspiring, but it seemed like a long shot.

While Ned and Pat were still formulating the bill that would fizzle out in the Washington legislature, Ty took a break during his second year of graduate school. Like Ned before him, Ty had doubts about the necessity of finishing his degree. "I went for a walk to a nearby basketball court to shoot hoops and clear my head," Ty recalled, "when I got this elated feeling. Allergy season hadn't quite arrived, the sun was shining, and I realized I didn't want my thesis to be a waste of time." Ty said that his "activist tools were guiding my understanding of policymaking and change," and for his thesis to be meaningful he needed to incorporate those impulses into his academic work.

He started reading George Lakoff's cultural-linguistic interpretation of US politics and found his way to deliberative theorists, such as Jane Mansbridge, James Fishkin, Francesca Polletta, and the first author of the book you're reading. Ty tried to work out connections among social psychology, deliberation, group decision making, and activism.

During the break from his studies, Ty went back into politics, a little older and wiser than before. He returned with a better understanding of the problems facing contemporary democracies. For the last several months of graduate school, he strung together internships, including one with a respected yet controversial attorney who led a campaign finance reform effort called Fair Elections Oregon. Ty led the Eugene office and enacted a membership development plan that yielded a direct mail and phone list of two thousand small donors.

Ty was still working on that campaign when he completed graduate school, married Natalie, went on a honeymoon to Greece, and took up rock climbing. Though his spirits were high, he returned to see his political efforts falter. "I assumed that campaign finance reform would have a better reception," he admitted. He didn't think it got a "fair hearing," not only from the business community but also from labor leaders. "I watched the heads of the campaign contort themselves for years to meet labor concerns," he recalled, "but labor informally pulled the plug."

Internal conflicts came to a head at a high-stakes campaign event at Cosmic Pizza in Eugene, where the guests sat around circular tables. They "wore nametags and had paperwork for their presentations." During one contentious exchange, a progressive organizer Ty hadn't met before leaned over and whispered in his ear, "I don't know if you know this, but this is a really bad measure being pushed by bad people." Ty told her that he was one of the campaign's supporters, and she blanched. Someone later argued that the campaign reforms were "being pushed by wealthy people who want to make it hard on Oregon's progressive community."

Ty remembered standing up in the meeting, and saying, "That's not true. You know that's not true." He said the proposal meant that "everybody had to abide by the same rules, so how is that a bad thing?" Nobody had an answer, but the organizer simply said he was wrong. Not for the last time, he witnessed strategic political pragmatism shaping activists' views of public policy. Idealism fueled his personal activism, but among professionals, he looked naïve.

The problems he debated in graduate school now became all too real, visible within his own campaign as much as they were within the opposition's. Even though he believed in the ballot measures for which he worked, Ty was plagued by a feeling that the campaigns from both left and right were hiding from the voters crucial information they needed to make good decisions. Too often, campaigns tried to scare voters into casting their ballots for or against an initiative. Dollars seemed to be the dominant factor in whether ballot measures passed.

Discouraged by what he perceived as dirty politics, Ty reconnected with Elliot Shuford in 2006 to learn more about the Citizens Jury that Ned and Pat were undertaking in Washington. After a productive conference call, Ty and Elliot drove up to meet Ned and Pat at a diner just off Interstate 5 in Castle Rock, Washington—midway between Portland and Olympia.

Ty recalled having no clear expectations. "I hadn't done my homework and didn't know they were wealthy. Elliot might have heard from Tom Atlee that Ned and Pat had spent too much money on their own projects." Perhaps that had created "some jealously in the deliberation community," which included few people in Ned's situation. However different their backgrounds, they hit it off. "We were there four hours," Ty said. "I had six cups of coffee. We all got to know each other and had a really quick bond. They wanted to make sure we were coming from a good place." The four gradually realized they shared many of the same philosophical concerns, practical experiences, and passion for reform. The result was a "genuine connection."

Ned smiled when asked about the Castle Rock meeting. He remembered the venue was a little "mom-and-pop" not far from Mount St. Helens. Though it was cavernous and largely empty, once they were seated in the back corner, the place had a "homey feeling." Of course, they were there for the people, not the atmosphere.

"Pat has a better judgment of people than I do," Ned conceded. "She's quicker at sizing up people. Pat took to them and saw their value. They asked if we could use the process we'd developed in Washington, and we said yes. I think we surprised them because we said right away, 'Sure, you can borrow the process, and we're ready to help.'" As Pat put it, "We didn't have to hem and haw and think very hard. We were discouraged with Washington. We were tired."

They connected at just the right moment. Ty and Elliot had grown more skeptical of conventional politics—even progressive politics. Ned had a plan to address those concerns but was unable to gain traction. He was ready for a new project. Three years after Elliot first attended Ned's speech, they had become unlikely partners.

Invoking the progressive traditions that first brought initiatives to Oregon, Ty and Elliot convinced Ned and Pat that the state legislature might authorize citizen panels to review initiatives. They began developing a legislative strategy to institutionalize citizen panels as a permanent part of initiative elections. Ty and Elliot acted as co-directors of a board that included Ned, Pat, and Oregon civic reformers. They also formed an advisory committee that included former secretaries of state from both parties, along with legislative and election officials. Their organization, which they called Healthy Democracy, had a clear mission: to establish the first Citizens' Initiative Review. ✺

Lobbying the Legislature

In 2007, Healthy Democracy introduced House Bill 2911, sponsored by Representative Peter Buckley (D-Ashland), to the Oregon State House of

Representatives. The bill would establish a CIR in a manner similar to the proposal in Washington. With legislators wary of implementing an untested process, however, the bill quickly died in committee. Even with this loss, Healthy Democracy pushed on. The bill found supporters in the legislature, including Democratic state senator Kate Brown, who fortuitously became Oregon Secretary of State in 2009, then governor in 2015.

In 2008, Ty and Elliot tested the CIR with the help of the League of Women's Voters and financial backing from Ned and Pat. This early prototype was held in Salem, the same city where Marion would experience the first official CIR two years later. For the pilot test, Healthy Democracy gathered twenty-four randomly selected voters to match the demographics of the state. For five days, the citizen panelists studied and deliberated on Measure 58, which would limit the use of English as a second language for K-12 instruction in Oregon. Neutral experts, along with proponents and opponents, provided testimony to the panelists, who used that information to create a statement identifying key facts and arguments relevant to the initiative. At the end of the week, Healthy Democracy held a press conference outside the state capitol building, where the panelists presented their statement. The League of Women Voters independently evaluated the process and found that both panelists and advocates were highly satisfied with the CIR and did not perceive any bias.

Behind the scenes, however, tension was emerging. To help design the details of the CIR, Ned had hired Larry Pennings, a consultant with a unique background that included an MA in management from Antioch University Seattle's Center for Creative Change and a doctorate degree from the San Francisco Theological Seminary. Larry had worked with many collaborators on a detailed manual for how to run the process—a blueprint that still shares the basic features of the CIR today.

Pat recalled that she and Larry "decided Ned shouldn't be telling Ty and Elliot how to fine-tune the process while the event was underway." Ned conceded the point. "I knew that I would be a pain in the ass," he said, "so Larry took on the role of being the buffer." Sure enough, Ned recalls, "I kept seeing things that I thought could be done better, but Larry was right that I shouldn't keep jumping in to change things." As Ty recalls it, nobody could keep their hands off the process details, before and during the CIR, and the agenda's details changed each day as a result of critical reflection by everyone on the team.

At the same time, Ty and Elliot tried to negotiate the CIR's design with potential allies beyond their inner circle. Seeking accommodation from outside interest groups often proved frustrating. Ty recalled that leading up to the pilot project, he met with Our Oregon "a couple of times." This powerful progressive coalition was cautious about the CIR, and Ty said that he and Elliot "worked really hard to satisfy their concerns." Our Oregon sent a representative to the pilot test, but only to counter the sponsor of the "English immersion" ballot measure. In the end, the progressive nonprofit didn't back the effort to establish the CIR.

Declining to support is not the same as opposing, however, so the pilot was an overall success. After it concluded, then Secretary of State Kate Brown suggested that Healthy Democracy introduce the CIR as a one-year trial run, with the goal of evaluating more extensively its quality and impact. Thus, House Bill 2895 was drafted to establish the Oregon CIR pilot process. In Ned's earlier attempts at institutionalization, legislators had balked at the idea of implementing citizen panels, in part because they required government funding. After negotiating the bill with legislators, its authors reworded the legislation such that the Oregon CIR would still be housed within the government but would be funded by private donations.

Optimistic to their core, Ty and Elliot began walking the halls of the state capitol armed with no more than a bill and a successful test run. Accompanied by citizens who served on the 2008 pilot CIR, Ty and Elliot went door to door, lobbying for the adoption of their proposal. As they gained momentum, organizations that had withheld support gradually came on board. When the League of Women Voters produced a report vouching for the CIR's fairness, that organization, along with Common Cause, offered the CIR their endorsement.

Recognizing that citizen support would put pressure on hesitant legislators, Healthy Democracy reached out to the public and circulated a statement in favor of the CIR, gaining upwards of thirty thousand signatures. They showed to any willing audience a short video that explained the design and purpose of the CIR.

Soon, the chair of the House Rules Committee, Representative Arnie Roblan (D-Coos Bay), signed on to sponsor the bill and began lobbying for its passage. A bipartisan group of legislators followed suit, with seventeen members of the state House of Representatives and ten state senators signing on as co-sponsors. The bill received its first hearing in the House Rules Committee in March 2009.

According to testimony provided before the House Rules Committee, the CIR would supplement the more narrowly focused explanatory statement and financial impact statements that already appeared in the state's *Voters' Pamphlet*. Its statement would serve as an alternative to the more inflamed rhetoric that came to voters through paid campaign messages in that same pamphlet. It also had an important tactical advantage: the CIR promised to improve initiative elections without infringing on anyone's rights to spend money or campaign any way they wished.

Legislative critics with a libertarian bent, however, argued that the CIR would amount to a government takeover of the initiative process. They also opposed increasing the size of government and feared that long-term implementation of the project would require using public funds to convene citizen forums. From the left came the concern that the CIR could alter an initiative process that progressive activists believed they could steer toward their own purposes.

Carefully navigating between these opponents, Ty and Elliot brought together a majority of legislators who believed the initiative and referendum process needed repair. In the CIR, they saw a way to put reason and evidence at the forefront of the electorate's mind when it voted directly on such legislation. The CIR offered citizens the same kind of consultation process that legislators themselves relied on when considering the range of proposals put before them each session.

On June 16, 2009, the Oregon legislature approved House Bill 2895 with a vote of 47–7 in favor in the House and 23–7 in the Senate. Both Democrats and Republicans voted in favor of the bill, yet all the "Nay" votes came from Republican legislators.

House Bill 2895 allowed for an official test run of the CIR. More important, it required that the Citizens' Statements produced by the CIR's panelists appear in the *Voters' Pamphlet*. Though the bill included a sunset clause requiring evaluation before considering a permanent renewal, this marked the first time a consequential, government-sanctioned, deliberative project of this scale had been adopted in the United States. On June 26, 2009, Governor Ted Kulongoski signed the bill into law and paved the way for CIR pilot panels in the 2010 statewide general election.

No longer an idealistic dream, the CIR had become a reality. The state that first entrusted their citizens with direct policy elections would once again place their trust in an unproven political institution. Would such trust prove warranted?

A Crucial Test

On the morning of August 5, 2010, Marion walked into the lobby of the Salem Convention Center as one of twenty-four randomly selected citizen panelists serving on the first official CIR. A happy young man at the check-in desk offered her informational materials and an "I ♥ Democracy" bumper sticker. Carrying her handouts, Marion entered the conference room where she'd spend the next five days with strangers discussing drunk driving and sex crimes—the twin subjects of a statewide initiative.

After fixing some tea, Marion found her name card on the U-shaped table arrangement in the center of the room. As she took her seat, the back of the room filled with reporters, researchers, and pro and con advocates, who would hope to sway the citizen panel.

Ty walked around the room to greet Marion and her fellow panelists. He checked small details with his staff, mostly to calm his own nerves. The day had arrived. An abstract idea was now about to come to fruition, or go spectacularly wrong.

Breaking the Ice

Elliot took the microphone at the front of the room. "Good morning folks. Can everybody else hear me okay? I can't tell if it's—a little louder? How's this?"

And so began the citizen review of Measure 73.

Elliot told the panelists they'd spend five days studying this initiative. They'd meet advocates for and against, along with independent experts. By the end of the week, they'd have crafted a one-page Citizens' Statement for the *Voters' Pamphlet*, designed to help Oregon voters decide how to cast their ballots on the measure.

Marion flipped through her binder, eager to dig into the details. Its thickness worried her. One challenge was that this was two issues rolled into one. Measure 73 proposed a mandatory minimum prison sentence of twenty-five

Hope for Democracy. John Gastil and Katherine R. Knobloch, Oxford University Press (2020). © John Gastil and Katherine R. Knobloch
DOI: 10.1093/acprof:oso/9780190084523.001.0001

years for repeat felony sex offenders, and it boosted the criminal penalties for repeat drunk driving.

Elliot handed the microphone to the moderators. Panelists first heard from Larry, who was dressed in suit and tie and rocked on his heels as he spoke. Larry's co-moderator Robin had a reassuring voice and dressed in natural fibers. Robin invited the panelists to introduce themselves.

As each panelist shared a piece of his or her life, Marion started to feel a connection. One panelist said she almost threw away her invitation letter, dubious that the state would sponsor such a thing. Another said that she'd be missing the doctor's appointment where she'd learn if her daughter was pregnant. A few seats down from Marion, another woman introduced herself as Ann Bakkensen. She'd just retired from her position as a library assistant, and she looked the part, with close-cropped hair and a pensive expression. Ann was frustrated with the increasingly partisan tone of politics and was looking forward to working with other Oregonians to improve elections.

The mix of panelist backgrounds was by design. The event's organizer, Healthy Democracy, had worked with a local polling firm to sort through the accepted invitations and balance the citizen panel by age, gender, ethnicity, education, partisan affiliation, and geography. Even with an honorarium of $150 per day (close to Oregon's median daily wage), plus transportation, lodging, meals, and expenses, organizers received only 350 replies to its ten thousand invitations. The response rate was low, but demographic stratification ensured a diverse panel of twenty-four persons.

Such recruitment strategies have become common in the practice of deliberative democracy. Deliberative Polls, Citizens' Assemblies, and similar processes aim to bring a representative cross-section of the public together for face-to-face discussion. Hundreds of citizens are chosen at random, then carefully balanced to mirror the wider population. Combining the random chance that ensured every wealthy man in Athens had the opportunity to serve in government, for example, with the desire to correct identity-based power imbalances, stratified random selection addresses one of the biggest problems in contemporary democracy—the lack of representation that persists for many social groups.

A simple look at office holders in the United States illustrates the problem. Even with historic gains for women and racial and religious minorities in the 2018 midterm elections, representative inequalities persist. Women make up roughly half of the US adult population but hold slightly less than a quarter of the seats in Congress. Structural racism, sexism, and homophobia are even worse at the executive level. In 2019, there are no black governors, and up to this point there have only been four. Barack Obama is the only non-white person to have held the presidency.

Public forums like the CIR try to correct those imbalances by inviting to the table participants that better represent the diversity of society. The system isn't perfect. No sample can ever capture the nuances of thousands—or millions—of individual perspectives. Twenty-four randomly selected citizens can hardly say that they speak for the entire Oregon electorate. Even so, the Oregonians who sat around the table at the first CIR *could* speak to a more diverse array of lived experiences than are generally given a voice in modern political systems.

An invitation to the table, however, isn't enough. Deliberative democracy also requires that all participants have an opportunity to meaningfully engage in the conversation. After an overview of the agenda for the week, Robin introduced the ground rules. The CIR asks participants to engage in a novel style of political discussion. A key difference is to focus on learning rather than winning. That means listening to people who are different than you.

Robin urged the panelists to stay in "learning mode" as long as they could. "We're all different people," she explained. "We come in with different perspectives already on life. . . . That's fine, but we really want to understand not only the interests and the views expressed by advocates and other presenters, but also from each other."

The moderators encouraged the panelists to disagree with one another but asked them to maintain a positive attitude and to be respectful of different experiences and opinions. They encouraged them to listen with care and focus on the issue at hand, to be diligent in their search for facts and to offer their own thoughts even when they worried that others might disagree. Panelists spent the rest of the morning practicing this new way of talking by working through a hypothetical historic preservation dilemma.

After lunch, Ty explained the details of the initiative process, including how the state titles and summarizes ballot measures. The quiet audience made Ty anxious, and he closed by joking that he "either put you all to sleep, or I did a really good job." A question from Marion about the finer details of the *Voters' Pamphlet* reassured him. Like a juror at a trial, these panelists appeared to recognize the stakes of their deliberations. They were processing as much information as they could, as fast as they could.

Larry and Robin got the panelists out of their seats and instructed them to walk around the room. On the walls hung broad swaths of blue fabric, which the moderators referred to as "sticky walls." Different parts of the *Voters' Pamphlet* appeared there, including Measure 73 itself. As they read through the information, panelists wrote down the questions forming in their minds, which were then placed on the wall next to the relevant passage and read to the full panel. Afterward, panelists read through written statements by the pro and con advocates and reflected on what issues were at the crux of the initiative.

At the close of an exhausting day, Larry and Robin asked the panelists to show up fifteen minutes early the next morning. Not a day in, and Marion felt rushed and exhausted. She returned to her room and hoped she'd feel refreshed the next morning.

Twenty-Four Hearts and Minds

Marion returned to the conference room Tuesday morning less nervous than she'd been the day before. Getting to know some of her fellow panelists helped, and she made small talk with them while they grabbed coffee and not-quite-stale pastries. At 8:15, Larry called the panel to order.

The first presenters that morning were representatives from the advocate teams. Retired district attorney Doug Harcleroad represented the Oregon Anti-Crime Alliance, which got Measure 73 on the ballot. Joining him at the front of the room stood his chief opponent, Gail Meyer—a legislative representative for the Oregon Criminal Defense Lawyers Association. They offered a joint response to panelist questions from the day before and defined key terms, such as "statutory counterpart" and "criminal episodes."

Marion squirmed uncomfortably when Harcleroad defined "sexually explicit conduct" with more graphic detail than she would have preferred. He let out a disconcerting laugh and said, "You can read the definition as many times as you want to."

As it turned out, Marion and the other panelists wouldn't need to do so. Proponents would remind them repeatedly of the horrific crimes and tragedies their ballot measure was designed to prevent. When it came time for his opening arguments, however, Harcleroad took a surprising approach.

"I'm a big believer," Harcleroad said, "that you can't make a good decision if you don't have the information you need. And this process scares me because you know very little about the criminal justice system, and you only have a week to learn a lot."

Perhaps Harcleroad meant the words for reporters in the back of the room, but to many panelists, it came across as a rebuke—of them, the CIR process, or both. Some picked up immediately on the irony: Even with a week of intensive study, the panelists couldn't possibly understand a measure that Harcleroad now put before the entire state electorate.

The most compelling witness Harcleroad introduced was Brittany Griffis. She sat down at the front of the room and related her personal experience of childhood rape. After recounting the details of the attack, she told the panelists that her assailant received only a little more than eight years. Every two years, she attended a parole hearing to keep him behind bars. If the measure passed, she explained, it would spare victims from having to sit with their perpetrators, at least "for that first twenty-five" years of a criminal sentence.

The mood in the room shifted. This wasn't the sound-bite rhetoric of professional politicians. Keeping herself in learning mode, Marion couldn't help but sympathize with a woman, not so unlike herself, who had to confront her attacker because of lenient sentencing laws.

When that was followed by testimony from a mother who lost a twenty-three-year-old child to a drunk driver, Marion could feel the force of the argument for this measure. The mother had received the news of her son's death on her own fiftieth birthday. "At that moment," she explained, "everything changed, right down to the tiniest speck of dust. I felt I had been skinned, and gutted, and left to die."

The measure's proponents closed with a sheriff passing around special glasses with distorted lenses. Panelists who donned the "fatal vision goggles" experienced the disorientation of a severely drunk driver. Begoggled volunteers drew laughs as they staggered about the room. The levity eased the transition into a cooler period of questions for the proponents. Already beginning to understand the complexity of the measure, panelists' questions ranged from rehabilitation options to parole processes to the strain the measure might place on the state's general fund.

After a short break, Gail Meyer began her pitch against the measure. She told the panelists that Measure 73 would upset the balance of power in the courtroom by removing the judge's discretion and the defendant's bargaining power. Mandatory minimums, she argued, give all that power to the prosecutor, who can use the threat of tougher sentencing to convince even innocent defendants to plead guilty to lesser crimes.

Meyer moved to what might have been an unintentional feature of the ballot measure, which was written by policy advocates, not professional legislators and their staff. She presented a hypothetical case in which a minor could end up in jail for twenty-five years.

> It can go like this: a sixteen-year old boy in the neighborhood sexually exploring some other kid in the neighborhood. There's one instance at the neighborhood picnic. Another instance a week later behind the tool shed. The sixteen-year old is now arrested. This measure means that if he goes to trial, this crime would merit a twenty-five-year mandatory minimum sentence, regardless of the age of the offender, as long as they're fifteen-, sixteen-, or seventeen-year-olds. He's in front of the judge for the very first time and had absolutely no opportunity for treatment.

Delicately, Meyer even defused the power of Griffis's testimony about confronting her attacker every two years. Oregon law had changed; parole boards no longer had the power to reduce a rapist's sentence. After introducing two other attorneys who affirmed the panel's concerns about fiscal impact, the opponents brought forward victims of their own.

Julie Smith was a victim of sexual abuse as a child, and she spent the last decade advocating for victims. Smith said, "I was twenty years old before I told anyone. And at that point, my life was pretty much of a mess. Ms. Griffis spoke so eloquently about the impact of crime and sexual violence, and I'm sorry to say that I went through a lot of similar experiences." Unlike Griffis, however, Smith favored devoting limited state funds to victims of abuse, who deserve better counseling, shelter, and prevention advocacy programs.

"Last year," Smith explained, "there were over 19,500 requests for emergency shelter from violence that had to be unmet because we just didn't have enough money to meet the need. Every day women and children are being turned away from services that can help them rebuild their lives."

As Smith spoke, Marion weighed the different perspectives offered by Smith and Griffis. Both had been victims of horrific crimes, but they were advocating for vastly different policies. And so it went again when the opposition brought a witness in a wheelchair; paralyzed by a drunk driver, she said she needed assistance more than any solace tough sentencing might offer. "My insurance will not cover this chair. Given the choice for where to spend the money, I have to choose a wheelchair over an attorney."

After another round of questions and answers, Harcleroad introduced the president of Crime Victims United to offer a rebuttal. Steve Dole shared his colleague's bare knuckle approach and impugned the opposition for misrepresenting themselves as victims' rights advocates. After arguing that Oregon already did a good job providing counseling and other services, he layered on top of that a more libertarian argument: "Government cannot continue to do everything for people." The legitimate purpose of government, he argued, is "not to educate people, pour concrete, or build parks. It's to protect our citizens."

All that, and it wasn't even lunch yet.

After a quiet period of reflection, Larry and Robin released the panelists. Over a heavy salad, followed by a rich chocolate cake, Marion continued to talk about the ballot measure. She and her fellow panelists recounted to each other the testimony from advocates and witnesses. Weighing the arguments she'd heard, Marion couldn't decide which way she might vote on the issue. If anything, she had more questions now than before she had arrived in Salem.

The afternoon offered less drama, as the panelists broke into small groups to study different aspects of the ballot measure and to distill the information they heard in the presentations. Following the discussion rules introduced the day before, participants listened to and learned from one another. They analyzed the information provided by the advocates, looked for the most reliable evidence, and noted any lingering uncertainties. They asked each other probing questions and told stories of their own experiences. When participants did get off track or had trouble working through disagreements, the moderators encouraged them to refocus the conversation and reminded participants of their discussion's ground rules.

Right outside of the room, however, a conflict began to surface that was not so easily placated. Harcleroad and Dole complained to Ty and Elliot that the panelists were misstating the facts, so—ever the forceful advocates—they demanded extra time to make their case.

Their frustration likely stemmed from a sense of dread. When the small groups reported back their findings to the full panel, it didn't look good for Measure 73's advocates. Ann offered a concise summation of the disparate arguments she'd heard in her own group that morning: "Mandatory sentencing may act as a deterrent in reporting cases of domestic violence within families—not a deterrent to violence itself." Another group reported its fear that the measure would ensnare juvenile offenders unintentionally.

Robin thanked the panelists for sharing their findings and told them to take a break. Technical difficulties and other snags had prompted unplanned breaks already, and panelists grumbled at Robin's announcement. Thinking quickly, she offered a point of praise: "I've never heard a group complain about having to take another break, but this group—you're very unique." When a ten-minute pause wasn't enough for staff to get ready—now, a printer had jammed—panelists resumed their discussions anyway, rehashing information they'd heard and trying to reconcile conflicting arguments.

The day closed with the pro and con advocates reinforcing what they considered their most crucial arguments. Harcleroad couldn't help squandering time berating the process. The initiative advocate couldn't quite distinguish the role of this quasi-jury, designed to help more than a million voters, from the formal procedures of a trial, where attorneys argue a case before a jury. The CIR "falls way below, way below what would be in a courtroom, and that's what I'm really used to."

After reviewing key financial and legal details, Harcleroad closed with a claim that jarred some panelists. Referring to an earlier ballot measure that established mandatory sentences, Harcleroad said, "Measure 11 has reduced just a huge number of crimes. What does that really mean? That means that at least my wife hasn't been raped. There's thousands and thousands of victims who have not occurred because of Measure 11."

Such stark language proved to be Harcleroad's rhetorical style, and panelists responded with furrowed brows, open mouths, and occasional grumbling.

When panelists deliberated, however, they rarely referenced these emotional appeals—instead responding with questions of fact.

The opposition took a subtler approach. They responded to proponent claims, then offered advice on which expert witnesses panelists should call the next day from a long list provided by Healthy Democracy staff. They wrapped up quickly enough to leave time for questions.

Ann raised her hand:

> I hope I can ask this question in a way that doesn't sound like I already have decided what my answer is. It's more coming out of a sense of confusion after hearing a lot of information. One issue in my mind is the victim versus the offender, and how do you balance out fairness to both of them? I believe, Gail, you said there was an unintended consequence—for example, if the beloved uncle or a coach may have been repeatedly harming a child—that if that person came up to the judge for the first time, the fact that he had done something repeatedly would kick in the maximum twenty-five-year minimum. Is that wrong? I'm not saying it is or isn't, but apparently you think it's wrong and I was wondering why.

Trying to stick by the rules Robin had given her the previous day, Ann added, "Again, I'm sorry. I don't mean this in an antagonistic way, but I want to understand your reasoning."

Across the table, Marion noted Ann's tenor. Whatever the advocates were doing, at least the panelists were staying in learning mode. In that moment, Marion became a little more hopeful. Here were everyday folks, coming together to discuss tragic crimes but digging into policy issues in a way she'd never experienced. Amid efforts to sway opinion with salacious detail, the panelists were making their way through the information. Empathizing with witnesses. Scrutinizing the evidence. Parsing the underlying arguments. Deliberating.

Sifting and Bickering

The panelists spent much of Wednesday seated at their U-shaped table listening to—and questioning—a parade of witnesses. The moderators controlled the flow of conversation, ensured that participants had equal opportunities to speak, and asked participants to reframe their questions when they sounded too much like argument. The fact that the citizens soon would have to summarize all this for an entire state electorate helped many panelists stay alert through economic projections, alternative treatment program analyses, and minute details about anything from prison beds to plea bargains. Even so, panelists became fidgety, distracted, even bored.

Panelists came back to life during a lively presentation by Craig Prins, the Executive Director of the Criminal Justice Commission. A self-proclaimed "data nerd," Prins gestured enthusiastically while standing in front of a detailed PowerPoint presentation that each panelist had in a binder. Prins maintained a conversational style even when covering difficult material. "Okay, so please look at Section 2," he said at one point. "I hope this doesn't make you uncomfortable, but I'm going to go into some detail [on] these types of sex crimes." At the close of his remarks, panelists erupted into spontaneous applause to show appreciation for his testimony.

After a lunch break at noon (dry but passable sandwiches with a key-lime pie), it was time for the panelists to start drafting the main section of their Citizens' Statement. The daunting task required panelists to extract a handful of sentences from information that now overstuffed their binders.

Leafing through her own papers, Marion felt overwhelmed. She'd begun to understand Measure 73, and was formulating an opinion of her own on the initiative. Transferring that knowledge to the state's voters was a different problem. How could a panel that had a week to study an issue share what they'd learned on a page that would take just three minutes to read?

Pushing aside such doubts, Marion picked out bits of information she'd found pertinent. Longer sentences imposed by a previous initiative had minimal effects on recidivism. The violent crime rate had declined since its passage, but that correlation didn't prove a cause-and-effect relationship. Robin interrupted this stream of thought to ask the full panel to break into subgroups, each of which would identify two things to include in the *Voters' Pamphlet*.

Each day, the CIR moved smoothly back and forth between a full panel and smaller discussion groups, but results varied. This time, Marion's group included Mark, a retired lawyer who relished the civic opportunity the CIR provided. He bristled when the professional moderators rejected his attempts to improve their process. Mark took a firm grip on the group leadership role, and Marion struggled to find her voice. When another panelist claimed Measure 73 would "disrupt the balance of power in the courtroom, putting all the power in the hands of the prosecutor," Mark questioned the phrasing.

Afraid that Mark was putting words in that panelist's mouth, Marion suggested, "Let's get the idea down, then we'll adjust it." A fellow female panelist backed her up: "I would say that we could just sort of brainstorm, put a lot of things down."

"No, I understand," Mark said. But did he really? His explanation left Marion flummoxed. "It's easier to brainstorm," he argued, "if we do a little wordsmithing. I mean, you're saying two things, and I'm asking, I'm not trying to dictate it. Would you think it preferable to say that it impacts the balance of power, or it inappropriately does something?"

Marion pressed the issue. "Yeah, but I don't want to get to that yet."

"I know that, but this is where the process begins, Marion. I hate to tell you, if we start making a lot of words, that's going to be too much."

The argument escalated enough to attract the attention of Larry and Robin. Prompts from the professionals didn't help. "Are you guys all"—note the *all*—"getting an opportunity to write some things down?" Even after the panelists turned their backs to the moderators, and Robin went to another group, Larry hovered over Mark like a schoolmaster. He rocked back on his heels, visibly displeased with Mark's directive style but without any license to intervene further.

At the back of the room, a higher stakes power struggle was taking place unbeknownst to the panelists. Harcleroad and Dole were more concerned than ever that the panelists had turned against their ballot measure. After all, their initiative was polling statewide with a two-thirds majority in favor. If these panelists were turning against it, perhaps the *process* was to blame.

These disgruntled proponents pulled Ty and Elliot into the hall for hourly chastisements. Their substantive complaints ranged from factual minutiae (a certain treatment program doesn't admit repeat offenders) to procedural flaws (no cross-examination, testimony isn't given under oath). At one point in the afternoon, when they disagreed with one particular expert witness, Harcleroad and Dole guffawed. Heads swiveled. Panelists shot them dirty looks.

Undeterred, Dole tried soliciting Mark, the retired attorney serving on the panel. During panel deliberations, Mark had made statements implying his opposition to the ballot measure, but at least he'd been fighting with the moderators. Mark listened politely as Dole rattled off process concerns, until Ty saw the scene and broke it up with a reminder: Panelists and advocates shouldn't interact outside of public sessions. Mark hit the snack table and fixed another cup of coffee, unperturbed by Dole's ham-handed tactic.

Closing Arguments

Thursday was the last chance the advocates had to speak to the panelists. This time, the opponents went first. They again praised the work of the panelists, noting that these citizens spotted the same problems in the proposed law that professionals had identified. Meyer said, "You guys have heard a lot of information—way more than any other voter ever, ever will."

With a few minutes to spare, Meyer returned to a question asked the day before about the legislature's ability to amend the law. She noted the legislature had to suspend the previous mandatory sentencing initiative (Measure

57) because it didn't have the resources to fund attached treatment program requirements. Changing the law required a two-thirds majority, and achieving that had created "epic warfare in the Capitol Building."

That claim was too much for Dole, who jumped up from behind his folding table at the back of the room. "You know, I have to stop this!" he shouted. The measure was *not* a mandatory minimum sentencing law—a point that was technically correct, though Measure 57 increased incarceration times for certain crimes. Moreover, he pointed out, the legislature's two-thirds majority threshold had been met four times in fifteen years.

Elliot rushed over to intercept Dole and calm him down. From the front of the room, Larry reminded Dole that his team would have their opportunity to address the panelists in just a few minutes. Though shocked by the outburst, the panelists turned their attention back to the measure's opponents, who simply ignored Dole altogether.

At this point, it should come as no surprise that when Dole and Harcleroad stepped before the panelists, they seized the opportunity to attack the process itself. "I got to start with this," Harcleroad exclaimed, "Ms. Meyer was wrong, flat out wrong." After reviewing the specifics, he offered this olive branch to his opponent. "She didn't *intentionally* lie to you folks," Harcleroad said. "She just doesn't know. And she was wrong."

When Dole's turn came, he, too, mixed contrition with rage. "I just want to apologize to Ms. Meyer," Dole said, "and to you for my outburst. But you know what? Enough is enough." Like a pro wrestler pleading to the audience after a crooked referee called the fight, he said, "I tell you what, I will debate anybody, anytime, about things I support. And I respect people who disagree with me, but I like to have a balanced debate. And you're not getting any balance here."

These same proponents who had pleaded for more time to lay out their arguments now rushed through the factual evidence they chose to review. They added handouts to the panelists' binders but hurried through them to ensure time for a video.

Cut to a long, gruesome slideshow, put to music.

Speakers filled the conference room with Bon Jovi's "It's My Life." The digital projector showed a slow-moving sequence of graphic car crash stills. Like jurors forced to study crime scene photos, the CIR panelists watched in awed silence the procession of automobiles in flames, bloodied pavement, amputated limbs.

Next, Garth Brooks's "The Dance" played over the aftermath of a drunk-driving fatality: dead bodies, gory head wounds, beer cans strewn across the highway. Some of the pictures were accompanied by text, which ranged from descriptions of how the crash occurred ("Leaving a [Minor in Posession] party") to drunk driving statistics. One slide highlighted the annual number of drug and alcohol-related traffic fatalities without providing information about the years in question or the geographic area referenced. The scant citations that did appear came in fonts tinier than those used for disclaimers during prescription drug commercials. No fact sheet was provided with the video.

As the slideshow continued, a few panelists teared up. One wept openly. Mark got up from his seat to talk to a colleague across the table. One panelist simply left the room.

For many in attendance, the jarring juxtaposition of this display against the rest of the CIR was too much. The panelists had accessed—and scrutinized— more information on Measure 73 than any voter would come November. They'd asked nuanced questions about the efficacy of treatment programs. They'd compared projected prison costs to potential law enforcement savings. They'd reconciled the fact that prison time can reduce the crime rate by keeping offenders locked up, even while making no dent in the likelihood that a crime is committed in the first place. In the context of such deliberation, the video felt jarring.

At the close of the day, Marion said as much to the staff. "Please pass on to the pro advocates," she said, "that certain tactics don't work. Scare tactics, in particular. Their time could have been spent in much more informative ways today. It made me angry that they wasted my time, when they could have been giving me facts."

Sending a Message to the Voters

Advocates weren't the only ones who needed to use their time wisely. Panelists still had to decide what information to include in their Citizens' Statement, and as Mark had warned, they risked rushing through the editorial review that the task required. Their page in the *Voters' Pamphlet* had to be concise, grammatically correct, and easily understandable for the average voter.

Anyone who has written a document via committee could have guessed that this final, crucial step was tedious. Panelists spent several minutes crafting just one claim: Measure 73 would tip the balance of power in the courtroom toward the prosecution. The panelists went back and forth, debating whether they should mention plea bargains, how they should talk about the shifting balance of power, and whether any of their revisions were actually making the statement more understandable to voters.

One panelist wrote a full revision down in his notebook, then read it aloud: Measure 73 "shifts the balance of power in court proceedings giving the prosecution additional leverage in plea bargaining and limiting the judge's discretion in sentencing individual cases." The panelists applauded the suggested revision, thankful to have made progress on at least one claim.

With one sentence of the Citizens' Statement written on the eve of the final day, the moderators decided to adjourn, but not before assigning homework. They gave the panelists a copy of the remaining claims they'd generated, asked them to review each one before the next morning, then dismissed the panelists for the evening.

After a restless night, Ty and Elliot conferred with staff over breakfast. The process was running behind schedule. Panelists still had to write the rest of the main ("Key Findings") section, draft arguments for and against the measure, and more. The hard deadline was a press conference, scheduled for 4 p.m. that afternoon.

Relieved that the end was approaching but wary about the work in front of them, the Healthy Democracy staff ran through the revised agenda. They'd built in some flex time for day five in case delays arose. Even then, all they could do was hope that the panelists could get the statement done by 3:30 p.m., when a chartered bus would take them to the state capitol.

Marion awoke that morning with a similar mix of optimism and trepidation. She'd learned a lot about the initiative. The previous day's testimony had solidified her stance on the issue, and she was eager to get to work. Still not quite sure they'd get the statement written in time, she'd already achieved something. The process had renewed a sense of pride—in herself and in democracy. Despite the doubts that lingered from her America*Speaks* experience, despite all the process frustration, and despite the insults from the pro advocates, Marion felt confident that she and her fellow panelists would prove equal to the challenge placed before them.

She walked through the lobby and into the conference room to find friendly faces. She talked with Ann, who confessed to being amazed they'd made so much progress. In Ann, Marion had found a kindred spirit, someone who could see past her own political affiliations and explore the issue and who wanted to make the best decision, whatever party it most closely aligned with. Marion learned that Ann and some of the panelists had formed an ad-hoc committee the night before. After eight long hours of deliberation, they'd stuck around and continued to work, editing and refining the most popular claims from the previous day. This would enable the panelists to more quickly edit their draft statement in the morning.

The final day of the CIR got underway by reviewing statements the ad-hoc committee had edited. After each claim was posted, the panelists worked together to make sure that it included each bit of necessary information while still being clear enough for voters.

Just as they had done the previous afternoon, panelists spent several minutes debating the inclusion of one word or the elimination of one phrase. When the claim, "Current Oregon law (ORS 137.700) provides mandatory minimum sentencing of 70 to 300 months for major felony sex crimes as listed in Measure 73," was proposed, several panelists spent time debating whether to reintroduce an "already" before "provides" that had been eliminated during the ad-hoc committee's editing. Some panelists thought this would make it clear that an existing law already met the concerns raised by the proposed initiative, but others felt this implied judgment that would be better left to the arguments in opposition to the measure.

Attempting to explain to the group how the ad-hoc committee had arrived at the decision to eliminate "already," Ann said, "We thought that by saying 'already provides' we were suggesting that we didn't need Measure 73 and we were trying to be more neutral by informing people that, Hey, we already have a mandatory minimum sentencing for the sex crimes as listed in Measure 73, so maybe people would think those were enough. That could be put in an argument."

"So, your intent was to leave it as neutral as possible by not saying 'already'?" Robin asked.

"But I'm not trying to impose my will on anybody by leaving 'already' out," Ann replied, "So, if people want 'already' in, that's the group decision."

Conversations like that continued for the next several hours, with panelists growing increasingly exasperated by the slow pace and the difficulty of collective editing. One of the biggest sources of disagreement about the statement was whether to mention Measure 11—a previous initiative that had established mandatory minimum sentencing for some violent crimes. Though several of the panelists thought that it would confuse voters unfamiliar with the initiative, others felt that it had been an important part of their conversation. At one point, Robin tried to end the conversation, after an informal vote revealed that most panelists didn't want to mention Measure 11.

Some panelists, however, felt that the move was presumptive. Alex was a middle-aged woman who often chimed in to share her personal experiences. She had a relative who was incarcerated under Measure 11 and insisted that they retain the reference to it so that people in similar situations could understand the relationship between the proposed measure and the earlier one.

At the end of a lengthy conversation about the reference to Measure 11, Alex seemed fed up with her fellow panelists' dismissive attitude. Referring to the current version of the claim in question, Alex said, "I've seen it and read it in the book, and it don't even jump out at me."

"Okay so let's keep working with it," Robin responded, "We haven't actually decided yet, so we need to hear from you what needs to be changed about it, Alex."

"If I was a voter and I'm reading this—I read it [last night] to my old man and he said, 'What? That don't even make sense.' So, it's not really jumping out. If we're going to write something, let it jump out at the voters. This is not jumping out, period."

"So, this is the opportunity if you have any suggestions for improving the statement let us know," Robin pleaded patiently.

"Well, let's go on to the next one," Alex reluctantly responded, "but we're not writing it yet, but that sentence right there is not jumping out. It's not making me feel like, 'Okay, I'm going to vote for this because it's going to shift the balance to the prosecution.' It's not jumping out. I didn't vote; that's why. Why should I? Because everybody's already taken over. If somebody says something and then it goes. This is supposed to be a group thing, and it's not."

"You are actually going to vote when we get the sentence fully crafted. You are going to vote on whether or not to put it in the pamphlet."

"Why should I vote? My vote don't count."

"It does if you say no," Mark said.

"You voted for it yesterday," said another panelist.

"Yeah, but then after I got to my room and I read it, it doesn't make sense."

Mark looked to Robin, "Point of order to the chair. I really think this is out of order." Turning to Alex, he said, "You're criticizing the whole group, and it's unnecessary now."

"I'm not criticizing the whole group."

"I'm offended," Mark went on, "and I really wish that you would stop it and you'd call her out of order. This is not appropriate. We talked about treating each other courteously and we've had a member of this group diss everybody in the group. And I'm sorry, that is not the way the rules are provided."

As Mark railed against Alex's interruption, Ann jumped up from her seat and ran over to Alex, putting her arms around her shoulder and bending down to confer with her.

"I'm not listening to him," said Alex.

Trying to calm things down, Robin intervened. "So, okay we are trying to strike a balance between making sure that all of the voices in the room are heard. And Alex, I think this is important for you to hear. Just a minute, Mark."

"I'm not dissing anybody," Alex replied. "You been taking over the whole group," she said to Mark, "so don't even get me started. Every time somebody talks, you take over the whole group. And I'm saying what other people are not going to say."

Sensing that Alex was feeling like an outcast, another panelist spoke up. "Alex, please don't feel like the lone ranger, because we've all had disagreements this morning already. That's the nature of bringing twenty-four individuals together to come to a consensus."

"All I'm saying is it's not jumping out," Alex replied. "We need to come up with something else. That's all I'm saying."

Robin took control of the conversation again. She told the panelists that they'd talk about it a bit more and that they'd have another chance to vote on it. After some back and forth, Ann spoke up. "I'm sorry if this is getting us further off track. I did not originally vote to have Measure 11 included in this language, but I would like to propose that we do have Measure 11 included in the language in some way to make everybody's voice be heard. And I feel like it's really important for all of us to feel valued and I think maybe all of us at some point in this process have questioned ourselves, and it's not a comfortable feeling. And I would like to do what I can, and hopefully everybody else can—well, anyway, how's this for proposed language? 'Measure 11, passed in 1994, (ORS 137.700) provides mandatory minimum sentencing.' Sorry if that's just making it more cloudy, but I want people to feel honored."

During the argument, a short woman in a gray pantsuit had entered the audience gallery at the back of the room and was engaged in quiet conversation with Ty and Elliot. When Ann had finished, Robin told the panelists that they'd put the conversation on hold because they were about to hear from a special guest. Kate Brown, the Oregon Secretary of State, was there to observe the process and talk to the panelists. Brown walked to the front of the room and addressed the panelists.

Good morning, everyone. . . . I think you know the Secretary of State oversees our campaign finance laws, and I've worked really hard on initiative reform over the last number of years and was very supportive of this concept of the Citizen's Review Committee. I am just so thrilled that each and every one of you took time out of your busy schedules to participate. I know this has been a challenging and interesting process, but your time and energy, I think, will really make a difference, and I'm really glad you were able to participate. I just came by to say thank you and you're almost there. You can make this happen. And we're just really excited. We're working to make sure that these statements get in the appropriate places in the Voters' Pamphlet, and hopefully it will have a huge impact in Oregon on the initiative process. I'm hoping we're going to be able to go national at some point. So, thank you. You guys are the pioneers.

After a quick round of applause, the panelists got right back to work. Reinvigorated by the secretary of state's encouragement, they were eager to make sure that their work got done, and done well. Once four or five statements had been edited, Larry stepped in and said that time was running out. He asked the panelists if they'd be comfortable using what they'd already produced without adding additional statements, noting that they'd have to take time from other parts of the process if they wanted to continue working on the key findings section. Most panelists agreed they were ready to move on, so Larry and Robin led the group as they voted on the inclusion of each individual statement that they'd just edited. While most of the statements had broad support from the panelists and made their way into the key findings, only one received all twenty-four votes in favor: "Passed in 1994, Measure 11 (ORS 137.700) provides mandatory minimum sentencing of 70–300 months for the major felony sex crimes defined in Measure 73."

When all of the claims had been approved, the group next had to vote on accepting the key findings as a whole. As the staff worked to pull up the slide to vote, the panelists, tired from their work and antsy for a break, began to grumble. Misreading the room, Larry asked the panelists to stand up and turn around three times in one direction and then three times in the opposite direction—an action they'd asked the panelists to do previously as a centering exercise.

This time, only about half the panelists complied while the rest remained seated. As the staff struggled to prepare the vote, Larry snapped his fingers in impatience. Immediately realizing his mistake, he apologized profusely, while some mischievous panelists shouted, "Take three deep breaths!" Finally, the panelists unanimously approved their completed findings before being dismissed for lunch.

When they came back from lunch, everyone had left the room except for the moderators and two staff members who would act as scribes for the next session. For the next hour and a half, the panelists were responsible for writing the statements in favor of and in opposition to the measure.

To protect the privacy of the panelists' vote, only they and the moderators would be allowed in the room. The moderators instructed those in favor of the measure to head to the front of the room, where a group of chairs had been arranged in a semi-circle in front of a projector. Panelists in opposition to the measure would work in the back. Slowly, each panelist went to a group, but only two panelists went to the front. Sensing those panelists needed more support, an undecided panelist joined them.

Ultimately, the panel voted twenty-one to three against the measure. The Citizens' Statement they produced, from the key findings on down, raised grave concerns about Measure 73. After reconvening and sorting through the final details, Robin and Larry invited the panelists to reflect on their five days together.

Mark was one of the first to speak, and he showed a self-awareness that might have surprised some of those who had spent the week with him. "I know I'm an outspoken person," he said, "and I want to apologize if, at any point during the course of these proceedings, I've offended anybody here." He made a point of looking around the room, from panelists to moderators to Healthy Democracy staff. "While I think everybody came in here with kind of some tentative views on this, I really felt that the process of hearing competent evidence on both sides became a catalyst for what I believe was forming a very substantial consensus." He was impressed to see that, if put in the right process, "people do change their opinions, and that's the best thing we can say about a healthy democracy."

Alex sat beside Mark, who she also joined for lunch. They had (mostly) worked through their earlier conflict, and she appreciated the honesty she saw in the room. "I'm glad I got to meet everybody here," she said. "Everybody has different opinions. You say what's on your mind." She hoped she hadn't "offended anybody," then joked that "Mark says I did, but I don't think so." With one last chance to needle him, she added, "*He* was the one hogging the group, so— nobody should get mad about this because we're all human, and we've all got our own voice. Some of you voted with, some of you voted against it. That's all I got to say."

Marion's turn to speak was fast approaching. She tried to figure out how to sum up her experience. When all eyes turned to her, she had one word in mind. "This has been an *amazing* week," she began. "I anticipated it would be amazing, but not this amazing. I'm so encouraged by the diversity of our group and the across-the-board intelligence that we all have brought to the table and all have contributed, whether in the small groups or the large groups. The attention to detail, the willingness to correct one another and to improve upon what we're doing—it's just been *amazing*." To make sure the panel saw the larger point of it all, she added, "I really hope that everybody takes this as an example of how we could do governance in a much better way than perhaps is currently happening."

Minutes later, she and the rest of the crew took a bus ride to their press conference. Marion wasn't born in Oregon, and she'd never visited the capitol building. Getting off the bus and walking up the steps, she said that she had a moment of quiet recognition. The magnitude of what they'd accomplished together struck her.

For a full week, a group of everyday citizens had come together, across party lines, to study an issue before deciding how to vote. In modern political life, if we vote at all, we often toe the party line or rely on campaign ads we know we can't trust. Rarely do we talk to people who might disagree with us, and if we do stumble into a conversation with a political adversary, we tune out information that contradicts our own opinions. Marion had the chance to try another mode of politics, and to share it with the whole state. The press conference wasn't really the point; only a handful of reporters were there to listen to their statement, and the news accounts that followed focused on the novelty of the process, not the substance of the panelists' insights. But just a few weeks later, the Oregon *Voters' Pamphlet* would broadcast to every voter what Marion and her fellow citizens had learned.

The inaugural Oregon CIR panel reading their Citizens' Statement in front of the state capitol. The inscription on the wall reads, "A free state is formed and maintained by the voluntary union of the whole people joined together under the same body of laws for the common welfare and the sharing of benefits justly apportioned." *Source*: John Gastil.

Marion, Ann, and the rest of the panelists boarded their bus and returned to the hotel, where they would gather their belongings and transition back to their daily lives.

For Ty, Elliot, and the rest of their staff, there was no time to rest. Their democratic experiment had passed its first test, but its second iteration would begin in just three days. After a hectic weekend of preparation, the process would start all over with a new issue, new advocates, and new panelists.

This first week, they'd barely made it through. The pro advocates had threatened to walk out. Right until the end of the last day, no one was sure if the Citizens' Statement would get written on time. Even if it ended well enough, much had gone wrong. To ensure success, the process had to be rethought and reconfigured. After a round of celebratory beers on Friday evening, Ty and his colleagues got some much-needed sleep. On Saturday, it was back to work.

The Best Argument Wins

In the forty-eight hours between the first and second CIR, Ty, Elliot, and their staff set goals for themselves. This time, advocates' expectations would be managed better, lest one side or the other vent their frustration in front of the panelists. The last two days of the process had to run more efficiently, or the panelists would be forced, once again, to rush through the drafting and editing of their all-important Citizens' Statement.

Most of all, panelists needed a clearer orientation to what at times became a confusing process. A week ago, the CIR was something no citizen had experienced before, but that was no longer true. Twenty-four Oregonians now had firsthand knowledge of it. Two of those citizens would address the second cohort of panelists, who would study a proposal to change Oregon's medical marijuana laws.

Ann volunteered to be one of the panelists to stand before her peers, and she began her remarks with a personal introduction: "When I came down here last week," she said, "I brought my knitting. But I left my knitting in the room because the week was so action packed. There was so much going on—listening, writing, thinking, discussing, disagreeing, trying to build a consensus."

"It's challenging," Ann explained, to be "on the edge of your seats all week." The panelists would thrive, nonetheless, if they remembered three things. First, "on behalf of the citizens of Oregon, listen for facts. Whatever opinion you come in with, that's fine, but when the final product is issued, whether you're for the measure or against the measure, tell some good reasons why."

Second, the panelists should enjoy the chance to hear different points of view. "There are too few times in our everyday life," Ann said, "where you can disagree with somebody, but then have the time to understand why, or understand where they're coming from." Everyone on the panel, and the advocates they'd meet, would get a chance to express their view "because that's what democracy's all about."

Ann added one last piece of advice. "Don't be afraid to speak up," she said. "You could be the smartest person in the world and have the best ideas, but if you

Hope for Democracy. John Gastil and Katherine R. Knobloch, Oxford University Press (2020).
© John Gastil and Katherine R. Knobloch
DOI: 10.1093/acprof:oso/9780190084523.001.0001

don't have the courage to speak up, your ideas will never be shared by the group, and the group will be a lot weaker. Whether you're a Republican, Democrat, however old you are, wherever you live, whatever your occupation, you are representing others, and it's your responsibility to them to speak up."

Ann concluded by saying that she suspected the panelists shared her frustration with politics and politicians. "Just about the only thing that we can agree on is that people can't agree on anything," she said. "But we can't rely on the politicians to change this." Her voice quavered. Ann paused to contain her emotions. "I get all choked up when I talk about this," she said, "because the change has to come from us. If we can work together to make the process better, then I'm hopeful that it will be an opportunity for others to see how it can work."

One week prior to her speech, Ann wasn't quite sure this type of democracy was possible. Now, she was leading the charge.

Do We Really Listen to Each Other?

After a week of neglecting her knitting, Ann believed that the CIR disproved the idea that "people can't agree on anything." She told the new crop of panelists to listen, learn, and let the best argument win because she thought that was what her pioneering panel had achieved. But had it?

The story recounted in chapter 5 suggests that Ann, Marion, and their peers deliberated. Even so, skeptics remind us that appearances can deceive. Some researchers might doubt the validity of what Ann claims to have witnessed. For instance, one decision-making theory—tested dozens of times on mock juries and all manner of odd laboratory groups—holds that initial majorities usually overwhelm minority opinions. Group members might believe their discussion was consequential, but they would have reached the same decision even if they'd never bothered to meet.

If discussions don't matter, why do they sometimes feel so compelling? Another theory has a ready explanation: People talk *as though they are listening*, but they really aren't. This account holds that, more often than we care to admit, we behave as though attending a high-stakes cocktail party. We want the guests to notice us and find us clever company. Thus, we opine at length while observing conversational norms that require us to at least feign attention. "That's interesting, and it reminds me of a story." Or, "It's funny you say that because just yesterday I saw the most amazing thing."

Theorists have the luxury of positing axiomatic rules that even they know amount to nothing more than insightful generalizations. Majorities do often prevail, but minorities can turn the tide. The dramatic story arc of *Twelve Angry Men* may overstate the likelihood of a single juror bending the will of eleven skeptics, but it does occur. And though all of us can stoop to boorish behavior, we can recall moments when we listened, learned, and changed our minds. Even the dead-eyed children who professed to "need no education" in Pink Floyd's *The Wall* probably learned a useful thing or two from their sadistic schoolmaster.

When it comes to listening, however, politics presents special challenges. Recall the discussion, in chapter 3, of the Cultural Cognition Project, a research program that shows how often people follow their political instincts when seeking and processing information. People watching the same video see different things depending on their cultural standpoint. When hooked up to wires that record an image of our brains, it's easy enough to see the footprints of credulity when we hear things we want to believe and resistance when confronted with inconvenient information.

Such brain scans became common only in this century, but even ancient historical texts note humanity's stubborn resistance to learning. In 399 BC, the good people of Athens saw fit to brew a hemlock cocktail for Socrates on account of his heresy against the religious dogma of the day. Scholars debate to this day whether the jurors who convicted and sentenced one of their city's greatest philosophers demonstrated the power of democratic judgment or mob rule, but when the American experiment was just beginning, human fallibility and the excesses of righteous mobs weighed heavily on the minds of the Founding Fathers. Harking back once more to a familiar colonial correspondent, John Adams noted that the ancient Greek governments were "subject to irregularity, confusion, and absurdity." They frequently devolved into "mob rule."

Modern reformers likewise recognized the public's capacity for resistance to reason. Ned Crosby knew of this liability when he conceived of the Citizens Juries process in the 1970s. Tyrone Reitman learned the same lessons working on initiative campaigns.

What gave them hope was the idea that citizens can defy conventional logic when placed in a special setting designed to encourage deliberation and discourage dogma. Time and again, Ned had witnessed the power of carefully crafted discussion procedures in the Citizens Juries, which routinely yielded sensible judgments. By the time the CIR became a possibility, Ned and Ty could also point to the success of Deliberative Polls, another innovation that had replicated many of the Citizens Juries insights about the potential for everyday citizens to produce a different kind of talk.

Political philosopher James Fishkin devised the Deliberative Poll when he sought a way for the general citizenry to reason its way through public problems that involved conflicting values. To get beyond the simplistic responses collected daily by pollsters, Fishkin created "a direct face-to-face society for its participants and a representative institution for the nation state." By meeting together for two or three days on a small set of issues, the citizens attending a Deliberative

Poll could arrive at an informed judgment "that begins to approximate what the public *would think*, given a better opportunity to consider the questions at hand."

Since its inception, more than a hundred Deliberative Polls have been held. Research on these polls has shown that meeting face-to-face with peers and experts can transform public opinion—sometimes in surprising ways.

Consider the example of the Texas Public Utility Commission, which sought to understand the policy direction that Texans would have them take. In a series of Deliberative Polls, the citizens of this oil-rich state shifted time and again in a direction that defied the common stereotype of Texans as hostile to environmental reforms. Fishkin found that "the percentage willing to pay more on its monthly utility bill to support renewable energy went from 52 percent to 84 percent. The percentage willing to pay more for conservation went from 43 percent to 73 percent."

More remarkably, the Deliberative Poll has caught on in China, where the government remains disdainful toward the very concept of "Western democracy." Professor Baogang He has studied China's adaptations of deliberative methods, which face special hazards in an authoritarian political system. For instance, he assessed the 2005 Deliberative Poll in the township of Zeguo, which played an advisory role on infrastructure spending, reminiscent of the Participatory Budgeting process discussed in chapter 1. As is often the case in such exercises, over the course of their meetings, citizens developed strong preferences for bolstering the basics—in this case, building new sewage treatment plants. The upside of such policy input in a country like China is that a central party determined to bolster its legitimacy can act quickly in response. Sure enough, the local People's Congress did just that by approving the top-rated projects that emerged from the poll.

In the Chinese context, public meetings have strict agenda constraints, in accordance with national political imperatives. From the perspective of an anxious authoritarian state, however, it makes sense to give local communities a strong voice on matters in which the Chinese Communist Party has little stake. "Deliberative democracy lets people add their voices to concrete policies," He explains, "and that can help the government make itself accountable, without taking political risks. Thus, the Eighteenth Party Congress in 2012, "emphasized that deliberative democracy is important for China." Deliberation draws Chinese people into decision making, He explains, "but does not change the power structure."

Whereas Deliberative Polls provide citizens with access to experts, an Irish experiment in public deliberation seated elected officials and citizens together to form a Constitutional Convention that ran from 2012 to 2014. The organizers of that process included legislative leaders to ensure the body had political muscle, but they worried that the members of parliament would strong-arm the randomly selected citizens seated among them. To their delight, the data suggested otherwise, with citizens having a clear and direct influence on the recommendations that body produced. The politicians themselves were so impressed that when it came time to convene a new assembly to continue their work, they recommended a body composed entirely of randomly selected citizens.

The bottom line? When brought together to deliberate, people—across a wide range of cultural contexts—can change their minds. Under the right conditions, political and policy experts can provide useful information to citizens without steering them to a preferred conclusion. Public opinion changes can follow a pattern that shows we can consider the wider context of issues and the complex connections even among people accustomed to disagreeing on all things political. Useful quibbling can be conducted over the details, but the evidence is there: We *can* listen. When given the right setting and incentives, we *do* listen.

Mapping Cultural Divides

But what of Ann, Marion, and their fellow CIR panelists? Did they listen to one another? Were they able to think beyond the limitations of the biases they brought with them to the conference room in the Grand Phoenix Hotel?

To answer that question, we return to the vocabulary of the Cultural Cognition Project introduced in chapter 3. This research program uses a shorthand terminology to describe the different cultural groupings into which people divide themselves. Along one axis lies the clash between individualism and collectivism—a continuum ably represented by Australia and the United States on one end and China and Nigeria on the other. Perpendicular to this axis lies the conflict between egalitarianism and hierarchy or traditionalism. In US politics, linguist George Lakoff channeled this dimension when he contrasted the "nurturing parent" metaphor for government's role in society used by political liberals with the "strict father" metaphor preferred by conservatives.

Every political ideology, party, and individual person has a location on this two-dimensional grid, and the Oregon electorate is no exception. To get a sense for how one can locate voters on this cultural map, put yourself in the shoes of a survey respondent. The phone rings and a friendly young voice—in this case a female college student—invites you to participate in a public opinion survey. She promises it will "only take a few minutes." Owing to politeness, boredom, civic duty, or for some undiagnosed condition, you agree. After some questions about the current election, the interviewer asks you to react to a series of statements.

"The government interferes far too much in our everyday lives," she says. "Do you strongly agree, agree, disagree, or strongly disagree?" When considering your response, you may notice that "neither agree nor disagree" is missing, because the interviewer wants you to commit one way or the other. You may also want to protest that "it depends," but she won't have it. On to the next item: "Sometimes government needs to make laws that keep people from hurting themselves." One by one, she walks you through six such statements. They seem to come at random, because they do, in fact, come at random. Your answers go into a database, then into a statistical dataset, from which will emerge your "individualism" score.

Another set of six items probe your hierarchical or egalitarian tendencies. How do you respond to the statement, "We have gone too far in pushing equal rights in this country?" How about, "Our society would be better off if the distribution of wealth was more equal?" Again, the result is a single score.

Multiplied over nearly two thousand phone calls, these data provided a portrait of where the Oregon electorate stood across the cultural map in the fall of 2010, just weeks after Ann gave her speech to the second CIR panel. As it happens, the cultural makeup of Oregon voters looks much like that of the US population as a whole, which has been measured in much the same way.

Figure 6.1 simplifies the statistical distributions and also overlays the locations of Oregon's political partisans. This cultural grid divides the state into four ideological quadrants. The top left represents hierarchical individualists, and the shaded area with the GOP elephant encompasses the 32 percent of Oregon voters who identify as Republicans. The opposite corner houses the egalitarian collectivists, within which a smaller circle holds most of the 37 percent of Oregon voters who call themselves Democrats.

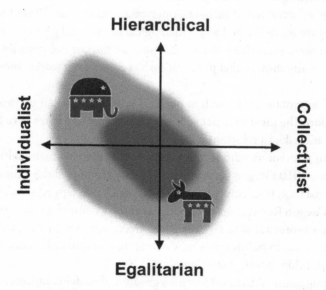

Figure 6.1 The Oregon electorate and the two main political parties on the cultural map.

Two other shapes in Figure 6.1 represent the bulk of the Oregon electorate. The larger gray blob covers the overwhelming majority of responses to the survey items, and the darker blob in the middle represents the central cultural tendencies in the state. There is no "true middle" to this graph, since there doesn't exist a perfect set of survey questions to ask, but enough survey data has come to confirm what the figure shows: most voters favor individualism, with a smaller majority leaning toward egalitarianism. Also, note the expanse of dark gray in the lower left quadrant. Those people are more commonly referred to as *libertarians*, an ideological group that has, from time to time, flexed its muscle, particularly within the Republican Party.

Figure 6.1 also shows that the central two-thirds of the two parties' memberships lie on opposite ends of the cultural spectrum, with a considerable distance between them. Thus begins the myth of the fully polarized US electorate.

Many political observers insist that Americans can't see eye to eye. In the context of the 2016 presidential election, it may seem hard to argue against that claim. Exploiting racial, religious, and educational divides, Trump captured four-fifths of white voters who reported attending religious services weekly. Clinton won the same share among whites with college degrees who had no religious activity. One can slice that year's vote many different ways, with the largest gaps being the least surprising. Nine out of ten Democrats backed Clinton, but Trump won over Republicans by the same margin, even with no major media endorsements and opposition from prominent GOP leaders.

The problem goes deeper than Clinton versus Trump. For example, a 2014 Pew study of over ten thousand Americans found that "Republicans and Democrats are more divided along ideological lines—and partisan antipathy is deeper and more extensive—than at any point in the last two decades." In 2017, a follow up study showed that polarization has gotten even worse since the 2016 election.

A small mountain of research in political science has taken on this polarization question. The most succinct summary is that partisan elites have grown farther apart and asked a reluctant public to follow them.

One can find voters who locate themselves at the two main cultural poles. Those in the 2010 Oregon survey who said they supported the aims of the Tea Party, for instance, formed yet another oval, which overlapped with the top-left corner of Oregon Republicans. For political elites, a cultural location on this grid shapes their professional fates. This is not necessarily so for the average voter. Most people turn to politics only now and again and otherwise attend to a daily life that has milder political overtones.

Returning again to Ann and Marion's group, and its deliberations on sentencing law, the question is whether they—and their peers—could render judgments independent of their preexisting cultural biases. And the CIR was not daily life. It was an exceptional *political* experience.

For Oregon in particular, the cultural map has a special meaning in regard to ballot measures. In anticipation of the 2010 CIR, a Western Oregon University public policy professor led a team that analyzed the twelve most important Oregon ballot measures from the prior decade. Figure 6.2 shows that half the statewide initiatives came from the egalitarian-collectivist quadrant, as measured by the rhetoric used by the measures' proponents. That same quadrant also played a role as either sponsor or principal opponent in every one of the important initiative campaigns during that decade.

What the students conducting the analysis of these initiative campaigns did not know was that their results would correspond with a reality well known to anyone who follows that state's politics. A political coalition had formed in the egalitarian-collectivist quadrant and dubbed itself Our Oregon. This not-for-profit organization saw its mission as "fighting for economic and social fairness"

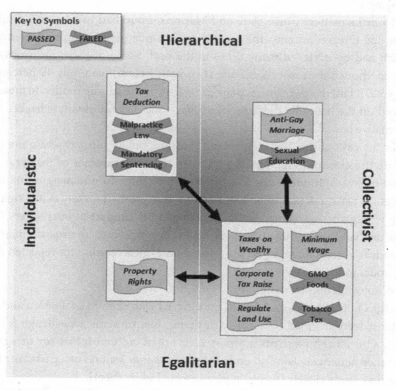

Figure 6.2 The cultural origins of twelve major ballot measures in Oregon from the ten years prior to the 2010 Citizens' Initiative Review.

and preserving "funding for our schools and critical services" and the Oregon environment.

As Figure 6.2 shows, that meant launching as many important initiatives of its own as it thought necessary to fend off those sponsored by opponents in the other three cultural quadrants. It also required taking a position on *every* ballot measure. Our Oregon opposed various laws championed by conventional Republicans (hierarchical-individualists). They fought against a 2007 libertarian (individualistic-egalitarians) measure that aimed to protect landowners against government restrictions. They countered social conservatives (hierarchical-collectivists), who opposed same-sex marriage and a curriculum regarding homosexuality in public schools.

Transcending Bias

As it turns out, the politics of ballot measures map onto the cultural grid quite well. In this environment, would it be possible for a CIR panel to do anything other than replicate the cultural clashes that typify statewide initiative campaigns?

To make matters worse, Ann and Marion's group had to take on a familiar issue for Oregon voters—the question of mandatory minimum sentencing, which had been visited many times in the past. Some of these measures had passed, though the most recent one (two years before) won only 49 percent of the vote. It faltered owing to its poor comparison with a more moderate measure placed on the ballot by the legislature. Sixty-one percent of voters backed that alternative law.

In the case of the 2010 sentencing measure, public support was quite high before the election. Preliminary polling in the early summer of that year had those in favor outnumbering those against by a three-to-one margin. Initiative designers place a premium on wording the "title" of their measures just right, to help with gathering signatures but also to win the support of busy voters. This measure had a compelling title, as it would simply require "increased minimum sentences for certain repeated sex crimes" and "incarceration for repeated driving under influence."

Who could oppose that?

Our Oregon could, and did. Many citizens who skewed egalitarian and collectivist were inclined to agree with them. This presents a challenge for the CIR: Can citizen panelists get past their initial cultural biases for or against "tougher sentencing laws" to understand the *specific features* of a particular law? Can they study closely the ballot measure put before them?

The description of the deliberation in chapter 5 would suggest that they did so, at least once. After all, twenty-one out of twenty-four panelists ended up opposing a still-popular measure—one that coasted to victory with over 56 percent of the vote in the final tally. Doubters could ask, though, if the result reflected not a deliberative shift but a skewed sampling of the electorate. Could it be that—in spite of the demographic stratification Healthy Democracy ensured for the panel—its cultural makeup was off-kilter?

Figure 6.3 provides the answer by matching up the panelists' final positions on the measure with their responses to a survey they completed two months after they completed their CIR duties. The panelists who attended the 2010 CIR on the mandatory minimum sentencing measure matched up well with the wider Oregon electorate, including representatives of the far right of the Republican party and the far left of the Democratic Party. Only three voters favored the measure: one was culturally centrist, with the other two representing opposing quadrants.

The pattern in Figure 6.3 matches with another perspective on Ann and Marion's panel. An end-of-week survey asked the panelists to recall what their views had been entering the CIR. Two-thirds said that they began their deliberations at a neutral position on the issue, with an even number starting out in favor or opposed (four on each side). The three who ended up favoring the measure consisted of one early supporter, one who began as neutral, and one who initially opposed it.

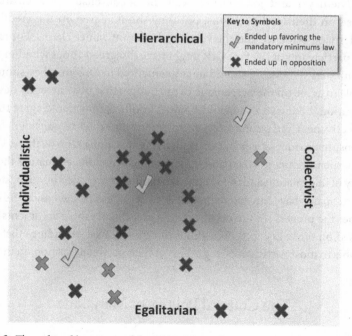

Figure 6.3 The cultural locations of the 2010 Citizens' Initiative Review panelists and their final position on the mandatory minimum sentencing measure.

Put simply, Ann was right. Her panel had listened to both sides and arrived at final judgments one could not have predicted—on the basis of either their deeper cultural orientations or their pre-deliberation assessments of the measure. The overwhelming majority of panelists, regardless of their cultural biases, simply found arguments for the mandatory minimum sentencing law inferior to those opposing it.

But should we expect this type of agreement regardless of the issue? If participants can't agree on a final judgement, has deliberation failed? On this question, it helps to step back from this particular CIR to consider the broader questions it engages.

For assistance, we turn to political theorist Jane Mansbridge, who argues that consensus might be an aspiration, but it shouldn't be a practical goal—not least because it is rarely achievable. Though competing political parties may sometimes agree based on their interest in the common good, different social groups often have interests in direct conflict. In such cases, deliberation can clarify those tensions so that participants can understand and respect one another, even if they ultimately disagree.

The CIR's design reflects this perspective. Rather than encouraging participants to arrive at a single judgement on a ballot measure, the CIR asks participants to seek agreement around questions of evidence and arguments, or what Simon Niemeyer and John Dryzek call "meta-consensus." Participants need not agree on their final decisions, but they should agree on the credibility of the underlying evidence and the validity of relevant values claims. For example, though participants at the first CIR might have disagreed about whether mandatory minimum sentencing should be implemented in Oregon, they should have been able to agree on the percentage of the budget that was currently devoted to incarceration. Likewise, even amidst values conflicts they could agree that both cost effectiveness and public safety were important values to consider.

To ensure broader agreement on underlying questions such as these, CIR participants spend hours in small and large group discussions evaluating the factual accuracy of information and the validity of arguments provided by advocates. Only after participants have identified the credible claims and pushed aside the dubious ones does the process shift to constructing a range of plausible arguments pro and con based on those key facts. The aim is to arrive at a set of findings that appears reasonable to most participants, regardless of their personal position on the issue.

The Cultural Politics of Marijuana

The first CIR had produced this result, but would the next week's panel succeed? The second CIR had a fresh set of twenty-four citizens, who had before them a new issue and a new team of pro and con advocates. This panel met August 16–20, 2010, to compose a citizens' statement on Measure 74, the title of which promised the establishment of a "medical marijuana supply system and assistance and research programs" and the "limited selling of marijuana."

Spoiler alert: Oregon voters rejected this measure, with only 44 percent in favor on the final count. Had it passed, the measure would have done many things, each of which the CIR panel had to consider. Oregon had already legalized medical marijuana through an initiative, but the previous measure prevented anyone from selling it. This new measure would have created a nonprofit system to license the production and distribution of medical marijuana and set up an assistance program for low-income patients. Under the measure, the state would be allowed to conduct and fund research concerning the medicinal use of marijuana, and certified growers and caregivers could increase the number of mature plants in their possession from six to twenty-four.

The advocate team for this measure included a mix of legal and medical professionals, along with moving testimony from patients using marijuana to alleviate the pain stemming from various maladies. The opposing side consisted of a sheriff and district attorney from Clatsop County, which encompasses the northwestern corner of the state.

One could tell as compelling a story about this deliberation as for the mandatory minimum sentencing CIR that preceded it. The advocates began with wide-ranging arguments for the measure but had holes blown through their case by a furious assault from the Clatsop duo, a pair that had worked together for years and were unrelenting in their argument that the measure lacked sufficient enforcement and specificity in its regulatory detail. Medical marijuana dispensaries, they argued, were a stalking horse for legalizing pot.

For a time, the opposition's criticism of the measure held sway, but in the final day of rebuttals, the proponents counter-attacked effectively on two fronts. They refocused attention on the needs of patients who have difficulty accessing a legal drug. Though Oregon already permitted medicinal marijuana, infrastructure was insufficient to meet demand. Proponents also revealed that the critics from Clatsop had crafted a ballot measure of their own, which was truly vague in its language. By comparison, the marijuana dispensary law seemed carefully crafted.

Though the tide swung in favor of the measure's proponents, they earned only a narrow victory, with a thirteen-to-eleven vote in their favor. Moreover, the Citizens' Statement these panelists wrote opened with an unwelcome sentence: "The language of the measure lacks clarity on regulation, operation, and enforcement. (23 of 24 agree)." Though super-majorities of panelists also signed on to more favorable words in that same statement, such as the new law's financial self-sufficiency and its recognized medical value, proponents had won only a partial victory.

This storyline, however, distracts from the question posed earlier about Ann and Marion's panel: Could one predict the outcome of the CIR's deliberations before it began? Did panelists' cultural biases underlie their judgments, such that the egalitarians and libertarians favored the marijuana dispensaries and the cultural conservatives opposed them?

As it turns out, the panelists *did* split along cultural lines. Figure 6.4 shows the distribution of panelists for and against the measure, with a horizontal white line dividing the midpoint in scale responses between hierarchical and egalitarian survey responses. All but one of those who ended up supporting the measure lie on the egalitarian side of that dividing line, and three-quarters of those who opposed the measure scored as hierarchs.

This pattern matches statewide survey data, which showed that of the two CIR issues in 2010, the strongest cultural predictor was the hierarch-egalitarian dimension on medical marijuana. Seventy-one percent of voters who identified as egalitarian said that they intended to support the measure, whereas a nearly identical percentage of hierarchical voters pledged to oppose it.

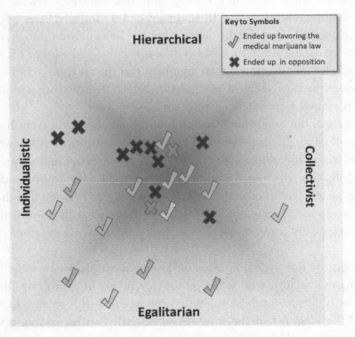

Figure 6.4 The cultural locations of the 2010 Citizens' Initiative Review panelists and their final position on the medical marijuana measure.

Moving Beyond the 2010 Panels

In a sense, the citizen panels conducted in the first year of the Oregon CIR show very different outcomes. The result of the mandatory minimums measure was striking, in that panelists from every cultural quadrant turned against a measure that had a large majority of Oregon voters behind it. By contrast, on medical marijuana the deliberation resulted in a pattern that split along the cultural divide between egalitarians and hierarchs. In sum, the CIR transcended culture and politics in one case, but perhaps not in the other. The two panels showed that deliberation could yield a cross-cultural consensus but such a result was not guaranteed.

Perhaps the reasoning is simple. In the case of the mandatory sentencing measure, panelists could reach near consensus across cultural divides because they were faced with a badly written law that had numerous unintended consequences. Regardless of whether one supported or opposed tough-on-crime policies, this measure seemed a poor means of implementation. A better written law, such as the one crafted by medicinal marijuana advocates, allowed panelists to grapple more readily with the values inherent in the proposed policy. In this case, the panelists could cast their votes based on their cultural predispositions. Here, votes reflected their different ideas of what Oregon's future should look like rather than a statement on the policy as written.

These mixed results introduce a new question: Are some issues better suited to deliberation than others? Was there something specific about mandatory sentencing that allowed participants to overcome their predispositions and shift their opinions. Does medical marijuana policy have a unique characteristic that encouraged participants to vote according to pre-determined positions?

An analysis of CIRs across several years suggest that it's difficult to predict what will lead to higher levels of participant opinion change. Even when measures deal with similar issues, such as genetically modified organisms, CIRs have resulted in split votes on some policies and overwhelming support on others. Parceling out which issues are more ripe for deliberation, however, is difficult to do prior to sorting through all the facts in a careful manner. In short, it takes a little deliberation to figure out whether an issue is *suitable* for further deliberation.

A study led by an undergraduate honors student at Pennsylvania State University explored this distinction between moral and technical issues in a clever experiment. Direct democratic elections often present voters with interlinked choices: voting for one measure could cancel out the effects of another one on the same ballot. For example, in 2015 the Ohio state legislature put forward a technical measure opposing state-sponsored monopolies to counter a marijuana legalization initiative. A survey experiment conducted with registered Ohio voters measured the impact of a CIR-style guide to see if it could help reduce the confusion these two ballot measures might produce. Sure enough, exposure to the issue guide substantially reduced the rate at which pro-marijuana voters inadvertently supported the counter-measure. To weigh competing values against one another, voters needed to understand that a vote against monopolies was, in this case, a vote against legalizing marijuana.

Results such as these suggest that the CIR's impact might vary across different electoral contexts and issues, but more pressing questions dogged the CIR itself. Foremost was the question of whether the legislature would renew the process, which had been established in 2009 on a one-year trial basis. With legislative hearings on the horizon, opponents would have the chance to kill this electoral reform before it became law.

Bureaucracy and Boycott

The 2010 CIRs had been a success. The panelists learned about the initiatives, deliberated respectfully, and wrote helpful Citizens' Statements that voters could use when casting their ballots. But with the close of the CIR on medical marijuana, Ty and his colleagues faced a new problem. The bill that had initially instituted the CIR, HB 2895, had included a sunset clause. The legislature had approved the inclusion of Citizens' Statements for the November 2010 initiative elections, but the continuation of the process required the passage of a new bill. If Ty, Elliot, and all the supporters they'd garnered along the way hoped to see CIRs implemented in the future, they had to get to work.

Making a Sales Pitch

Before the elections on mandatory minimum sentencing and medical marijuana were complete, Healthy Democracy had already begun lobbying the state legislature for the passage of a new bill. House Bill 2634 would renew the CIR in perpetuity and include the statements produced by its panels in the *Voters' Pamphlet* for future initiative elections. In addition, the bill would create a state commission responsible for overseeing and eventually implementing future CIRs.

Building on the momentum garnered when passing HB 2895, Ty and Elliot returned to the halls of the state capitol relying on old allies and identifying new legislators who might be willing to lend their support. They began with the original fourteen state legislators who had sponsored the pilot bill. As they branched out to others, they alternated their requests for support between Democrats and Republicans to ensure that the bill wouldn't receive a flood of support from one party that aroused suspicion in its counterpart.

The highest priority was convincing the legislature that the 2010 CIRs had worked as intended. The House and Senate Rules Committees welcomed testimony to assess the quality and statewide impact of the CIR. In late 2010 and

Hope for Democracy. John Gastil and Katherine R. Knobloch, Oxford University Press (2020).
© John Gastil and Katherine R. Knobloch.
DOI: 10.1093/acprof:oso/9780190084523.001.0001

early 2011, legislative hearings featured Ty and Elliot, citizen panelists, initiative advocates, and independent researchers evaluating the CIR.

Marion was one of six participants whom Healthy Democracy asked to advocate on behalf of the CIR bill. When identifying panelists to testify on their behalf, the Healthy Democracy staff looked for a cross-section of participants, just as they had done when selecting panelists for the CIRs, selecting a mix of Democrats and Republicans as well as rural residents and city dwellers. More important, however, was that the participants had the chance to speak in their own words. Ty and Elliot were careful not to coach the participants or tell them what to say. In a few cases, they provided feedback on written testimony, but only at the request of the participant. Recognizing the passion that the citizen panelists felt for the process and the intelligence they'd brought to the CIR, they simply asked participants to speak honestly about their experience.

When Ty asked Marion if she could testify for the CIR in front of the legislature, she wasn't quite sure that she was up for the task. Such duties seemed beyond the realm of an average citizen. Sure, Marion had enjoyed her time in the CIR, but relaying her story to her state senators and representatives seemed far more daunting. Seldom do everyday citizens have the opportunity to interact with their elected officials in ways that matter. They might write their senator a letter or attend a rally when their preferred candidate runs for office, but actually providing input on important policy questions rarely happens. More often, citizen input is tallied by a staff person who may or may not tell their boss that twenty-three people left angry voicemails in opposition to a contentious bill, or that they'd received a flood of form letters favoring some new proposal. This would be much different.

On an overcast morning in early February, Marion drove from Portland to the capitol building in Salem to speak in front of the House Rules Committee. The committee would be deciding whether to add any amendments to the bill and ultimately whether the bill would go to the full house for a vote. Driving down the hour-long stretch of Interstate 5, as the Portland metropolis and its bridges gave way to twisting highways, farm lands, and thick forest, Marion went over her testimony. Approaching the state capitol, she once again looked up to the top of the capitol building where the statue of the golden Oregon pioneer resides. Only six months ago she'd entered the building for the first time after the CIR press conference on the capitol steps. Back then, that trailblazer had been awe-inspiring—the manifestation of the pride she'd felt upon completing a week of deliberations that had renewed her faith in the power of democracy. Today, it evoked trepidation.

Searching for the committee room in the labyrinth of halls that contained legislative offices and meeting rooms, Marion was relieved when she turned a corner and saw familiar faces. Pausing his conversation with another CIR panelist,

The Oregon state capitol building in Salem. *Source:* Healthy Democracy.

who was also there to testify, Ty turned and smiled at Marion as she approached. Marion hurried toward the group, eager to meet again with some of the people she'd come to know so well only a few months prior.

When the time came for their hearing, Marion entered the room with Ty and Elliot and the other presenters who were there to testify. She followed Ty to the row of seats in the audience section and settled in, looking around at the raised platform where some of her state representatives would sit in a semi-circle looking down at her as she provided testimony from the table in the center of the room.

Soon after, the hearing began. The committee chairperson called the session to order. First on the docket was amending HCR10, a resolution to honor the U of O's football team—the Ducks had played in the BCS National Championship and deserved special recognition. The matter was quickly settled, with even those attending the rival Oregon State University voting in favor. Next up was HB 2634, the measure that would establish the CIR in perpetuity.

Ty and Elliot were the first to provide testimony. At this point, both men were seasoned pros who had been working with members of the legislature since 2006 to establish the CIR pilot process. Ty gave a brief overview of the CIR and argued that the state needed it. "As all Oregonians know," he began, "ballot measures often deal with very complex issues, significant fiscal tradeoffs, significant policy implications. Given that the stakes are often so high . . . a lot of money is spent to sway votes one way or another. That's not necessarily the same thing as informing voters. That's where the CIR really steps in. The idea is to provide voters with clear, useful and trustworthy information about ballot measures."

He and Elliot then showed a video they'd created about the 2010 pilot, which explained how panelists sorted through information and how their Citizens' Statement was distributed through the *Voters' Pamphlet*. Next, Elliot talked about the CIR bill itself. Passing this bill, he argued, simply continued a proven process, while improving oversight to ensure its integrity into the future.

The committee then began digging into the bill. "Does the bill require that panelists be screened for potential bias?" "Would the vote count continue to appear in [their] statement?" The committee was particularly concerned that the vote count would indicate that the government itself had come out in support or opposition to the measure. Ty and Elliot reassured the committee that the Citizens' Statement stood apart from other sections of the pamphlet.

Despite that reassurance, legislators remained apprehensive about bias in the CIR process spilling over into the Citizens' Statement. One representative noted that his spouse had received an invitation to participate. Given her relationship to a sitting legislator, could she have remained unbiased? He asked if there was "some way of weeding out people" with a vested interest.

Next came a member of the research team who had been tasked with evaluating the pilot process. She and her academic colleagues had compiled an evaluative report of the CIR that assessed its deliberative quality and its net impact on the electorate. Though the report noted specific areas for improvement, the evaluation concluded that the CIR lived up to the deliberative ideals that inspired it. A key element of that report was the "CIR Report Card," which graded the different elements of the 2010 CIR panels as earning marks ranging from "A" to "B."

The researcher noted that the Citizens' Statement had a significant impact on the voting decisions of those who read them. As many as 25 percent of readers learned about new arguments or information regarding the initiatives, she noted; voters who read the statement strongly opposing mandatory minimum sentencing were much more likely to vote against the otherwise highly popular initiative.

After the research slideshow concluded, it was the panelists' turn to provide testimony. A man that Marion didn't recognize spoke first. He'd served on the medical marijuana CIR panel and believed that the statement he and his fellow citizens wrote provided a valuable service to voters. The CIR might have been a new idea, but it was "as American as apple pie."

Finally, it was Marion's chance to address the committee.

"I'm Marion Sharp, and I live in Tigard." Knowing her audience, she added, "I want to go on record saying that I'm at Portland State. Playing the Ducks is an incredibly painful experience."

After the chuckles died down, Marion told the committee that she was thrilled to speak at the invitation of Healthy Democracy. "I have been surprised by the ongoing impact of the Citizens' Initiative Review," she said. "I experienced this process almost like an infrastructure project. It's changed my personal infrastructure—how I think about things and the confidence I have that, using the right process, all of our citizens can participate effectively in solving any problem."

Marion explained that the CIR's procedures shaped the way participants reached a decision. She and her panelists moved away from a discussion "that is conflicted to one that is effective, and I believe that it ultimately can change the infrastructure of how this state operates." Institutionalizing the CIR, she argued, will create an "engaged, capable citizenry that can bypass the polarization that we so often see today." She added that the process gave panelists a new kind of opportunity to participate in their democracy. "It gives us something we don't get anywhere else."

Not all impressions, however were so positive. During the first CIR, the frustrated proponents of mandatory sentencing had threatened to leave during the CIR deliberations. The Healthy Democracy staff convinced them to remain, in part by making it clear that the CIR would continue with or without their involvement. By the end of the week, however, the proponents were still unsatisfied, arguing that the panelists needed many more hours to study the issue and that advocates had insufficient rebuttal time.

Doug Harcleroad, the chief proponent for mandatory minimum sentencing, attended an earlier legislative hearing for that very reason. During his opportunity to address the committee, he unleashed a torrent of arguments in opposition to the CIR. He argued that it could not produce a high quality, factually accurate statement and that the process amounted to the government telling the citizens how to vote on initiatives. He said he remained concerned that the panelists may have pre-developed opinions on a measure under review and that organizations could use donations to the CIR to advance their particular causes and influence the process.

These arguments gained little traction in the legislature, though some of these concerns were used to amend the bill by regulating more clearly who could donate to the CIR and what stipulations they could place on their donations. When Harcleroad argued that the panelists couldn't learn the information that they needed to make a good decision, the representatives responded with incredulity. As Representative Vicki Berger (R-Salem) noted, "I wish I had a week to sit with the members of the committee and deliberate about the important things that we talk about."

The bill received bipartisan sponsorship with initial backing by ten state representatives and five senators, and in early June 2011, was approved by both the

House and the Senate. Figure 7.1 shows the breakdown of the vote across the two parties and in the two chambers. As in 2009, every Democrat in the state legislature supported the CIR, and they were joined by a minority of Republicans. Republicans made up over one-quarter of the CIR bill's support in the Senate and one-fifth of its support in the House. Looked at another way, almost one-in-four Republican state representatives supported the CIR, whereas closer to half of Republican state senators took that position. In sum, the CIR sustained broad support from 2009 to 2011, and it managed to pass in a House split evenly between the two parties.

For the bill to officially become a law, however, it needed the governor's signature. Two weeks after the bill's passage in the senate, Healthy Democracy staff and supporters returned to Salem to stand alongside the bill's legislative sponsors and a handful of former CIR panelists, including Marion and Ann.

For Ty, this moment seemed the culmination of five years of work. When he and Elliot first began to dream about the CIR, they imagined it developing in a series of steps. They had to gain funding, test the process, lobby for the pilot bill, run the 2010 CIRs, then return to the legislature to advocate for its permanent implementation. Ty and Elliot never quite thought they'd actually be where they were now—at the state capitol about to have the process they'd brought to life become a regular part of Oregon's elections.

Ty had been in the governor's signing room only once before. Back in grade school, he and his fellow classmates had collected change for the pioneer that

Figure 7.1 Votes in the Oregon legislature to create a Citizens' Initiative Review Commission.

Oregon Governor John Kitzhaber signing a bill on June 16, 2011, to make the Oregon CIR permanent. Tyrone Reitman stands to the left with his wife Natalie, son Rohan, and Senator Arnie Roblan. Elliott Shuford stands to the right—his family were standing just outside the photo. CIR panelists and moderators flank the governor, including Marion Sharp and Ann Bakkensen. *Source:* Healthy Democracy.

stood atop the capitol building. Each nickel and dime went toward putting up a new piece of gold leaf, so that collectively Oregon's school children could take part in encasing the statue in gold. Like Marion on the morning of her testimony, Ty looked up at that trailblazer as he entered the building, remembering every step that had gotten them to this point. On June 16, with Ty and Elliot and all their supporters looking on, the governor signed the bill into law. "It was a wonderful moment," Ty recalled during an interview years later. "It felt like the end of a chapter." With the benefit of hindsight, he added, "It was also a jumping off point. We had no idea how to do what we had to do next."

Becoming a Bureaucracy

Though the bill had passed, actually implementing the new legislation required continual political persistence. One aspect of the bill—the creation of a commission to oversee the CIR—would prove particularly challenging. The commission would be composed of former CIR panelists and moderators, as well as the neutral members of the committees who write the explanatory information already included in the *Voters' Pamphlet*.

Commission membership is a key CIR feature because it keeps control in the hands of the citizens. Though deliberative events are designed to put power back into the hands of the people, they often face a deeper problem: maintaining the public's will in the face of process complexity. Who decides the topic for deliberation? Who sets the agenda? Who chooses the information panelists should use to reach their decisions?

The wrong answer to any of these questions could undermine the purpose of deliberative democracy. If these decisions are taken away from the public, how can we truly say that the process alone grants citizens more power? If the panelists are given biased or inaccurate information, how can the CIR help better inform voters? An oversight commission would help solve these problems by ensuring the integrity of the CIR and preventing its capture by special interest groups and initiative advocates.

Though the bill had required establishing such a commission, Ty and Elliot soon learned that bureaucracy doesn't move on its own. Months went by, and the commission was no closer to forming than it was when the bill had passed. Without an invested leader in Salem or external political pressure, the CIR had authorization but remained a low priority.

Looking back, Ty recognized the naivety of assuming he and Elliot had completed their jobs. "We did what we thought was correct," he explained, but "we didn't know what we were doing."

More than that, Ty and Elliot were simply tired after five years of fighting against uncertainty. Feeling burnt out, Elliot was ready to look for something new—something that would allow him to step back from the pressure of lobbying. For his part, Ty was struggling to balance a young family and a new governing institution. Natalie had been pregnant throughout the legislative session. Though Ty was proud to bring his baby to the governor's bill signing, the pressures of family distracted him from the demands of work.

Compounding the exhaustion was a lack of political will on the part of the legislature. Ty and Elliot had been the primary champions of the CIR, attending every legislative session and personally garnering every sponsor, supporter, and funder. Though the bill's sponsors likely would have lent support, had they asked, the young directors of Healthy Democracy were simply too inexperienced with this side of bureaucracy to realize they needed to ask for help. They just assumed that once a law was passed it would be implemented. Without political pressure or a legislative champion, however, the bureaucracy stalled.

The law required that some members of the committee be appointed by political leaders; the governor would appoint four members who had served as the neutral fifth person on the initiative explanatory statement committee and legislative leaders for both Republicans and Democrats would each appoint a member as well. With the 2012 CIRs fast approaching, Ty and Elliot reached out to a friend in the Department of Administrative Services, which was tasked with setting up the commission. At the eleventh hour, the political appointees were selected.

The law also required that former CIR panelists and moderators make up the remainder of the eleven-person commission. Marion became one of the first appointees to that commission. She was joined by Ann, whom she had befriended during her own CIR, and two other citizen panelists. With only a few months before the CIRs set for August 2012, the commission had time to do little more than select the initiatives to be reviewed that year. As stipulated in HB 2634, the commission had to prioritize those initiatives with the greatest potential impact on the state constitution or the budget. With those criteria in mind, the commission chose two initiatives for the 2012 CIR: Measure 85 would repeal a corporate tax refund and direct the revenue to K-12 education, and Measure 82 would establish non-tribal casinos in Oregon.

An Institution Without a Constituency

Taxes and casinos have constituencies. Individuals and corporations will profit, and some will lose profit, from the passage of such laws. Ballot measures also have stakes for public-spirited interest groups, which aim not to count dollars but to save lives, forests, fetuses, freedoms, and so much more. Both private and public interest groups have memberships, funds available for campaigning, and a mix of volunteer and professional staff to see their will be done.

One problem for the Oregon CIR is that it lacks such a constituency. Its mission is not to achieve a particular policy outcome, but rather to change the dynamics of the policymaking process by giving every citizen the chance to make a more informed vote during initiative elections. This spirit of deliberation may—to quote *The Simpsons*—"embiggen us all," but politically speaking, the concept arouses no passion.

In this respect, it has much in common with other "good government" efforts, such as campaign finance reform—another one of Tyrone Reitman's causes. Harvard law professor Lawrence Lessig recently became one of the most visible champions of that cause, and he has introduced ingenious variations on conventional finance restrictions. He raised eleven million dollars in a national campaign to create a Super PAC (political action committee) that would fight other Super PACs. Even after targeting just a handful of key races, he didn't get results. One *New York Times* reporter summed up the problem with this understatement: "As an election issue, money in politics is rarely a top concern of voters." Again, no constituency.

Civic reforms have another, more serious problem: Every time they *do* get implemented, there's usually a winner and a loser, at least in the short term. Some political party, advocacy group, or corporate sector usually experiences real losses as a result of cleaner elections, realigned districts, or improved candidate

debate systems. Even merely *anticipating* those losses can be too much for critics who want to stop a reform before it becomes a law—or undo a law before it
becomes an institution.

The CIR arouses suspicions in the same way that other deliberative processes
have in recent decades. For some, replacing the passion of direct action with a
more sober public debate sounds politically conservative. Why slow down to
talk if a cause has gained enough momentum to get on the ballot?

To understand these fears, two scholars interviewed activists from around
the world and recorded their concerns about Citizens Juries, Deliberative Polls,
and other forerunners to the CIR. A feminist activist who worked across several
continents doubted that even stratified random selection can generate a discussion that would incorporate diverse points of view. "A person's dominant visible
identity," she explained, "doesn't mean they represent the consciousness of that
identity group. . . . Women, young people, and Latinos don't all have the same
viewpoint." Even if the right people are present, she argued, that doesn't "guarantee a diversity of views and critical analysis," nor does it "ensure that people will
feel comfortable about speaking their mind."

Worse still, those who do speak are likely to reinforce the views of dominant social groups. As a South African activist said, "I get the feeling that deliberation is an elitist discourse." People need to have "a certain level of maturity
and . . . power in order to deliberate." Given the reality of political struggles,
"We don't necessarily want to have a unified discourse. We do want a divided
discourse."

Even if participants entered into a deliberative forum as equals, the process may have a bias built into it. An Indonesian activist worried most about
"neutrality" and "rationality," concepts he didn't believe in because of how
they are deployed. "Knowledge isn't power," he argued. "Those who have
power can define what knowledge is." Put simply, *power* is power, and requiring informed judgments can amount to requiring judgments that favor the
powerful.

From there, the worries spread to the motivations of the organizers, the
machinations of the government behind the scenes, and the ephemeral public
support for the decisions rendered in forums like a CIR. The last criticism came
from two Brazilian activists who had worked on Participatory Budgeting in their
country but found it lacking. This process had leveraged substantial participation by poor and working class Brazilians into real changes in their quality of
living, yet it had neither the fervor of a genuine social movement nor the power
of a robust political institution.

The fate of the CIR, however, did not rest in the hands of activist critics.
The Oregon legislature had run out of patience with the status quo method of
conducting initiative elections and had established a CIR Commission to make

CIRs a regular part of Oregon politics. The CIR's critics couldn't stop the CIRs from returning in the next election. They could, however, try to subvert it.

Boycotting Citizen Deliberation

The first permanent iteration of the CIR took place in August 2012. Healthy Democracy was again tasked with implementing the CIRs, this time with less funding than before. Ned and Pat believed that if Oregonians wanted the CIR, the state should find a way to pay for it. In 2010, they had pledged a three-year commitment to Healthy Democracy, with their financial contribution decreasing significantly each year.

Tasked with setting up a new commission, implementing the CIR, and raising funds for its implementation, the small staff of Healthy Democracy was stretched thin. Elliot had stepped down and left Ty as the lone executive director.

Ty turned to old allies for help. Larry Pennings would once again develop the agenda for the process, and four moderators would facilitate the CIR, three of whom had experience from the 2010 CIR. Looking to increase efficiency, this team managed to reduce the cost per CIR to approximately $100,000. They again sought funding from civic organizations, this time receiving the bulk of their funds from the Omidyar Network, a "philanthropic investment firm" created by the founder of eBay. Panelist recruitment followed the 2010 protocol, though this time the invitation was stamped with the official state seal. Perhaps due to its official nature and voters' greater familiarity with the CIR, the survey had a response rate of approximately 8 percent, more than twice the result from 2010.

The highest hurdle Healthy Democracy had to clear for the 2012 panels was the advocates. In the wake of the 2010 CIRs, the process had drawn the ire of some initiative advocates, who worried that it would diminish their power. Moreover, in its short tenure, the CIR had developed a bit of a reputation as an initiative killer. CIR panelists had voted in favor of establishing medical marijuana dispensaries by the narrowest of margins—a near tie that didn't look anything like an endorsement. The prior CIR panel had soundly rejected a popular mandatory minimum sentencing initiative.

The first CIR in 2012 would focus on Measure 85. Compounding an already complex tax structure, Oregon tax law required that when the government collected a considerable surplus in tax revenue relative to projections, the treasury was required to return those additional taxes. This particular refund is referred to as a "kicker." Because Oregon does not collect sales taxes and only collects property and income taxes, this kicker had exacerbated an already unstable tax structure, wherein the state collected less money during economic downturns and could not compensate for that by collecting more money during economic booms. Measure 85 would repeal the kicker for corporations and divert the excess revenue to K-12 education.

The primary proponent for the measure was Our Oregon, the progressive alliance first mentioned in chapter 3. In conversations and email exchanges with Healthy Democracy, Our Oregon had agreed to participate in the CIR on Measure 85. One week before the CIR was set to begin, however, the organization instead opted for a boycott. Within minutes of calling Ty to tell him that they would not be participating, Our Oregon sent out a press release to the major news organizations in the state to explain their decision and skewer the CIR.

Their withdrawal sparked a story that ran in the state's biggest newspaper, the *Oregonian*. Our Oregon insisted that the "output" of the CIR "has zero impact on shaping the opinions of voters." The basis for this claim was the 2010 report written by the authors of this book, yet our research had demonstrated the opposite. In the age of Trump, such a misreading—willful or otherwise—might seem unremarkable, but for Ty and the other progressives who had worked to establish the CIR, it was disheartening.

Ty was stunned by the sudden withdrawal of Measure 85's advocates. He was accustomed to infighting within the political left, but Our Oregon had voiced no direct opposition to the CIR. Believing that it had amassed enough political clout to pass initiatives in the state at will, perhaps Our Oregon saw only unnecessary risk in endorsing a process that could end up giving its measure an unfavorable analysis.

A 2016 interview with an official from Our Oregon tacitly acknowledged this political logic. Deputy Political Director Courtney Graham explained that "the decision was little more than a calculation of where limited campaign resources would be best spent. At that time, it did not make sense to devote campaign resources to a two-sided process when there was no organized opposition." Referring to the con advocates that Healthy Democracy recruited for the CIR, she noted that the organizers had to "manufacture an opposition in order to move forward."

True enough, Our Oregon's refusal to participate meant that Healthy Democracy had to assemble both the pro and con teams. Given that the unofficial advocate team included members of the Our Oregon coalition, the organization's tactic was akin to that of a wary opposition party in a fledgling democracy. Such groups sometimes choose to officially stand apart from an election (while participating wholeheartedly) in case the party chooses to protest any unfavorable results.

In response to Our Oregon's stance, members of Healthy Democracy's board including former secretaries of state and a former attorney general wrote a rebuttal, arguing that the CIR was an important addition to initiative elections. "Voters routinely express frustration with our electoral process," they argued, "feeling disconnected and turned off by 30-second advertising and sound bites. This frustration translates into apathy, robbing our initiative process of one of its founding principles—to provide a voice for everyday citizens. We can do better than this, and we deserve far better than this."

Our Oregon's claims directly contradicted the research that had been funded by the National Science Foundation. The lead researcher studying the 2010 CIRs wrote his own editorial rebuttal, pointing out that the CIR did, in fact, have a clear impact on voters' knowledge and preferences—a result explained fully in chapter 9.

To understand Our Oregon's actions, one can look to the details of their 2012 ballot measure. The state government had given their initiative an inelegant ballot title. If passed, the measure promised to allocate "corporate income/excise tax 'kicker' refund to additionally fund K through 12 public education." To get a feel for the legalese a busy voter would have to parse, try quickly reading the Oregon Attorney General's summary of Measure 85:

> Before each biennium, the governor must prepare an estimate of revenues expected to be received by the General Fund for the next biennium. The General Fund is the primary funding source for schools, prisons, social services[, and] other state-funded programs/services. Current law requires an automatic "kicker" refund to taxpayers of corporate income and excise tax revenue that exceeds estimated collections by two percent or more. Measure allocates the corporate income and excise tax "kicker" refund to the General Fund to provide additional funding for K through 12 public education. Measure does not change the constitutional personal income tax "kicker" provision that requires a refund to individual taxpayers when personal income tax revenue exceeds estimated revenue by two percent or more. Other provisions.

Our Oregon was talking to voters because voters weren't sure what to make of such a proposal. To be precise, a SurveyUSA poll in September of that year found that two-thirds of respondents were undecided on the issue, with the remainder more inclined to oppose than favor it. The problem with the initiative was parsing what *precisely* it did and didn't do.

The public face of the pro campaign was Defend Oregon. Its website's claims were straightforward: "Measure 85 will reform the corporate kicker by putting money into Oregon K-12 classrooms, rather than back into the pockets of large, out-of-state corporations. That would mean lowering class sizes and restoring important school programs. These funds would also help get Oregon schools off of the financial roller coaster and provide more stability, even in economically tough years."

Those claims made for strong talking points. Who would give a refund to outsiders, rather than supporting Oregon's public schools? Who doesn't want their children to learn in an ideal environment, where there are smaller classes, better art supplies, and an all-weather track for the running team? And everyone knows that stable revenue is better than erratic funding. Who could oppose such things? Framing the issue this way makes for an easy argument, and the pro campaign outspent the opposition handily in making this case through paid advertising.

This is precisely the kind of situation in which a CIR can help to scrutinize laws and see if there aren't questions behind those questions. A CIR asks whether there might be another way to look at the law, or if there are even good reasons to oppose it. But how to design a CIR when one side of the debate walks away from its lectern?

Without the participation of the measure's advocates, Healthy Democracy had to figure out a way to make the CIR work. They set about contacting other supporters of the bill, ultimately creating an advocate team that included tax reform and education advocates only loosely affiliated with Our Oregon. Thus, on August 6, 2012, at the conference center in Salem where the 2010 reviews were held, the first permanent iteration of the CIR commenced.

The panelists again met for five days, utilizing a similar format to that which had been used in 2010, though slight adjustments had been made based on Healthy Democracy's internal critique and recommendations provided by the research team. The 2012 process improved the CIR in many respects, particularly by permitting more time for feedback on the final statements from the advocates and panelists, the embrace of values-centered discussions, and via the new "Additional Policy Considerations" section added to the Citizens' Statement.

Our Oregon's strategic gambit appalled the rank-and-file membership of the association, yet the CIR panelists took it in stride. Aware of the editorials running in the *Oregonian*, panelists broached the topic on the second day, demanding that both the Healthy Democracy staff and the advocates explain why Our Oregon had decided to boycott. For their part, the initiative's advocates said that they were associated with Our Oregon and represented many of the same interests, essentially side-stepping the question. Wary of biasing the panelists against the measure, the moderators informed the participants that they had simply provided them with the advocates who had been willing to participate.

But the CIR panelists couldn't let go of this concern. On the fourth day, the final pro witness, Laurie Wimmer from the Oregon Education Association, explained the initiative using language that sounded like her organization had written it. When a panelist asked why the erratic revenue raised by the measure wouldn't go into a "rainy day fund," Wimmer claimed that "our research shows" that voters wanted the funds earmarked, in principle, for education. "So," she explained, "we gave it to them the way they preferred."

Another panelist jumped on that phrasing: "You say we gave it to the voters. What affiliation do you have with the people that actually put this measure forward? And, do you have any idea why they refused to come to the panel?" What followed from Wimmer was equivocal at best: "Well, I certainly can't speak for others, but . . . the Oregon Education Association is allied with the progressive community, and they all participate in [Our Oregon]."

That didn't satisfy the panelists, many of whom remained frustrated by the boycott. In the end, however, panelists pushed those concerns aside when evaluating the measure on its own merits. Throughout the week, this fresh batch of randomly selected citizens heard from unofficial advocates for the measure and listened to criticisms from state legislators, who favored putting the recouped tax revenue into a rainy day fund rather than dumping it into the vast education budget.

The absence of the official advocates may have even benefited the panelists. As demonstrated by the exchange above, Measure 85's replacement advocates veered from Our Oregon's talking points to have more honest and open exchanges with the panelists. When questioned as to why the money would go into education rather than the state's rainy day fund, where most economic experts agreed it would be more useful, the unofficial advocates admitted that this decision had been made on the basis of polling. The measure was more likely to pass, they confessed, if tied to education than if tied to the rainy day fund.

In the end, the panel voted 19–5 in favor of the ballot measure and wrote a sophisticated statement that reflected the panelists' growing understanding of their unique political role. The CIR and Healthy Democracy had once again faced down political opposition and pushed through.

With only a week of rest however, the CIR was about to face a new threat. The next panel would study a proposal to establish non-tribal casinos in Oregon. Proponents of this initiative had millions of dollars in their war chest, owing to financial backing by casino operators interested in moving into the state.

Would the CIR be able to maintain its integrity when one side in a policy debate could outspend its opponent by a wide margin? If the CIR failed to meet this challenge, it would be a failed experiment—one more example of political victory going to the highest bidder.

Back in the Wind Tunnel

The boycott of the first 2012 CIR was a surmountable challenge, but the subsequent CIR faced a more serious threat. What if instead of walking away from the CIR, Our Oregon had stayed? If the panelists had turned against repealing the corporate excise tax, could its advocates have controlled or undermined the CIR's deliberation?

As interest groups become more aware of the power of processes like the CIR, such questions become less and less hypothetical. One scholar who has noted this danger is Genevieve Fuji Johnson, a political science professor at Simon Fraser University—the same institution that hosted the BC Citizens' Assembly in its Centre for Dialogue. Johnson has witnessed firsthand exceptional processes such as the assembly, but she finds her eye drawn to what she calls "democratic illusions."

Previous chapters in this book have showcased the success of Deliberative Polls, Participatory Budgeting, and consultative processes in which governments have turned to well-structured bodies of deliberating citizens to inform policymaking. But what if the power, or even the deliberative sophistication, of such processes is illusory? Just because the public speaks with a clear voice doesn't mean it will have an impact. Just because that voice is clear doesn't mean it is well-informed or genuinely reflective of the values at stake on a given issue.

Johnson explored four Canadian cases in which the best of deliberative designs and intentions proved powerless in the face of powerful interests that favored maintaining the status quo. From public housing in Toronto to a public utility in Nova Scotia to national issues of nuclear power and vanishing indigenous languages, Johnson saw concentrated interests twist promising deliberative experiments into sophisticated disguises for the conventional exercise of political power. "In each of the four cases," Johnson explains, "elites framed their procedures as a significant step in reshaping relations with their affected public. Elites created high expectations that their procedures represented a new approach to decision making—an approach that would enable participants to have a meaningful say in policy."

Hope for Democracy. John Gastil and Katherine R. Knobloch, Oxford University Press (2020).
© John Gastil and Katherine R. Knobloch
DOI: 10.1093/acprof:oso/9780190084523.001.0001

What distinguishes the CIR from these cases, and many more like them cited by democratic theorists and government scholars the world over, is that by 2012, the CIR process had a standing authorization from the state legislature, which did not play even an indirect role in the content of the CIR itself. Also, the CIR's power came not through influencing elite decision makers but from shaping the judgments that individual citizens can make about the ballot measures the CIR examines.

What the CIR does have, however, is one of Johnson's main risk factors for becoming an illusion: it accepts and even welcomes into the heart of its deliberative process groups that have private interests and the motivation to advocate for them by whatever rhetorical means necessary. Such interests have been quick to recognize the value of winning in initiative elections, which can set the rules for entire industries. In the 2014 election cycle, more than a quarter billion dollars was spent on advertising for ballot measures in the United States, with a single medical malpractice measure in California accounting for over twenty million of those ad dollars. Among the biggest spenders in 2014 were private casinos, which sponsored or fought ballot measures across the country from Colorado to Massachusetts.

In 2012, the casinos took their shot at the CIR process in Oregon. Their participation tested the resiliency of the CIR against the gale-force winds of one of the most concentrated and powerful commercial interests in the United States.

Confronting the Casinos

Rather than trying to avoid or discredit the CIR, the backers of a private casino measure approached the 2012 CIR as a serious business opportunity and hired professionals. This CIR was their best chance to make the case for establishing casinos outside tribal lands, and they crafted their arguments, evidence, and overall message like a team of high-priced lawyers and lobbyists. In fact, they *were* a team of high-priced lawyers and lobbyists. Over the course of the election, their campaign would raise over five million dollars.

The CIR was the first to be held in Portland, which was appropriate because the issue before the citizen panel was authorizing private casinos, the first of which would appear in Wood Village, just east of the city. A Canadian investment firm led the effort to build a "125-room, four-star hotel, a water slide, bowling alley, concert hall and theater," with a "130,000-square-foot casino" that included two thousand slot machines and a hundred card tables. Trying to appeal to the sensibilities of Portlanders, the developers promised to "incorporate local foods and drinks as much as possible" and "re-use the wooden beams from the 1950s-era grandstand of the Multnomah Kennel Club." Re-use, recycle, and expand dramatically—or something like that.

The proponents of private casinos had to win two ballot measures: one to authorize them constitutionally (Measure 82) and a second to begin the Wood Village project (Measure 83). The focus of the CIR was the first measure, which had provisions that aimed to preempt the concerns voters might raise. For instance, the measure permitted new casinos only within cities and only with explicit voter approval for each project. Twenty-five percent of casinos' adjusted gross revenue would go to the state government. Finally, new construction couldn't occur "within 60 miles of a tribal casino that was operating on reservation land on January 1, 2011."

Not surprisingly, the opponents included those same tribal casinos, who hardly viewed the sixty-mile rule as a concession. Leading the opposition at the CIR was Justin Martin, who spoke on behalf of the Oregon Tribal Gaming Alliance. Justin himself was a member of the Confederated Tribes of Grand Ronde, and he'd used both of those connections to build a team that would explain the tribal perspective on the issue and match the private casino advocates fact-for-fact. The fiscal details of the ballot measure, however, were inscrutable. Even the state's official fiscal impact statement for the measure took a pass by telling voters that "this measure has an indeterminate financial impact."

Focusing on Justin's experience at the CIR helps show how the process operates from the standpoint of a policy advocate. Justin had given considerable thought to how he would approach a CIR because the casino measures had almost come to the ballot in 2010, and would have but for missteps by the proponents during the signature gathering phase. Had the casino question made it to the ballot, Ty had assured Justin that the CIR might select that issue for the CIR owing to its potential social and economic impact. As a result, Justin and his colleagues had already "tested public opinion" and done enough opposition research. He was confident that he "knew who they were and what their motives were."

What was frustrating to Justin, however, was *who* worked on behalf of the casinos. In an interview, Justin admitted to feeling betrayed by who he would have to oppose in the election. "Our Oregon had boycotted the previous week," he recalled, "and two of their folks were consulting for the other side." Justin said that fellow Democrats "making millions of dollars to work against us" left "a bad taste in my mouth. . . . When you get paid enough you can be on the wrong side of the issue. I can't, but they can."

To take on these opponents, Justin knew he had to cover every angle, and he believed that the citizen panelists would need to be "educated from the ground up." In particular, he made a point of emphasizing the unique legal context of the ballot measure. "We took a tribal and governmental perspective," he explained, which meant "taking the time to let them know who the tribes are and how they differ from other governments." In doing so, he could make the case that the indigenous tribes in Oregon held a moral high ground given their history of mistreatment by successive federal and state governments. He could appeal to the panelists' sense of fairness.

Would that be enough? Justin wasn't at all sure he would sway the twenty-four strangers assembled in Portland to hear his case against the ballot measure. More than once, he asked himself, "Why are we doing this?" He felt confident he had a "winning message," and if the panel "comes out favorable, great." But laying out their case against the private casinos in this way was "a scary proposition." To him, the panelists were "almost like a jury: they're going to vote one way or another."

What scared him the most was the sequence of the arguments. Panelists would hear from "the pro side, then the no side, then there's no interplay or ability for me to challenge when they throw out bullshit information" in their closing rebuttal. Looking back on the CIR after it had concluded, he recalled one day where the proponents "were up there spewing information" both sides knew were false, and all he could do was watch and wait for his next turn to speak later that afternoon. "Things like that were frustrating," he said.

Justin and his colleagues "weren't thrilled" with how the measure's proponents behaved during the CIR. "My clients saw it as a real affront to what they were doing." He said the atmosphere felt "charged" because of his opponent's style of argument. "My colleague on the other side [is someone] I've been dealing with for fifteen years. She was saying terrible things."

Such tension was not apparent to most of the panelists. Interviews with them supported some of the fears Justin had expressed about battling the information juggernaut of lawyers advocating for the private casino industry. The only tension one panelist felt, for instance, was "racing the clock." Throughout the CIR, his "opinion sort of vacillated. Initially, I was on the opposed side. Later, as I considered things, I went in support of the measure." He was impressed by "the presentation by the experts and the proponents and opponents. An awful lot of matter of fact had to be cleared up and explained, because I think a lot of people didn't quite understand the factuals. Even within the presentations, there were statements made that could be very misleading."

When the fourth day of the CIR began, it was not only misleading statements that worried Justin but also the layers of legalese. For example, when the lead advocate explained how the state estimates fiscal impacts, she read from statute. "As part of the Fiscal Estimate Committee," she said, "the Legislative Revenue Officer shall prepare on behalf of the Committee an impartial estimate. The Financial Estimate Committee shall incorporate relevant parts of the estimate prepared by the Legislative Revenue Officer . . . and incorporate those into the estimate prepared by the Committee."

And so it continued, with one after another expert advocate for the casinos building their argument in a methodical fashion. The panelists would go into their group deliberation shortly after hearing from the measure's proponents. When the panel turned the floor back over to the advocates just before lunch, the proponents would again get the final word. Justin would have to make a strong closing case that cut through what he viewed as a bewildering jumble of facts and falsehoods arrayed by his counterparts.

Justin decided that the best way to break through this wall of sound was to make himself fully present as a person, rather than trying to out-lawyer the lawyers. Fortunately for Justin, the CIR affords both sides in a debate more time than they have in any other political context, and that luxury of time permits one to array arguments with an exceptional level of creativity.

In conventional political debates—even in the presidential debates broadcast on every network—candidates get just a minute or two to address complex policy questions, such as healthcare reform or foreign intervention. Worse still, frequent interruptions are the norm. As the *New York Times* explained during the 2012 election cycle, a debate's winner "may be the one who best grasps when an interruption is a bold assertion of his conversational rights, and not an offensive violation of his rival's."

By contrast, Justin knew he could relax. Fifteen minutes were set aside for his closing statement, then ten minutes to field questions. In his allotted time,

Plenary deliberations during the 2012 Oregon CIR on private casinos. *Source*: Healthy Democracy.

Justin delivered a speech that spanned more than one thousand eight hundred words—roughly the equivalent of reading seven double-spaced pages. To get a feel for the relaxed posture Justin assumed, listen as one of the CIR's facilitators introduced him.

FACILITATOR: I think our con advocate is ready. So, Justin will speak for the con.
JUSTIN: Thank you. It takes a while to get used to that—"con."
FACILITATOR: I know. You're not a "con."
JUSTIN: No, I'm not.

From that bit of banter, Justin slid into a friendly, personal greeting. Smiling at the twenty-four panelists, Justin said, "Well, good morning, everyone. Nice to see what is now familiar faces around the room." He joked that he "took yesterday off so you guys wouldn't get too tired of seeing me in and around this room." What sounded like a confession allowed Justin to present himself as not only an advocate but a regular person:

I hope I'm not too groggy. I went to a rock and roll show last night. Saw ZZ Top out in Troutdale. The nice thing about these bands is they're getting older. They actually went on at 7:45 and were done by 9:00. So I knew I would be going to a rock show that would be over very, very early.

A smooth transition brought the focus back to the issue at hand. "So, you guys have been overrun with information," Justin said. "I'm sure that's been a very difficult task to try and absorb so much of this into one week, but let me give you some more. . . . I will get right to the point: The bottom line is that Measure 82 is bad for Oregon."

A flurry of counterpunches followed, attacking the proponents' arguments from a dozen different angles. One recurring insight at CIRs held before and since the casino panel was that there is more to a law than what appears in the official ballot summary. Justin built on that.

Let me give you a concrete example. If you look closely at the fine print within these measures, you will find that casino proponents have rigged the rules in their favor by writing in a loophole that exempts them from paying taxes on those machines. Yet all the small businesses, all the retailers, all the mom and pops, all the local businesses that have those six Video Lottery Terminals pay those taxes on that machine. So, what does that mean? That means one foreign-owned casino would get a constitutionally protected special advantage that hundreds of Oregon's struggling retailers and Video Lottery businesses do not get. Simply, that's just not fair.

A subtle effect of this argument was reinforcing a related theme conspicuous for its absence in Justin's closing rebuttal. His very presence as lead advocate was enough to underscore the tribal sovereignty argument, which panelists had cued into since the beginning. During the second day of the CIR, for instance, a small-group discussion led one panelist to raise the issue, albeit tentatively.

"It's not what we're supposed to talk about," said the panelist, "but I'm thinking the same human thing of the tribes and stuff. . . . The Native Americans, you know, were the first ones here. . . . That's something that helped them, as people weren't doing well before they had casinos." After a back-and-forth discussion with another panelist, who had seen a documentary about the variation in how indigenous people had fared over the centuries, the same panelist concluded her thought. Native Americans "just were in this kind of hole they couldn't get out of. In Oregon we said, 'It's your land. You actually can do gambling.' It saved them."

Would that same sentiment be able to save Justin's case? After his closing statement, it was the panelists who picked up this theme during the question and answer session. A panelist reminded Justin of his claim that "about 13 percent of your employees . . . are Indians. . . . Who trains them to be dealers and whatever?"

Justin thanked the panelist for the question and offered a gentle correction: "The overall number is 12 percent of our one thousand five hundred employees, approximately, are tribal members," but taking into account other tribes, "about 16 percent are Native Americans." As for oversight, Justin explained, "the great thing about all tribal facilities in Oregon is we are managed by ourselves. We don't rely on Las Vegas interests or other large companies that come in and do that management. So, we do the training. We provide that onsite."

When the advocates' final statements were done, questions of fairness remained on many panelists' minds. After the facilitator broke the panelists into pairs to help each member decide whether to vote for or against the measure, one panelist asked her conversation partner, "So, you're against it?" The woman seated beside her answered, "Yeah, yeah. I really do feel in my heart that the Native Americans deserve their casino." For her, it wasn't a question of "free enterprise." Rather, "I just think they need it, and this has done great things for their people."

Had Justin overheard that exchange, he might have had more confidence in the coming result. Instead, he confessed to being anxious about what the panelists would say in their final Citizens' Statement. He couldn't read the panel, and he wasn't sure he had reached them. "It wasn't like a debate," he explained. "I couldn't just stand up there and dispute what they were saying." Though he felt confident in his own closing statement, it was followed by one just as long. "They went first and went last," and he worried that advantage was too great. He even recalled "wrestling" with Ty about "how they were choosing who speaks when." Losing that procedural argument, he feared, could mean he would lose the more important panelist vote.

When the panelists began to craft their key findings, it seemed he had reason to be concerned. The opening sentence was as tepid as the official state fiscal summary: "Economists disagree on the long term economic impact of private casinos in Oregon." More promising for Justin, however, was this finding: "Private casinos could negatively affect the gaming revenues of the tribal casinos and the communities they support."

Seventeen of the twenty-four panelists ultimately sided with Justin, and they restated this concern in starker language: "Measure 82 will negatively impact the revenue generated by tribal casinos traditionally used to support tribal communities, nearby rural areas, nonprofits and charitable organizations throughout Oregon." They also decried the threat of "outside influence on gambling" on the state constitution and the likely negative social impacts that would ensue, including "addictions to gambling, alcohol and drugs."

The proponents of the measure could see a crushing defeat coming, and they tried to forestall the CIR's conclusion. Looking back, Ty recalled that during the CIR, the lead advocate for the casino measure was practically "robocalling" Ty's assistant, who finally "couldn't take the vitriol." It still smarted him that these were people he had worked with as allies. "They were the same people that consulted with Our Oregon," he recalled. "It's a small world in Oregon." He had tried to give them the benefit of the doubt that "they decided to participate because they wanted to have a deliberation."

By the fourth day of the CIR, however, he felt differently. "Their tactics were clear," he said. "What they probably saw was that their messages, which work in a campaign ad, were a bit too simple. When the panelists started discussing their views, the advocates freaked out." Thus ensued their desperate stalling tactics on the final day, when they insisted that they had the legal right to respond formally, again and again, to every iteration of the panel's Citizens' Statements. Behind the scenes, Ty said, "We had been dealing with their rage for two days."

"The panel did a great job under the circumstances," Ty recalled. They kept their composure even when that final day "took on a quasi-nightmarish feel. Had a bit of a Twilight Zone toward the end." In desperation, the measure's advocates "provided two pages of insulting material for the panel," an approach that reminded Ty of Doug Harcleroad's flailing rhetoric on the mandatory minimum measure in 2010.

"They were hired guns," Ty said, "doing what they were paid to do." Their self-destructive behavior "just blew my mind. It's reflective of how shitty politics can

be. Twenty-four people taking a week out of their lives to provide a public service, and the best you can do is insult them because they don't agree with you."

The final day of the process dragged into the night until the panel left the conference hotel to perform their last duty, a bleary-eyed reading of their Citizens'
Statement at a press conference. For Justin, that moment crowned a victory—but
it also made him realize that the CIR had a less obvious value for his campaign.

Initially, Justin had found the CIR to be a "bummer." It was "cumbersome,
a little bit long, and a little bit kind of bureaucratic." Before it began and during
each day, "You had to write to stuff and respond to stuff, on top of the presentations." Overall, it was "somewhat frustrating but also helpful for getting ready for
the campaign." The challenge of articulating arguments during the CIR "forced
us to do work early in the campaign that we didn't have to do later on. It was
burdensome but helped me out in the long run."

Returning to the theme that opened the chapter, there is no question that
Justin represented a concentrated special interest of his own. The tribal casinos
in Oregon had much at stake and opted to participate in the CIR not out of civic
obligation but out of necessity. "It's something you have to do," he explained.
His partners "discussed it strategically. I didn't want to turn it down." If they did,
Ty and his staff "could assign people" to represent their side, "and that was a red
flag." Justin decided that "the better option was to have the true experts present
this thing so we can control the environment and the situation."

The proponents of Measure 82 had a very different experience. A month
before election day, the private casino campaign suspended its operations, essentially conceding defeat. Justin almost giggled when recalling the social media
blowup that appeared the following day. "Their lead consultant got in a huge
pissing match with another consultant working for another tribe. They got in
this epic Facebook-off. It was awesome. *Willamette Week* ran a big story on that."

Given how poorly the private casino advocates had comported themselves on
the last day of that CIR, Ty also admitted to being amused at their implosion. When
asked if he thought the panelists' statement opposing the measure led to the sus-
pending of its campaign, however, he pointed out that their campaign had myriad
problems already, including opposition from prominent public figures across the
political spectrum.

Instead, Ty suspected that the CIR process may have been gamed by the
professionals running the measure's campaign. Back in 2010, when it looked as
though casinos might appear on that year's ballot, casino advocates "said they
would try to screw us if the measure was selected" for a CIR. So Ty was "shocked
they participated" in 2012. Looking back, however, he noted that "campaign
consultants charged upwards of a million dollars" for their work related to the
CIR. In effect, consultants may have agreed to take part "as a ploy to escape
blame" if the measure failed, "while still getting hired to do work."

Even beyond the financial incentives, however, Ty wondered if the advocates had begun to believe their own bullshit. "I was told by an advocate," he recalled, "that there were no valid points against their measure. I sat on the phone asking them if they seriously thought that." They persisted and claimed "no one should feel any opposition. There was no valid debate." Ty conceded that this mentality was common. "Whether it's for show or what you really believe," he said, "that is where a lot of initiatives come from."

Expansion and Experimentation

The 2012 casino CIR marked the fourth iteration of the CIR process, but in 2014, five more were held, including two more statewide in Oregon, plus pilot projects that tested the process at the city level (Phoenix, Arizona), county level (Jackson County, Oregon), and in the state of Colorado.

In 2014, Healthy Democracy received a matching grant from the Democracy Fund, a national non-governmental organization, to expand the CIR's reach. This permitted a measure of experimentation, which brought significant structural changes to the CIR. Recall that Justin had called the CIR "cumbersome" and "a little bit long." To address that, and reduce its overall cost, the process was reduced from five days to four; the panel from twenty-four to twenty; and the number of third-party background witnesses to zero, or close to it. Another major change concerned how the sections of the Citizens' Statements were written. Rather than independently developing findings and arguments for the statement, as had been done in years past, participants began deliberations with a set of claims developed by advocates and largely worked to prioritize and edit these claims for inclusion in the Citizens' Statement. Finally, the statewide Oregon CIRs were the only ones to have their statements appear in the official *Voters' Pamphlet*. Because the other CIRs were pilot tests, their organizers distributed their statements through unofficial means, such as websites, direct mail, and media coverage.

The first CIR in 2014 took place in Medford, Oregon, in April, examining Jackson County Measure 15-119, which banned the growth of genetically modified organisms in that county. Organized and conducted by Healthy Democracy, with twenty Jackson County voters facilitated by local professionals, it was the first such examination of a local, rather than a statewide, ballot measure. It was also the first to test the new process design: shorter, with fewer panelists, no neutral background witnesses, and moderation of all small-group sessions. The Jackson County Citizens' Statement was disseminated via Healthy Democracy's website and the local media, though many voters likely were exposed to the CIR through a survey researchers sent through the mail to roughly one-fifth of the registered voters in the small county.

Two more Oregon CIRs addressed statewide initiatives in 2014, including an open primary election system and a requirement that food manufacturers and retailers label packaged foods that contain genetically engineered ingredients. Both CIR panels opposed these measures; both measures went on to lose on Election Day. That same year, the University of Colorado-Denver hosted the first review held outside Oregon—again on the subject of labeling foods containing genetically modified organisms. Advocates who had gained experience advocating these issues before the Oregon CIR had a second chance in Colorado, but they only persuaded half the CIR panelists and lost at the ballot box. Finally, Phoenix conducted the first city-wide CIR, at which panelists expressed skepticism toward a pension plan reform that the city's voters ultimately rejected.

In spite of the changes introduced in 2014, the process maintained its integrity across each of the new CIRs. One indicator of the quality comes from the citizens who participated in them. At the end of each review, panelists are asked to rate their "overall satisfaction with the CIR process." When looking at the reviews across those four years, satisfaction levels have been very high: over 90 percent have rated their satisfaction as "high" or "very high." Even for the lowest-rated CIR, the most common response was "high" satisfaction, with 95 percent giving it that rating or higher.

Likewise, the researchers evaluating the CIR each year, including this book's authors, have continued to assign solid grades for the process' overall quality of issue analysis, the democratic character of its panels, and the quality of the Citizens' Statements they produce. The typical CIR process has received an A- grade on its deliberation, with some performing better than others but none (so far) earning straight As on these evaluations. As for the statements produced by CIR panels, the typical grade has been a B+, since the CIR panels have produced accurate and substantive Citizens' Statements.

Nevertheless, producing a one-page guide on ballot measures that explains the facts and key arguments in a way that is most useful for a voter who has not had the chance to study the issue as closely as the panelists is a challenge. One difficulty panels run into is conveying complex information in the simplest language possible to improve readability.

The concept of readability has spawned multiple measurement techniques. The numbers in Figure 8.1 use one such approach, called the "Fog Index." This score judges a text's reading level based on the length of both sentences and their individual words, with special weight given to those words having three or more syllables. By this measure, the Citizens' Statements have a linguistic complexity appropriate for a high school senior, or slightly higher.

Expecting readers to approach a Citizens' Statement at the twelfth grade level may not be prudent. The state of Oregon itself has set tenth grade as the maximum reading level for state government information. Then again, in the

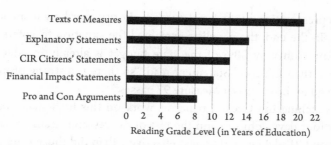

Figure 8.1 Readability of Oregon CIR Citizens' Statements versus other voting guide materials for the same statewide ballot measures, 2010–2014.

official *Voters' Pamphlet,* the state fails to meet its own rule when it comes to the Explanatory Statements it writes on ballot measures, which typically require a level above that of a college sophomore. Worst of all are the laws that citizens must judge: those clock in above twenty, meaning that a JD or PhD would be appropriate training to understand what an Oregon ballot measure *really* says.

Independent Judgment

Reading levels and satisfaction scores aside, the more fundamental question for the CIRs takes us back to the process integrity questions raised by Johnson at the outset of this chapter. Too often, Johnson found that power imbalances among key players compromised the deliberative quality of public consultation. For example, during one such process, Canada's Nuclear Waste Management Organization flexed disproportionate muscle relative to aboriginal nations and organizations. Dissenting groups concluded that the regulatory body "drew from its dialogues with aboriginal peoples only what supports its recommendations." In the end, Johnson agreed with such critical assessments and hoped that future efforts at deliberation would better manage power imbalances between competing interests.

As it would happen, Johnson got the chance to apply her criteria to the CIR in 2016, when a panel of twenty Oregon citizens assessed the "Oregon Business Tax Increase," an initiative sponsored, once again, by Our Oregon. Arguably, this was the highest stakes of any CIR process, with the proposal estimated to raise the state budget by as much as 25 percent by removing a cap on corporate taxes for gross sales in excess of twenty-five dollars.

Given the progressive intent of the measure, it shouldn't surprise anyone that Our Oregon was the prime sponsor. Once again, they had worded the initiative to promise that the legislature would allocate the new revenue to specific purposes, and as described in the previous chapter, critics made hay of this misrepresentation of the legislature's authority over how it spends general revenues. In the end, the panelists explained the situation to voters in simple terms: "Approximately 80% of the state budget is already in education and healthcare," their Citizens' Statement read, "so there is a strong propensity for money to go to those areas if Measure 97 passes."

After watching the Oregon panelists work on this high-stakes ballot measure over four days, Johnson and the rest of the research team concluded that this Oregon CIR deliberated no less effectively than did those from years past. Held during the height of the 2016 presidential election, tensions flared among panelists—and between panelists and moderators. Staff managed those tensions effectively enough and moved the panel through a routinized process that ensured the citizens weighed the testimony they heard before drafting their final Citizens' Statement for the voters. Most of all, the CIR that Johnson observed exercised independent judgment. Just as it did in the case of the 2012 CIR on casinos, it appeared that the CIR process could not be bought or bewildered.

Does such stubborn independence fit the overall pattern of CIR panels? To answer that question, Table 8.1 shows the full slate of fifteen CIRs from 2010 to 2018, including the official Oregon CIRs and pilot tests held in different states, counties, and cities. CIR panels have neither a clear bias for nor against ballot measures in general, with eight panels coming down in favor of a measure and seven against. The panels are capable of reaching near-consensus judgments, with the strongest votes being 21–3 (against the mandatory sentencing, discussed in chapter 6) and 19–5 (for removing the corporate "kicker" tax, discussed in chapter 7), but panelists can also reach split judgments. Seven of the panels favored the pro or con side by only two to three votes. (Close votes are one of the reasons that CIR pilot tests outside Oregon typically do not include a panel vote tally in the Citizens' Statement distributed to the electorate, lest voters misinterpret a narrow win as a definitive recommendation.)

CIR panels on the sale of genetically modified seeds and foods, mentioned in chapter 6, also offer insight into the process. In the case of Jackson County, Oregon, citizens reached a nuanced judgment in favor of banning genetically modified seeds for the simple reason that "there's no practical way to stop genetically engineered pollen and seed from trespassing onto traditional farms, since there's no way to stop the wind and other sources of pollen transport." The particularly strong winds in the Rogue Valley made "contamination of traditional crops . . . very likely," and that contamination means local farmers couldn't replant seeds from their own farms without risking legal action against them.

Two other panels in two different states reviewed the related—but distinct—issue of whether to require food labels to indicate that a product included genetically modified organisms. The results were essentially similar Citizens' Statements, with one panel splitting 11–9 in favor and the other 11–9 against.

In other words, where one would expect reasonably similar CIR results, they occurred. The two food labeling initiatives were roughly equivalent proposals, and sure enough, the CIR panels convened in Oregon and Colorado gave both measures lukewarm reviews. The divergent result for regulating seeds in Jackson County, Oregon, however, suggests that panelists take more than simple presumptions about "genetic modification" into their decisions.

Table 8.1 also juxtaposes the results of the CIRs with final election results. Eight times, the CIRs have taken the same side as the balance of ballots on

Table 8.1 **Voting results from all fifteen CIR panels, 2010–2018**

Year	Election	Ballot Measure	Subject	Panel Vote	Election Results
2010	Oregon general	Measure 73	Sentencing	Against (21–3)	57% For
		Measure 74	Marijuana	For (13–11)	56% Against
2012	Oregon general	Measure 85	Kicker	For (19–5)	60% For
		Measure 82	Casinos	Against (17–7)	71% Against
2014	Jackson County local	Measure 15-119	GMO seeds	For (14–6)	66% For
	Oregon general	Measure 90	Top 2 primary	Against (14–5)	68% Against
		Measure 92	GMO food labels	Against (11–9)	51% Against
	Colorado general	Proposition 105	GMO food labels	For (11–9)	66% Against
	Phoenix municipal	Proposition 487	Pensions	Against (11–8)*	57% Against
2016	Oregon general	Measure 97	Excise tax	For (11–9)	59% Against
	Arizona general	Proposition 205	Marijuana	For (12–9)*	51% Against
	Massachusetts general	Question 4	Marijuana	For (12–5)*	54% For
2018	Portland Metro	Bond measure	Affordable housing	Against (12–8)*	59% For
	California general	Proposition 10	Rent control	For (12–8)*	59% Against
	Massachusetts general	Question 1	Hospital regulations	Against (10–7)*	70% Against

Note. "GMO" refers to genetically modified organisms.
* No official vote was taken but the result presented was recorded via a survey at the end of the process. Some of these tallies include abstentions or undecided responses.

election day, but seven times the panelists have taken the opposite position. That ratio might be about what one would expect from a deliberative body. A panel that deviated *consistently* from the general public might show signs of undue influence from advocates during the CIR process; however, a panel that mirrored public sentiments would do little more than replicate the surface opinions collected in a poll.

The CIR, however, must do more than guess at what a public would decide after deliberating. James Fishkin, who has overseen dozens of Deliberative Polls, argues that such bodies have a "recommending force." Their first job is to deliberate, but their second job is to advise. The same was true of the BC Citizens' Assembly, which explicitly recommended that voters in that Canadian province support the new electoral system it had designed.

Thus, a critical question for the CIR is whether its Citizens' Statements inform and advise the wider electorate. We will return to the personal narratives of the CIR's creators and its panelists, but we must first widen our focus to look at the general public. We invited voters to share their perception of the CIR through one-on-one interviews, focus groups, and large-scale surveys. The next chapter reveals the results of these investigations.

Can Voters Deliberate?

The preceding chapters provide ample evidence that a small group of citizens can get past their political and cultural biases when given the same time, resources, and respect more commonly given to expert panels or legislative bodies. The CIR produced thoughtful one-page analyses of mandatory sentencing and marijuana laws in 2010 and wrote even sharper statements regarding tax reform and private casinos in 2012. All this would be for naught, however, if the findings of those CIR panels went nowhere.

That result had been the norm for the dozens of Citizens Juries Ned Crosby had organized since the 1970s. To take one example among many, a 1993 Citizens Jury analysis of President Bill Clinton's healthcare proposal reached a conclusion that papers across the country found newsworthy. The *Chicago Tribune* captured the main findings in the words of one panelist:

> Odds are Lenny Nelson Jr. knows more about healthcare than you do. Thursday, the Minneapolis custodian finished up the last of five days of analyzing national health-care plans. He and 23 others were selected at random to come to Washington as a "Citizens Jury" to figure out if the Clinton plan is right for the country. By a vote of 19–5, they said it is not. The jurors instead said they prefer the single-payer style plan presented to them by Sen. Paul Wellstone (D-Minn.)—a plan that has been virtually dismissed in Washington as politically unworkable. "Wellstone's plan, most of us agreed, seemed like the way to go," Nelson said.

That particular result was among the most striking from decades of Citizens Juries, with the citizen participants zeroing in on an alternative solution to the healthcare crisis that was not even the focus of their deliberations. So dissatisfied were the jurors with both the Clinton plan and the Republican proposal that they called back Wellstone for an extra round of testimony to hear more about the single-payer alternative. In the end, however, Crosby found that the jury's

Hope for Democracy. John Gastil and Katherine R. Knobloch, Oxford University Press (2020). © John Gastil and Katherine R. Knobloch
DOI: 10.1093/acprof:oso/9780190084523.001.0001

voice carried little weight in the national debate. The Clinton plan died, to be sure. But the single-payer option also fell by the wayside.

The limited impact of Citizens Juries was the standard for deliberative innovations, not the exception. Consider the experience of one particularly timely Deliberative Poll. Recall that these special events bring together hundreds of citizens to meet face to face and query experts on a topic of national concern. A decade after the healthcare jury, Stanford professor James Fishkin and his colleagues convened a Deliberative Poll on a pressing question—whether the United States should invade Iraq to seize their weapons of mass destruction. A Brookings Institution article summarized the main findings of the 343 US citizens who deliberated on this question for three days:

> By the end of the weekend, the participants were more likely to see Iraq as a threat but also far more insistent that the threat be dealt with only within the framework of the United Nations Security Council and on the basis of evidence from UN weapons inspectors. . . . Only 46 percent, compared with 57 percent of the control group, wanted to shift America's focus from Iraq to terrorism. . . . More generally, the participants grew warier of go-it-alone approaches, and not just with respect to Iraq. Support for acting alone to stop the spread of weapons of mass destruction fell from 58 percent to 44 percent, for acting alone to stop terrorism from 67 percent to 52 percent.

The judgment of that 2003 deliberative body had no discernible impact, and it failed to reach even the attention of civic reformers such as Ned and Ty. To succeed, the CIR had to do better. It had to reach Oregon voters and hold their attention long enough to make a difference in how they understood the issues on their ballots. If voters didn't read the CIR's statements, or if they disregarded what they read, the CIR panels could become yet another failed experiment in political reform.

When one of the initiative proponents due to testify at the 2012 Oregon CIR withdrew just days before it got underway, as described in chapter 7, their spokesperson cited precisely this concern. Our Oregon's official skepticism may have stemmed from the fact that the first two CIR panels in 2010 gave unofficial "recommendations" that contrasted with the actual electoral outcomes. One 2010 panel had endorsed medical marijuana dispensaries by a narrow margin, yet the measure failed. All but three of the twenty-four panelists who scrutinized proposed sentencing laws ended up opposing them, but that measure passed easily.

Did Our Oregon reverse its position in 2012 after CIR panels sided with the election results that year? Certainly not, and for good reason. Elections involve dozens of forces that impinge on voters' decisions, and the CIR introduces only one such influence. With the right research tools, however, one can assess a CIR's impact even in the midst of a statewide election.

Changing Votes

The experimental approach provides the best place to start. Carefully designed experiments randomly assign participants to different conditions so that one can isolate the impact of the experimental treatment. Given the experimental spirit of much modern deliberative innovation, too little experimental work takes place. A handful of laboratory studies have been conducted to show the degree to which unsuspecting undergraduates or other research subjects respond to various stimuli, but the most compelling experiments have what researchers call "ecological validity." That is, they occur in compelling settings with real stakes for the participants.

During the final weeks before the 2010 election, the authors of this book designed such an experiment to test the efficacy of the CIR's one-page critique of the proposed mandatory minimum sentencing law. The experiment used 431 Oregon voters who hadn't yet voted, nor even read the official *Voters' Pamphlet* mailed to them by the Secretary of State. Before those respondents answered the main survey questions about the sentencing law initiative, they were placed randomly in one of the following four groups:

(1) a control group that received no further instruction;
(2) a modified control group that read a bland letter from the Secretary of State that describes the *Voters' Pamphlet*;
(3) a standard *Voters' Pamphlet* exposure group that read official summary and fiscal statements; and
(4) the main treatment group, which read the CIR's one-page Citizens' Statement.

After receiving their experimental treatment, respondents answered the following question: "One of the issues in this year's general election is statewide Initiative Measure 73, which would increase mandatory minimum sentences for certain sex crimes and DUI charges. Do you plan to vote YES or NO on Measure 73, or have you not decided yet?" Figure 9.1 shows the stark difference in results across the four experimental groups. In the first three groups, roughly two-thirds of voters intended to vote for Measure 73, but in the group that read the Citizens' Statement, only 40 percent of voters said they planned to vote for the measure.

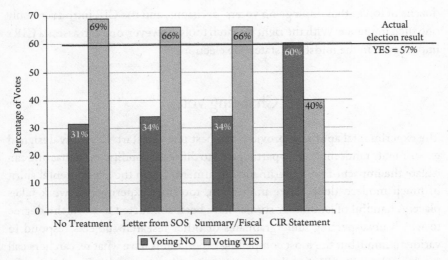

Figure 9.1 Effect of reading the Citizens' Statement on a proposed mandatory minimum sentencing law in 2010.

These data came from an online panel survey, so a large subset of the experiment's participants had given us answers to the same question about the sentencing initiative back in August, months before election day. Among those initially opposed to the measure, 93 percent remained opposed across the four experimental conditions. Of those initially inclined to vote for the measure, only 71 percent still held that position after reading the Citizens' Statement (compared to 88 percent in all other experimental conditions).

The key issue was that a significant proportion of Oregon voters reported in August that they were unsure how they would vote on the measure. In the first three experimental conditions, these initially undecided respondents split nearly 50/50, with a bare majority ultimately supporting the mandatory minimum sentencing measure. What happened to the quarter of the undecided voters randomly assigned to read the CIR's analysis? More than three quarters—fully 78 percent of those who saw the Citizens' Statement—ended up opposing the measure.

That single result was the most striking initial evidence of the CIR's impact on voters. The strong statement that the panelists wrote regarding the mandatory minimum sentencing law had not swayed most of those who initially supported the initiative, but it peeled away some of the measure's broad support. Among those whose opinions were not fixed the summer before ballots arrived in the mail, the statement had considerably more potency.

Even Oregonians couldn't help but take notice of the evidence from this initial experimental test. When Our Oregon claimed in their 2012 op-ed that the

CIR had "zero impact," one of the state's residents fired back in a letter to the editor that referenced this same experimental finding, as it had appeared in an evaluation report submitted to the state legislature.

> It's disappointing to read that Our Oregon has chosen to boycott the Citizen's Initiative Review. . . . Our Oregon . . . claims that the CIR is a waste of time and money, [but] the National Science Foundation disagrees. The NSF measured a dramatic impact on voting behavior among voters who read the 2010 CIR statement . . . , [and] Measure 73 passed, not because the CIR wasn't of value, but because too few Oregonians were aware of the process and read the CIR Statement in their *Voters' Pamphlet*.

National Science Foundation staff doubtless cringe at their portrayal as opinionated authors of a report. It bears repeating the boiler-plate language the foundation asks its grant recipients to memorize: "The opinions, findings, conclusions or recommendations expressed in this material are those of the authors and do not necessarily reflect the views of the Foundation." Fair enough, but to the average Oregon voter, it mattered that a national research foundation saw fit to support the study of their state's electoral innovation.

One might wonder if the striking result of the first CIR was an anomaly. To see whether other Citizens' Statements influenced voting choices to the same degree, the same basic research design was repeated across eight different ballot measures from 2010 to 2014.

Figure 9.2 shows that a somewhat linear pattern emerges, though not without some bumps in the road. This graphic shows difference between those voters shown the Citizens' Statements and those *not* shown them, and it arrays the eight CIR issues by the proportion of panelists who ended up supporting each ballot measure. On the far left, one can see that reading the Citizens' Statement on the 2010 mandatory minimum sentencing law reduced survey respondents' support for that measure by 26 percent. As one moves from left to right in the figure, CIR panelists' support for a proposition goes up. In parallel, the line tracing the Citizens' Statement's effect rises, to a point. Though the statements generally tend to decrease overall support for initiatives among their readers, the effect diminishes as the measure gains support among CIR panelists.

The two issues deviating from this trend are the CIR panels on labeling food containing genetically modified organisms in Colorado and the 2012 Oregon initiative to remove the corporate "kicker" tax refund. The Citizens' Statement on the kicker measure expressed some strong reservations about that initiative, which had overstated the certainty with which these new state funds would go to education. In the end, the panelists concluded that passing the measure was

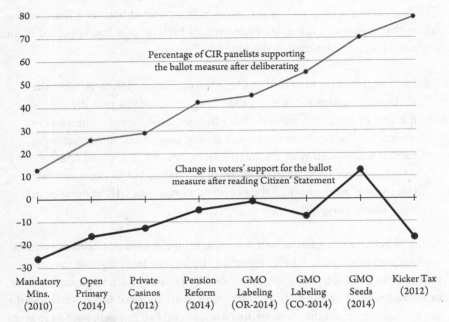

Figure 9.2 Effect of reading the CIR Citizens' Statement on voting in eight survey experiments, 2010–2014.

better than the status quo, but that subtle judgment may not have come through in the Citizens' Statement. In the case of labeling food containing genetically modified organisms in Colorado, the CIR panel that evaluated that proposition split almost evenly, and panelists raised some red flags, such as the fourth key finding: "Approximately 2/3 of the foods and beverages we buy and consume would be exempt." In both cases, the statements amounted to what might be considered lukewarm support rather than a clear endorsement.

The bottom line is that how a CIR panel votes gives *some* indication of its likely effect on the electorate. What really matters, though, is the content of the panel's statement. In fact, two of these CIR survey experiments used statements that didn't show voters how the panel split. The panelist vote tally wasn't shown in the surveys on pension reform and genetically modified seeds. The latter issue, however, saw the largest *positive* CIR impact on voter support for a ballot measure.

Voter Reflections on the CIRs

More statistical evidence awaits, but let's first hear what the CIR meant to voters in the words of two of the many Oregon residents we interviewed one-on-one.

A typical experience was that of a panelist we'll call Rebecca. She first learned of the CIR while reading the *Oregonian*, the state's largest circulation newspaper based in Rebecca's hometown of Portland. The article came out "shortly after the process was initiated, just letting the world know that this was happening."

When she read her first Citizens' Statement, she liked that "it cuts to the chase." The one-page statement "gets a lot of good information out but is concise and well-thought-out and well-formatted." It doesn't necessarily include any unique information, but thanks to the CIR, "each of us individually doesn't have to go through and do it on our own."

In the course of studying and filling out her ballot, Rebecca used the Citizens' Statements as a tool. Once the election was over, she put it out of her mind. When the interviewer asked if she remembered what the CIR addressed in the 2012 election, Rebecca paused. "We vote on so many initiatives," she said, "that I'm trying to remember the two or three that they actually published findings on. . . . I can't remember the issues themselves."

When reminded that the 2012 CIRs concerned taxes and casinos, Rebecca nodded. "I'm not sure they changed my mind," she said, "because I was probably leaning towards the outcome that they recommended, but I thought that the process was good. If I had been an [on the] fence person on either of those issues, it certainly would have made me vote—more likely to vote—along the lines of the recommendations."

A common theme in the voter interviews was that the CIR process itself impressed voters. It offered an alternative information source, even if they couldn't find the right words to describe it. When an interviewer asked a Salem resident we'll call Harold how the CIR "compares to other information provided in the voters' guide," he paused to think. "Well, I think it's fair and, you know, I hate to say 'fair and balanced,' because that's FoxNews, but . . . " Harold took a moment to chuckle. "But that's what I think about it."

"How do you think it compares to political ads?" the interviewer asked.

"It's much more reliable than the ads," he said. "The political ads can't be trusted at all." Again, Harold laughed. "They've all got some axe to grind, and you can't really depend on what they say."

Rebecca agreed with this assessment. She'd even spread the word about the CIR to fellow voters. "I know it's come up in conversation a few times, mostly for me saying, I just love this process." As Harold had noted, the CIR stands out from alternative sources. "It's refreshing," Rebecca said, "to be able to trust some information in the hearts and the heat of a political environment, and that's how I feel about the information that comes out of this."

The most striking voter feedback came from in-depth interviews we conducted in 2014 with sixty voters in Oregon and Colorado. Each of these individuals was a likely voter, and the intent was for each to come into a research lab for an hour before they cast their ballot. Every Colorado voter who came into the lab had no prior knowledge of the CIR, which was an under-publicized pilot project in their state. When given the chance to read what the CIR panel had concluded about their state's genetically modified food labeling proposition, some participants said that reading the Citizens' Statement didn't cause a change of opinion, but it made them want to explore the measure further. As one person said, "It raises more questions in my mind, which is a good thing." Other participants indicated that reading the Citizens' Statement changed their mind or helped them form an opinion on the proposition. Another said, "I feel more enlightened."

The most poignant moment came from a session with a woman who had already voted in her state's first all vote-by-mail election. The participant began by answering the interviewer's questions. When asked to read the Citizens' Statement on labeling food containing genetically modified organisms, she did so willingly and carefully, even though she had already cast a "Yes" vote on the measure. After reading quietly to herself, she told the interviewer that an insight in the Citizens' Statement surprised her:

VOTER: It says two-thirds of the food and beverages we buy would be exempt. Meat and dairy products are exempt, even if they're from animals raised on GMOs [genetically modified organisms]. Alcoholic beverages. So, why are they exempt? *[long pause, as she continues to read]* I wish I would have read this before I voted. Wow!

INTERVIEWER: Why?

VOTER: Because I would have voted differently.

INTERVIEWER: Okay. *[another pause]*

VOTER: Yeah. I would have voted differently.

What Voters Already Know

These voter interviews represent a small sample of the Oregon and Colorado electorates. Though these individuals were excited to read the Citizens' Statements, their experiences might not have been typical. Perhaps the typical voter feels more than ready to mark their ballot without the aid of a citizen panel's issue analysis. To get another measure of the CIR's value for the average voter, we conducted a statewide phone survey of more than two thousand Oregon households during the CIR's first year of existence.

The typical Oregon voter values the opportunity to vote on statewide initiatives every other year: 76 percent say their initiative elections are "a good thing," with less than 7 percent holding the opposing view. To get news and information about ballot measures, 30 percent of Oregonians turn first to local TV news, and nearly as many read the *Oregonian* in print or online. For another 14 percent, the official *Voters' Pamphlet* is the go-to source for information, a fact worth revisiting later.

Being a vote-by-mail state, the Oregon initiative campaigns heat-up well before election day. Figure 9.3 shows that the peak for hearing information and arguments on ballot measures in 2010 came in mid-October, when roughly half of voters heard what they considered pro, con, and objective information on that year's mandatory minimum sentencing initiative. Equivalent figures on the medical marijuana dispensary initiative were considerably lower, with a maximum of one-third reporting that they'd heard neutral or pro-marijuana messages and fewer hearing con arguments.

Put another way, most of the Oregonians surveyed reported that they hadn't heard anything one way or the other on these two ballot measures, both of which had profound implications. Nonetheless, four in five of those who had

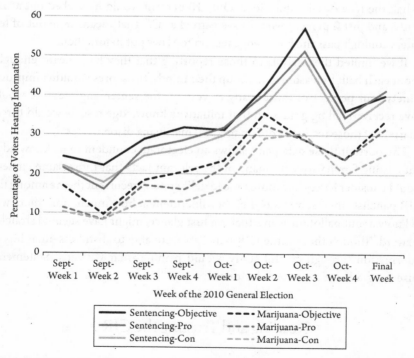

Figure 9.3 Percentage of Oregonians hearing neutral, pro, and con arguments on two ballot measures during the nine weeks leading up to the 2010 general election.

completed and mailed in their ballots said they'd "received enough information" about these two measures.

How warranted was such confidence? We read voters a series of statements about these two ballot measures and asked if the statements were true or false. A follow-up question asked how confident respondents were in their answers, so that we could distinguish certainty from guesses. For example, one important feature of mandatory sentencing is how it affects prosecutions, and we asked whether the sentencing measure "would shift the balance of power in court proceedings by giving the prosecution additional leverage in plea bargaining." It would, and 7 percent of Oregonians knew it. Another 43 percent guessed correctly that this would occur, with the other half of the electorate either unsure of their answers or giving ones that were wrong.

This was among the *highest* knowledge scores obtained for the twenty-two true-or-false items included in our survey. For half the statements, the most common response was a correct hunch, but equally common was either an incorrect guess or complete uncertainty.

The sum of those hunches and doubts may be surprising. We reassured respondents that they wouldn't be graded after answering our questions, but what if they had been? Even if one looked only at those who had voted before the survey, 74 percent of voters didn't know (or couldn't guess) the correct answers to half the true-or-false questions. Only 10 percent would have eked out a "D" grade, and just 2 percent would have earned a "C." That means nine out of ten voters couldn't pass the knowledge test on the laws put before them.

If we limited the analysis to those reporting that they had "heard enough" about each ballot measure to make up their minds, the scores wouldn't improve. Ninety-four percent of those ready to vote on the sentencing measure would have received failing grades on that initiative's knowledge test, as would three-quarters of those ready to vote on medical marijuana dispensaries.

The portrait these data paint shows an electorate confident in its knowledge but lacking familiarity with many of the relevant facts that those same citizens would consider if they had more time to deliberate. A recurrent theme among the CIR panelists themselves was their bewilderment at how much more there was to know about ballot measures that, on first glance, might have seemed straightforward. Though those same CIR panelists were able to distill essential bits of information through careful study, would reading their Citizens' Statements raise the grades of the wider electorate?

Reading and Trusting the CIR

First, that wider electorate would have to become aware of the CIR. Each election cycle, the CIR's statement has to catch the eyes of busy voters already navigating a river of political information. One would hope that anyone who reads the *Voters' Pamphlet* carefully would discover the CIR pages therein, but the 2010 pamphlet ran 136 pages long, and subsequent editions were even longer.

Our initial statewide phone survey found that during the CIR's first year, a majority of Oregon voters didn't even hear of its existence. Though only 40 percent of Oregonians knew about the CIR by the time they had completed their ballots, phone surveys in subsequent years show that figure rising to between 52 and 54 percent in 2012 to 2016. The consistency of the numbers over the last three general elections suggests that this awareness level may plateau unless publicity for the CIR changes dramatically in the future.

Awareness of the CIR generally translates into use of the Citizens' Statement. In 2010, only 29 percent of those who had turned in their ballots at the time of their survey interview had read at least one of the statements, but that figure rose to 43 percent in 2012 and 44 percent in 2014.

The 2014 phone survey also included a question asking respondents how they first learned of the Oregon CIR. The results underscore the importance of distributing the Citizens' Statements via the *Voters' Pamphlet*: 58 percent said that they learned of it from that source; 17 percent credited their awareness to radio/television; 11 percent said "word of mouth"; 8 percent said newspapers; and the rest were spread across other categories.

Those who found their way to the Citizens' Statements generally liked what they saw, and the CIR's reputation improved from 2010 to 2012. In its inaugural year, two-thirds of Citizens' Statement readers found its analysis of mandatory sentencing useful, with 47 percent rating the medical marijuana statement as at least "somewhat useful." In 2012, two-thirds or more found that year's Citizens' Statements useful, with at least a quarter of all readers rating each "very useful."

A variant on that question appeared in the 2012 and 2014 surveys, in which we asked a more pointed question: "In deciding how to vote on [the measure], how helpful was it to read the CIR Statement?" Figure 9.4 shows a dip in the percentage who found the statements useful from 2012 to 2016. In 2012, around 70 percent of voters reported finding the two statements at least "somewhat helpful"; 65 percent thought the statement on non-tribal casinos was helpful; and 73 percent found the statement on a corporate tax reform helpful. The equivalent figure hovered around 57 percent in 2014 and 60 percent in 2016.

Those statistics square with the in-depth interviews we conducted in Oregon. Voters generally see the Citizens' Statements as useful complements to what they already get in the course of an election. The key idea is that it *adds* to what voters already have at hand. Thus, when the 2014 survey asked voters to rate how much new information they got from Citizens' Statements, most rated them as "somewhat informative," with roughly a third saying they brought "no new information."

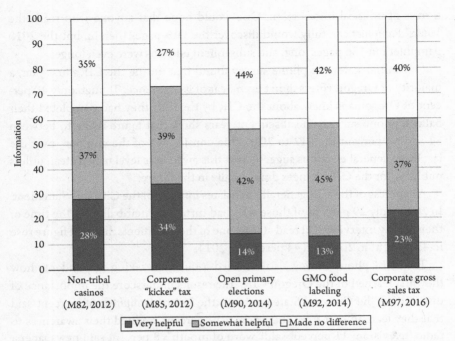

Figure 9.4 Percentage of Oregonians who found the Oregon Citizens' Statements helpful when deciding how to vote, 2012–2016.

The preceding discussion generalizes across all Oregon voters, and one might have expected those with more education or other distinct demographic markers to be more frequent Citizens' Statement readers. To date, no strong predictor of who reads or appreciates the CIR has surfaced. All that turned up in 2014 was younger voters finding one statement more useful than did older voters, and younger voters rating another statement as more informative than their counterparts did. Otherwise, zilch.

Increasing Voter Knowledge

If deliberation can shift people's understandings of *facts*, however, one might worry about who tells the voters what's true and false. When elites strategically misinform a subgroup of voters, they can create what political scientists Jennifer Hochschild and Katherine Einstein call the "active misinformed." To take one example, they found that in 2010, 54 percent of Republicans with college degrees were "engaged and misinformed" about the Affordable Care Act, which meant they intended to act in the upcoming election on the basis of inaccurate information. Fewer than one in five Republicans without a college degree fell into this category, which underscores the fact that people don't just invent lies—they *learn* them.

This concern ranks high on a long list of the things that troubles the mind of US Senator Ted Cruz. When he became a Republican presidential candidate in 2015, he published *A Time for Truth*. Cruz warned about the danger of information sources that feign objectivity to hide their political agenda:

> There is . . . a new, particularly noxious species of yellow journalism that is beginning to infect what passes for modern political discourse. It's called "PolitiFact." Through this website, left-wing editorial writers frequently dress up their liberal views as 'facts' and conclude that anyone who does not agree with their view of the world is objectively lying. Then, left-wing hacks immediately run out and say, "Look! The conservative said something that PolitiFact calls a lie. He wouldn't know the truth if it him with a two-by-four!"

Yes, this is the same *PolitiFact* that earned a Pulitzer for its 2008 campaign coverage, then provided a stark contrast between the accuracy of statements by Trump versus Clinton in the 2016 election. Those who appreciate poetic irony would also want to know that Cruz used a factually inaccurate example to support his claim. He asserted in 2013 that Americans had been credited with inventing Pong, Space Invaders, and the iPhone. Though he got two out of three correct (a Japanese coder brought Space Invaders to the arcade), he complained the liberal elites at *PolitiFact* tagged his claim as "Mostly False." Problem is, their actual rating was a begrudging "Half True."

The Pulitzer committee might wince at what merits investigation between elections, but there are two larger points about which Senator Cruz was correct. First, fact-checking has become a mainstay of journalism, with both independent websites and newspapers such as the *Washington Post* providing timely assessments of public discourse, such as overnight ratings of major speeches or candidate debates. Second, such sites will always be subject to accusations of ideological bias, as has been the case for the editorial boards of newspapers, magazines, and broadcasters.

Political scientist Mark Warren, who helped coordinate the research on the BC Citizens' Assembly, abstracted this problem into a diagram, a revised version of which appears in Table 9.1. When Warren looks over the political landscape, he sees what he calls "motivated reasoners" who are subject to the same cultural cognitive biases detailed in chapter 3. Those motivated reasoners with limited knowledge end up as the kind of unpleasant ideologues we instinctually avoid, unless we seek the cultish comforts of a political fringe group. Those who *do* become issue experts hold public office and fill the ranks of interest and

Table 9.1 **Trust-relevant qualities of political actors within democratic systems**

Issue Knowledge and Deliberative Competence	*Goal-Oriented ("Motivated") Reasoning*	
	Low	*High*
Low	Apolitical or "independent" citizens	Highly partisan citizens and fringe advocates
High	Citizens' Initiative Review	Legislators, policy advocates, interest groups, and partisan media

advocacy groups. The media also fall into that cell when taking a political stance, as one sees with Fox News or MSNBC. Nonpartisan media don't appear in the table because they cannot take partisan stances, by definition.

Thus, citizens have no ready source of political advice that provides more issue-relevant information than they already possess. Into the otherwise blank cell in the diagram, however, drops the CIR. Those voters who happen to live in Oregon and who seek guidance on a ballot measure can turn to a Citizens' Statement and expect competent judgments relatively free of biased reasoning. Warren also knew about the CIR, which he called a form of "trustee democracy." Trustees enable citizens "to participate more knowledgably and effectively" by giving them timely and relevant information.

This is precisely what Ned had in mind when he designed the CIR, and it's also what had drawn Ty and Elliot to the idea. It's what Marion and Ann experienced as panelists, and it's what they hoped to sustain as members of the CIR Commission.

For consistency's sake, this abiding faith in the CIR must remain subject to careful study. Has the CIR made voters more knowledgeable about the issues put before them? Or do ideological and cultural biases make voters resist the factual information that a CIR provides?

Every year of the CIR, survey experiments have tested the efficacy of a Citizens' Statement as an educational tool. The 2012 voter survey, for example, included ten knowledge items that corresponded to the critical issues addressed by the CIR on corporate tax reform. Reading the Citizens' Statement yielded true/false test scores (60 percent correct) more than twice as high as those of the other experimental conditions (25 percent correct). Just as the earlier data on voting and values suggested, Oregon voters exposed to the Citizens' Statement appeared to read it carefully enough to become more knowledgeable about the measure.

Even more encouraging was the reach of this effect across cultural lines. Positions on the corporate tax initiative split along cultural lines, yet egalitarian voters improved their knowledge scores by 14 percent compared to a twenty-point jump for their counterparts (hierarchs). To look across a wider set of issues, one can locate the corporate tax initiative at one end of an ideological continuum, with its opposite being the mandatory minimums measure strongly favored by conservatives. At various points along that spectrum lie the other six CIR issues studied in a similar manner.

On every one of the eight CIR survey experiments conducted from 2010 to 2014, voters gained knowledge when exposed to the Citizens' Statement relative to the control group and the other experimental conditions. More importantly, across the ideological spectrum of issues analyzed by the CIR, what voters learn does not reflect how their politics align with an issue.

When expressed as a percentage gain in issue knowledge, the CIR's effect may appear modest. Across the 2010–2014 surveys, reading a Citizens' Statement increased the rate at which voters gave correct answers by just 13 percent, as compared to the control group. That boost looks more impressive when considering that college graduates' knowledge scores were only 9 percent above those for voters with a high school degree or less. Likewise, the CIR knowledge bump is greater than the 11 percent gap between those who follow politics "most of the time" versus "hardly at all."

Though the Citizens' Statement has a clear effect on voter knowledge for those who read it, the survey experiments on this phenomenon reveal many other intriguing findings, which lie beneath the overall pattern. One of these is the difference between asking voters to assess a true statement versus a false statement. Across our surveys, voters started with far better knowledge scores for true statements than for false ones. The CIR had a comparable effect on both true and false statements, but it did not often convince voters that false statements were incorrect. Rather, it more often made voters uncertain of such statements' veracity.

Sharing Information

For maximum impact, the CIR would need to do more than make its readers knowledgeable. To become a "trustee" of public information, as Warren dubbed it, the CIR would need to persuade its readers to *share* the CIR's findings and resist other attempts to undermine the accurate information it conveys.

For the 2016 election, we examined these two questions in regard to the Oregon CIR on Measure 97, which proposed removing a cap on excise taxes. We asked respondents about four factual claims, each of which had been adapted directly from the Citizens' Statement.

- *Second Key Finding*: The Oregon legislature would have the authority to use the revenue generated by Measure 97 according to the priorities it identifies.
- *Third Key Finding*: The estimated 6 billion dollars Measure 97 could generate biennially would represent a 25 percent increase in overall state revenue.
- *Third Pro Argument*: Oregon state expenditures are growing faster than the state's tax revenue.
- *First Con Argument*: Measure 97's tax could increase significantly what consumers pay for essential goods and services.

In the previous section of this chapter, we showed that reading Citizens' Statements from 2010 to 2014 increased respondents' confidence in the accuracy of valid factual claims. After replicating that result with an experiment built into the 2016 survey, we narrowed our focus to only those respondents who had not yet voted but who had seen the Citizens' Statement on Measure 97 during our online survey. This section of the interview began by revealing to respondents the origin of the four claims and posing a question: "Each of the following four statements appeared in different sections of the Oregon Citizens' Initiative Review Statement on Measure 97. Which, if any, of these pieces of information would you like to share with friends, family, acquaintances, or others before they vote on Measure 97?"

For each of the four knowledge claims, survey respondents could indicate that they would "definitely not share," "probably not share," "probably share," or "definitely share" the information. (Those who chose a "don't know" response were dropped from the analyses, but this had a minimal effect on sample size.)

In each case, a majority of respondents said they would "probably" or "definitely share" what they had learned from the Citizens' Statement. More interesting were the variations in these responses across different voting groups. A voter's eagerness to share knowledge depended on the specific claim, as well as on respondents' positions on the ballot measure. Table 9.2 shows that Measure 97 supporters were more eager to share the information about a revenue increase the measure might bring than the costs it might entail. A large majority of the opponents of the measure were inclined to share each fact, but that majority was smallest regarding the revenue increase the measure would engender. For all four items, more than three-quarters of the undecided voters were ready to pass the information along to others.

These results make clearer what it means when voters say that they "trust" the CIR. Majorities want to share what they learn from the Citizens' Statements— sometimes including information that goes against their own voting preferences.

Table 9.2 **Percentage of respondents who would probably/definitely share four claims from the Citizens' Statement on Measure 97**

Voter group	KEY FINDING: Legislative authority (%)	KEY FINDING: Revenue increase (%)	PRO CLAIM: Expenses rising fast (%)	CON CLAIM: Raise costs for consumers (%)
Opposes Measure 97	77	59	69	85
Undecided	80	77	78	87
Favors Measure 97	75	80	80	44
Overall	77	71	75	69

Fulfilling a Narrow Purpose

The CIR was neither the first nor the only attempt to link a small deliberative group to the general public, but its relative success may reflect its modest ambitions. As a comparison, consider the June 2011 Deliberative Poll that brought together 412 California voters to establish priorities for governance reform in that state. For three days, these citizens discussed problems in the initiative process, legislative representation, local government, and tax and fiscal policy. Behind the citizen body stood a formidable array of co-sponsoring institutes and nonprofits, such as Common Cause, as well as a panel of legislative, policy, and public engagement experts. They helped bring the citizens' recommendations to the electorate in the form of Proposition 31, which appeared on the 2012 statewide ballot. Alas, the multifaceted proposition met opposition from both left and right. In the end, it won less than 40 percent of ballots statewide.

Whereas that process, like the BC Citizens' Assembly before it, aimed to create an electoral outcome, the CIR's sole purpose is to better inform voters. As the official CIR Commission explains, it provides "an innovative way of publicly evaluating ballot measures so voters have clear, useful, and trustworthy information at election time."

Previous chapters showed that CIR panels can render sensible judgments and explain the key issues and arguments voters must weigh when deciding how to vote. The question that had remained for this chapter to answer was whether the larger public would take up the challenge to consider the complexities their fellow citizens put before them. As it turned out, the CIR has succeeded in not only summarizing but also *conveying* that information to voters. A succession of

Citizens' Statements have clarified for many voters key facts and caused them to re-evaluate the principal arguments for and against ballot measures.

In fulfilling that task, however, the CIR has played a fleeting role in people's lives. Recall the voter who cheered the CIR as an invaluable source of information, even telling her friends about it. Once the election was over, she couldn't remember the issues it had addressed. Even if the CIR prompts a whole public to deliberate, that deliberation comes to a natural end each election day. Once the ballots are tallied, the voter returns to being a citizen. Initiatives cease to be questions in the voter's mind. They become either law or failed campaigns.

Yet deliberative processes that bring citizens together only briefly can have a more lasting effect. Researchers have found that jurors who serve for just a few days often come away more committed to participating in future elections, following public affairs, and working with others to improve their local communities.

Even deliberative processes that fail to realize their intended purpose can leave a lasting impression on those who deliberated. The Californians who participated in the Deliberative Poll mentioned earlier certainly saw the world differently after their three days together. When asked beforehand to assess "the system of democracy in California," 61 percent said it functioned "extremely poorly," with 21 percent saying it worked "extremely well." After deliberating, the proportion of those rating it favorably nearly doubled, with only a minority still giving it the lowest rating.

Could the same kind of transformation occur for the two dozen people who participate in the CIR panels? Might these kinds of effects radiate out further, to shape how Oregonians at large view themselves, their fellow citizens, and their political system? Could the CIR not only improve the quality of voter decision making but also bolster the legitimacy of democracy itself? Could it transform the way people think about politics by inspiring a more deliberative norm to replace the extreme partisanship we take for granted today?

Such feats might seem too grand for small citizen panels built to carry out a more modest task. Yet, this may not be beyond the CIR's reach. After all, reshaping democracy itself is the more fundamental aim of nearly all deliberative experiments. The next chapter will present new data that shows whether the CIR serves that greater purpose.

Restoring Public Faith

After her first experience serving as a CIR panelist, Marion reported feeling something change inside her. She felt a political awakening.

> [The CIR] changed my perspective dramatically. Going in, I was curious but not at all hopeful that this would turn out well. Previous experiences . . . [had shown] that no viable conversation could be had [about] political issues. And the CIR completely turned those experiences on their heads—I now *know* that it can be done. . . . A safe space can be achieved and that safe space brings out the individual and collective intelligence of all of us. . . . I have hope that we could in fact reclaim our democracy. I don't know if we will or not, but I know that we have the ability and the intelligence. And I saw the commitment that everyone brought to the process. I would never have believed it if I hadn't been there. But I saw it, and there is no doubt we can do that.

Marion didn't just believe that citizens could reclaim democracy, she wanted to help make it happen. When asked to sit on the CIR Commission, the official state body that oversees the Oregon CIR, she didn't hesitate. As a commission member, she helped decide which measures panelists would review for the *Voters' Pamphlet*. She brainstormed process modifications to strengthen the quality and efficiency of the CIR. She's met with state officials and testified before the state legislature on several occasions. During her stint on the commission, Marion at times expressed frustration that state government too often lacks the respect and reflective decision making that she experienced at the CIR, but she remains hopeful that the CIR offers a chance for a different kind of democracy.

Though the high arc of Marion's story is exceptional, study after study has confirmed the transformative power of citizen deliberation. By giving citizens the opportunity to cross political divides and engage in informed and respectful political decision making, processes like the CIR have the potential to change

Hope for Democracy. John Gastil and Katherine R. Knobloch, Oxford University Press (2020).
© John Gastil and Katherine R. Knobloch
DOI: 10.1093/acprof:oso/9780190084523.001.0001

how citizens think about their role in governance, take part in political conversations, and engage in public life. If political life socializes us into accepting our role in conventional partisan politics, experiences such as participating in a CIR panel can *re*-socialize us into a new ways of thinking and acting.

This chapter presents evidence of precisely how the CIR, and civic opportunities like it, can change us. Before getting into the details, though, it's useful to take a step back and ask how it is that fleeting experiences such as these can leave a lasting impression.

What Juries Do for Democracy

Recall that the CIR has its roots in the Citizens' Jury process that Ned Crosby developed in the 1970s. Ned used juries as a kind of metaphor partly because it is only within the jury context that most Americans use or hear the word "deliberation." As it turns out, the jury has a subtler parallel with the kind of political deliberation Ned wanted to encourage. Ned had hoped that the experience of deliberating together would give participants a spark of civic inspiration, and as it turns out, even the humble jury system can transform a private individual into a more passionate and powerful democratic citizen.

Statistics bear this out, but consider first the experience of a juror who served near the city of Seattle, Washington, in 2004. Maria was a middle-aged homemaker who told an interviewer that she was "fascinated by the process" she saw at her county courthouse. The modern building impressed Maria, but she was even more pleased by what happened inside it. While serving as a juror on a two-month trial, Maria kept reminding herself that the defendant "was on trial for murder." Maria said she was careful to "pay attention, remember everything, and keep a clear open mind." She recognized that her decision would "affect this person for the rest of his life."

Maria described her twelve-person jury as "an amazing group." Once her jury began to work inside a cramped room at the courthouse, however, their deliberations became stressful. Driving home after the first day of deliberation, Maria confessed that she had "burst into tears" and "cried all the way home." The next morning, Maria argued with the foreperson about the murder charges, and then another juror stepped in and explained how the jury was supposed to deliberate. The juror reminded her that "we all have to come to a consensus together." The jury gradually worked through its disagreements and returned a verdict of murder in the first degree.

Long after her trial concluded, Maria told an interviewer that she changed as a result of the experience. "After it was over," she said, "I realized how much I liked the law, how much it meant to me to put all the pieces of the puzzle together, and how important it was to get my verdict in." After two weeks in the courthouse,

Maria wanted to make a bigger difference in her community. She began doing local volunteer work and became politically engaged. The jury experience even made her decide to "go back to work" outside the house. She said that serving on a jury made her want to do "something with passion and purpose."

Maria was certain that her jury experience made her more active in politics and civil society, but how often does it have this effect? As it turns out, Maria's story was one grain of sand in a study funded by the National Science Foundation to collect public records in eight different counties across the United States, including mostly medium-sized cities, such as Omaha, New Orleans, and El Paso. Thousands of juror service records were combined with county election records to figure out how often these individuals voted before and after serving on a jury.

To understand this study, remember that even after being selected for a criminal jury, there are many reasons that a person may never get to participate in jury deliberation. A person can be named as an alternate, or the trial may end without jury deliberation for legal reasons, such as when charges are withdrawn, a mistrial is declared, or a defendant changes to a guilty plea.

Thus, due to forces beyond their control, this study's large sample of empaneled jurors were split into two groups—those who got to deliberate and those who did not. Comparing these two groups showed that serving on a criminal jury trial increased a person's odds of voting in elections during the years that followed. The "participation effect" of jury service added up to roughly a 5 percent increase in voter turnout for several years. Put another way, the voting effect of even just a few days of jury service was as powerful as an entire semester spent in a civics course, or a whole year serving in student government.

Moreover, the study showed that the participation effect can come from *any* deliberating jury, regardless of whether it reached a verdict or became a hung jury. Only one in twenty juries end up as hung juries, but their experience of democratic deliberation is as powerful as it is for other juries. The civic effect of deliberating appeared for trials weighing both minor and more serious crimes, but it was stronger when juries had to return several verdicts for multiple charges. After all, juries weighing more charges face a more complex deliberative task as they make *more* decisions often involving interlocking judgments and mixed verdicts.

How Deliberation Re-Educates Us

In this sense, a CIR panel represents a kind of supercharged jury, which makes not only one overall decision for or against a ballot measure but also a series of important decisions about each sentence that goes into a Citizens' Statement.

To understand how the CIR might have a civic educational effect, start by thinking of the CIR as a classroom. The organizers and facilitators play the role of the teacher, particularly on the first day of orientation. The panelists play the part of the students as they soak up the information presented to them. The neutral witnesses and policy advocates who enter the room assume the role of guest lecturers, with their contributions managed carefully by the rules of the classroom.

As the week unfolds, however, the panelists take on other roles as well. They act as teachers for one another. They start to control the flow of guest lecturers. Even the purpose of the course shifts from learning about a ballot measure to practicing the skills of deliberating to conceptualizing a different kind of politics.

Stanford University psychologist Albert Bandura provides an educational model that encompasses these different kinds of learning. Bandura's career has spanned more than half a century, and his thinking shows the influence of theories that extend from the mechanistic behaviorism that Ned Crosby endured in graduate school to the more dynamic learning theories that superseded it. Supported by hundreds of studies, Bandura's model posits that people learn behaviors and attitudes in four ways: "direct experience of the effects produced by their actions, vicarious experience of the effects produced by somebody else's actions, judgments voiced by others, and derivation of further knowledge from what they already know by using rules of inference."

Bandura labels these four processes enactive learning, observational learning, verbal learning, and inferential learning. The CIR context provides apt illustrations of all four. Panelists learn the skills and habits of deliberation by enacting them for five straight days. They learn deliberative norms by observing each other and particularly the facilitators, who consciously aim to model active listening, respectful talk, and rigorous issue analysis. The bulk of a CIR panelist's verbal learning comes in the form of oral testimony from witnesses, along with the printed materials on the ballot measure that they review together. They also get instruction in the art and purpose of deliberation, from organizers, facilitators, and especially the former panelists who play a key role in their orientation on the first day.

The fourth method of learning, however, plays a special role in the CIR. Inferential learning takes us far beyond rote learning of rules or the mimicry of observed behavior. Bandura viewed inference as the foundation of human invention and freedom—our creative ability to look beyond what the world lays out in front of us. It is through our "capacity to manipulate symbols and to engage in reflective thought," Bandura argues, that "people can generate novel ideas and innovative actions that transcend their past experiences." We can conceptualize and learn previously unseen behaviors by combining or adjusting those we've experienced, observed, or been shown.

For a CIR panelist, the inferences drawn from the experience enable a reimagining of oneself. A panelist can infer new possibilities for their role in democracy after the close of the CIR panel itself. Based on the powerful experience of the CIR, a panelist might change not only their attitudes toward democracy but also their estimation of their own political capacities. They might also change the habits they had formed prior to the CIR and try to become a more engaged citizen.

This returns us to the idea of a civic re-socialization, or re-learning the responsibilities, attitudes, and habits of a democratic citizen. Different conceptions of good citizenship abound, but one can conceptualize the deliberative citizen simply by reversing the forms of political alienation that plague modern democracies.

Table 10.1 shows five facets of political alienation. The CIR can't change the structural reality of modern politics, but it can show another way of engaging in civic life. As the beating heart of that deliberative process, citizen panelists practice that new kind of politics and feel its power. They experience the formation of a considered judgment through a fair process, and they become connected to the entire state electorate in a way that can powerfully reshape the course of an election. Such a rare experience likely packs considerable weight as a tool for civic re-education. Or, at least, that's the theory.

Personal Transformation

As for the evidence supporting that theory, a growing body of research has found that participation in deliberative experiments—even ones less spectacular than the multi-day CIR panels—can reduce the public's sense of political alienation. These findings have been summarized in multiple academic reviews, some of which have noted the importance of providing citizens with some measure of real influence, as with the CIR. As political scientist Heather Pincock explains, a key variable is "whether participants are asked to reach a collective decision. The psychological conditions produced by collective decisions," she explains, "are conducive to educative effects on deliberative skills and dispositions. When the stakes are real for participants, and when they must reach a decision through discussion, they are more likely to engage in the process in a way that can foster deliberative skills."

Even if past studies have shown the educational impact of deliberation, too few have shown anything more than short-term changes. Fewer still have tried to assess participants' subjective experience of such changes. Do participants in a deliberative forum sense themselves changing? Do they attribute that change to the forum itself? These are particularly important questions because in any

Table 10.1 **How participation in the CIR moves participants from political alienation to engaged citizenship**

Facet of alienation	What citizens learn through the CIR	Attitude shifts triggered by the CIR	New habits citizens learn by participating in the CIR
Commodification One's opinions and judgments get reduced to a political commodity	The panelists' judgment, as well as the reasons underlying it, get crystalized in a Citizens' Statement distributed to the full electorate.	Citizens feel an increased sense of political self-confidence.	Panelists become more likely to share their knowledge and views with fellow citizens and public officials.
Social isolation Weak connections to fellow citizens and community networks	Panelists work closely alongside two dozen fellow citizens for a week and also get connected, via the *Voters' Pamphlet*, to every other registered voter in Oregon.	Panelists come to identify more with one another, including with those who hold different views.	After meeting other panelists, citizens may become more engaged in community life and develop more diverse political networks.
Meaninglessness One gets presented with false choices and develops only limited political knowledge	Though panelists can't change the question put before them, they can study it fully and even comment on the larger problem it was designed to address.	Panelists not only gain issue-relevant knowledge but also develop a firmer grasp of politics and democracy.	To attain more balanced current knowledge on other issues, panelists pay more attention to public affairs, possibly turning to more diverse sources in pursuit of another CIR-like experience.
Normlessness Public institutions appear to perpetuate partisan warfare, rather than democratic self-government	Panelists learn and practice a deliberative model of politics, which they can carry with them into other venues.	A positive experience with the CIR heightens panelists' faith in the efficacy of a more deliberative politics.	With newly honed deliberative skills, citizens seek to find or create other ways to use those skills in their communities, and perhaps at work and at home.

Table 10.1   **Continued**

Facet of alienation	What citizens learn through the CIR	Attitude shifts triggered by the CIR	New habits citizens learn by participating in the CIR
Powerlessness One feels incapable of influencing government or addressing pressing community problems	The panelists exercise tremendous power in clarifying for the electorate the key considerations on an important statewide issue.	Panelists recognize that the power they exercised came from state government, which created the CIR to address a public concern.	Though the CIR stands in contrast to mainstream politics, panelists become more willing to take part in conventional political processes to make their voices heard.

public debate on democratic reform, citizens are more likely to advocate for deliberation's educational potential only if it is experienced as such.

Previous studies on deliberation also suffer from focus on single events, rather than multiple public forums. If deliberation is what changes people, results should show up across specific experiences. Fortunately, data collected in recent years with funding from the National Science Foundation and the Australian Research Council make such a comparison possible.

Toward that end, it's first necessary to make the acquaintance of another democratic experiment, the 2009 Australian Citizens' Parliament. This parliament convened a representative body of Australian citizens tasked with creating and evaluating policy proposals for the Australian federal government. Bearing some resemblance to two other deliberative processes mentioned in chapter 9—California's Deliberative Poll on governance reform and the BC Citizens' Assembly—the Australian Citizens' Parliament brought together one member of each federal electorate to address the question, "How can Australia's political system be strengthened to serve us better?" Participants were selected through stratified random sampling, with a special effort made to include Aboriginal participants.

After convening in brief regional gatherings and then again online to develop a set of initial proposals, the 150 citizen parliamentarians met over four days in February 2009 at the Old Parliament House in Canberra, the nation's capital. Parliamentarians divided their time between large plenary sessions and facilitated, small-group discussions, and they stayed focused on their task even as deadly brush fires raged in the nearby state of Victoria. More than one citizen remarked that the gravity of their task as parliamentarians required their full attention, even as the fires claimed the lives and homes of too many of their fellow Australians. On the final day, the citizens presented a set of recommendations to the Prime Minister's parliamentary secretary, then each returned to their daily lives.

One testament to the enduring significance of serving on the Citizens' Parliament, or on the CIR panels, was the remarkable response rate of these citizens to a survey conducted a full year after their participation had ended. Eighty-seven percent of the Australians completed their surveys, as did 77 percent of the CIR panelists we contacted.

And the results of those surveys? Figure 10.1 tells the story for the CIR panelists. The citizens who deliberated in Salem, Oregon in the summer of 2010 believed, one year later, that their experience had changed them. They had become more politically self-confident, had more faith in politics, and greater faith in deliberation. They came to view themselves more as "Oregonians"—members of a common political and cultural unit. This same pattern appeared for the 2010 panelists when we surveyed them just two months after their participation. In other words, the CIR had both an immediate impact and a lasting one. Even with a small sample size of thirty-seven complete surveys, the likelihood that most of these changes were due to chance was less than one in one thousand.

The one non-significant change is telling. A year after their remarkable experience deliberating together, 57 percent of the panelists did not change their view on the question of whether "people have the final say, no matter who is in office." Of those who did change their mind on that particular claim, more of them were

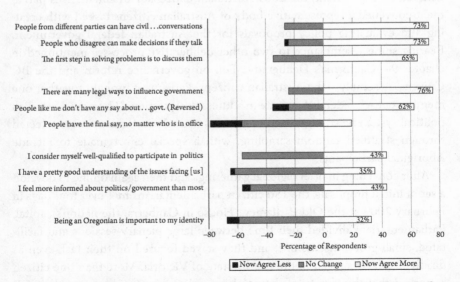

Figure 10.1 How 2010 Citizens' Initiative Review panelists believed their civic attitudes changed one year later.

likely to doubt it than to believe it. One could chalk that up to a healthy skepticism since previous research has shown that at some point too much faith in government and the political process can actually dampen civic engagement by way of a passive acceptance of the status quo. Talking to the panelists tells a more nuanced story: after transcending their own biases and learning to work across political differences with their fellow citizens, panelists were often disappointed that elected officials couldn't, or wouldn't, do the same.

Would the same attitude shifts occur as the result of a deliberation more than 7,770 miles away from the capitol building in Salem, Oregon, in the Old Parliament building in Canberra, Australia? In a word, yes. The 115 Australians who completed their surveys showed precisely the same pattern of differences—even with the same lone non-finding. When surveyed a year later, most Australian citizen parliamentarians hadn't changed their mind about the statement, "People have the final say, no matter who is in office," with 27 percent agreeing with it less than they did before (and 24 percent agreeing with it more than they did before). They did, however, report that the Citizens' Parliament experience made them more politically self-confident, more optimistic about the power of deliberation, more hopeful about democratic government, and even more attached to their Australian identity.

Aussies and Oregonians also saw their civic habits changing in similar ways as a result of deliberating with their fellow citizens. Figure 10.2 shows the results for CIR panelists. After their experience, participants thought they were much more likely to pay attention to the news and turn to their fellow citizens to discuss issues and candidates. They also saw themselves becoming more active in community affairs, but not in traditional politics. Though panelists said they

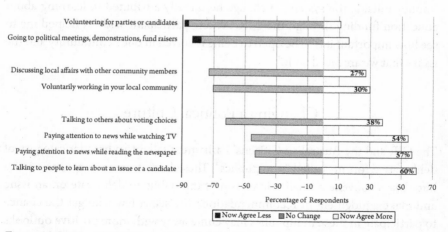

Figure 10.2 How 2010 Citizens' Initiative Review panelists believed their political behaviors changed one year later.

were more engaged on every other measure, the uptick in volunteering for candidates and attending political events was too small to count as a statistically significant result. (With a larger sample size for the Australian study, a similar result for attending political events did reach significance.)

Follow-up interviews with the 2012 CIR panelists asked for their perspective on the process two years after serving. The focus this time was on hearing their reflections in their own words. Many panelists discussed the lasting value of the deliberative skills they had acquired. One panelists said that he became more inclined to keep "an open mind until I know all about an issue." Another noted that because of the CIR, he became "willing to look at positives going on in current government." He now had "a more full understanding of how two sides can be equally valid," and this gave him "less negative judgment about things and more curiosity and interest at what may be motivating the opposing view." Another veteran panelist put it this way:

> Learning how to think the issue through [and] hearing the other side really helped me see how I can make biased automatic judgments. The review helped draw out the pros and cons to make more informed decisions. . . . I am so grateful for this idea, I am tired of not knowing the whole truth when I make decisions, it is more like gambling without things like the CIR.

Consistent with the 2010 survey data, some 2012 panelists reported becoming more involved in their local communities as a result of the CIR. One noted that he utilized his deliberative skills in his position on a city council, and another said that he had started organizing a high school alumni association to help find "money outside the system," a change he directly attributed to learning about education funding through the CIR. As one participant said, "It helped me to see how important it is to be open to being involved in one's community and the issues that we are faced with."

Changing a Political Culture

The CIR and the Australian Citizens' Parliament fall into a broader category of deliberative forums called "minipublics." These bodies come in many varieties but always convene a small microcosm of the public to deliberate on an issue and make a judgment or recommendation. The select few who get the chance to participate in these minipublics may come away with more positive outlooks and civic habits, but what about the rest of society?

The goal behind many deliberative experiments is systemic political change—not a few compelling personal transformations. The hope is that deliberative bodies will forge policy consensus on difficult issues, alter the focus of media coverage, or bolster the legitimacy of bona fide democratic institutions. Even if the CIR has achieved one such macro-level goal, by making voter judgment in initiative elections more informed and reflective, the question remains as to whether it can have more lasting effects on the larger public.

One particular purpose receives the focus here. Political theorists have speculated that the conspicuous presence of a deliberative minipublic connected to macro-level decision making could change the attitudes of those who did not get the chance to directly participate in its deliberation. In the case of the CIR, this means that convening deliberative citizen panels and posting their findings in the *Voters' Pamphlet* could have statewide effects on civic attitudes for those citizens who become aware of the CIR's structure, purpose, and outcomes. Those who become aware of the CIR are, in a sense, engaged in a kind of deliberative process if they can incorporate a minipublic's findings into their own internal reflections and political conversations.

Minipublics like the CIR could reshape the wider public's civic attitudes in some of the same ways they influence the few who participate in them directly. After all, a government's establishment of inclusive minipublics may signal to the wider public the development of a more legitimate and deliberative kind of politics—a sign that governing officials care about what citizens have to say. Seeing fellow citizens competently perform the tasks normally left to professionals may also increase the public's confidence in their own political abilities or even bolster one's confidence in the capabilities of one's neighbors.

To see if the CIR has such an effect, we turn again to survey data. The first of these came in 2010, when we conducted a two-wave online panel survey of the Oregon public that permitted us to measure their general political attitudes before and after voters learned about the CIR for the first time. Between August and October, many Oregonians appeared to change in response to the CIR's arrival. The top row of Figure 10.3 shows that voters came to see their government as more responsive once they recognized that it had created the CIR. Voters who took the time to read one or both of the 2010 Citizens' Statements became more confident in their own political abilities.

What makes those results particularly compelling is that they measure real change in attitudes over time—not perceived change—and they control for many other factors, such as age, education, political party, and so on. Those control variables also show that the magnitude of the CIR's impact compares favorably with the effect of educational level and political knowledge. These findings parallel those from chapter 9, which showed how reading the CIR gave a knowledge boost equivalent to the gap between high school and college educated voters.

This was the first time a deliberative process had shown such effects on a wider population, and some scholars who saw the 2010 survey data were reluctant to believe them unless a second study replicated the findings. For the following round of CIRs, we had sufficient funds to survey those Oregon voters with valid email addresses. After controlling for the same demographic and political variables, the same pattern of effect appeared for confidence in oneself and one's government. In addition, this cross-sectional survey featured a new item, which showed that both awareness and use of the Citizens' Statement boosted Oregonians' confidence in their initiative voting choices.

Open-ended interview questions gave a clearer sense of why these changes occurred. Regarding confidence in the state government, one voter felt good about being part of a governing process that adopted the CIR: "I would have a better feeling about living in a place where they had a lot more of these than I would some place that didn't have any. . . . It offers a more independent view."

Another voter favorably compared the CIR to their experience with New England town meetings, like those described in chapter 2. "I'm experienced in direct democracy," he said, "and I kind of miss it. They'd actually stand up and look the other guy in the eye and talk things out, you know? It really was an

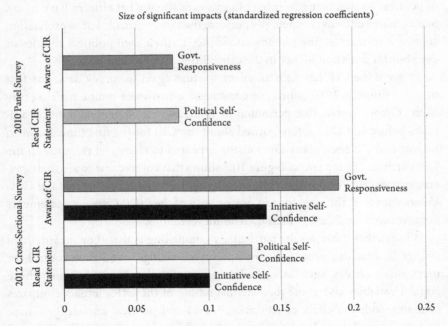

Figure 10.3 Impact of learning about the CIR and reading a Citizens' Statement, 2010–2012.

amazing experience compared to your typical at-a-distance politics." For these voters, the presence of the CIR was evidence of a different—and better—kind of politics, one less swayed by strategic campaigns and more responsive to thoughtful consideration and the will of the public.

Inspiring Citizens to Vote

Such statistical results are encouraging signs that even just appreciating the CIR and reading its voting guides can make a difference in how the public sees itself. Boosting the public's confidence in its own capacity to influence policymaking goes a long way toward reducing its sense of alienation. It would be something else, however, to show that the CIR induces both attitudinal and *behavioral* change for the wider public. The grandest ambition of minipublics like the CIR is to heal and empower an alienated public, such that it can act more decisively.

When thinking about the CIR's behavioral impact, there may be a kind of parallel with the civic impact of jury service, which led off this chapter. Just reading a Citizens' Statement is unlikely to turn a non-voter into a voter since few people would read such a statement unless they had already decided to participate in the election. But, there is a sense in which even a voter must still be persuaded to vote, all the way down the ballot. This gap between how many people show up to vote and how many complete their ballot on a given item is called the "undervote."

A recent study assessed the cause of undervoting by way of a clever natural experiment. Each year, voters across California have the chance to vote on the same statewide initiative, but how long it takes a voter to get to that initiative on the ballot depends on where that voter lives. By statute, California's statewide propositions appear after not only federal but also state and local offices on the ballot. Voters living in areas with many local contests have to wade through more voting choices before getting to the statewide ballot questions. After setting up statistical controls to address other factors in the data, the authors concluded that "choice fatigue" accounted for 8 percent of the total undervote. The study also found that measures further down the ballot tend to get more "No" votes, as weary voters fall back on a status quo bias against any proposed legislation.

Worse still, the average undervote across a decade of elections was found to be over 21 percent. In other words, one in five voters skipped whatever appeared at the midpoint of their ballot. Granted, California's ballots are notoriously long, with an average of over thirty candidates and propositions appearing on ballots in the decade studied.

With that in mind, consider what one of the Oregon voters interviewed about the CIR said when asked whether it helped with completing their ballots: "It definitely makes me want to vote more, because it helps you understand the issues." This idea was intriguing enough to investigate further in a statewide survey. How many voters might, as a result of reading the Citizens' Statement, cast a vote on a measure they might have otherwise left blank?

Our 2014 Oregon statewide online survey approached the subject with a question that acknowledged the reality of undervoting: "Some people choose to skip over particular ballot measures while filling out their ballot. Did reading the Citizens' Initiative Review statement . . . make you more likely to mark your ballot on this particular measure, less likely to do so, or did it make no difference?"

Figure 10.4 shows the results from this online study for two different survey populations. The two sets of columns on the left include those respondents who intended to vote but who hadn't yet read the *Voters' Pamphlet*. In the course of completing their survey, those voters were shown the Citizens' Statement: nearly 40 percent of them said reading it made them more likely to vote. The two sets of columns on the right include voters who had already read the statement on their own before taking the survey. The result was similar, with a third being more likely to vote after having read the Citizens' Statement.

A critic might object that results such as these reflect self-conscious survey respondents' unwillingness to disappoint their interviewers. This "social desirability bias" can cause surveys to overestimate voter turnout, for example. Though the experimental aspects of these surveys gives us confidence in interpreting the differences in responses between treatment categories, it does make us unable to estimate precisely the magnitude of the CIR's boost on voter turnout.

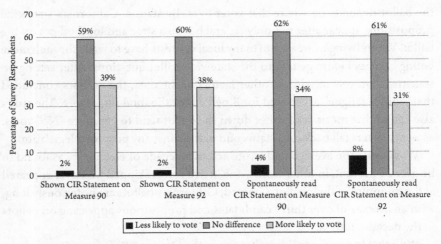

Figure 10.4 How often reading a Citizens' Statement changes willingness to vote on the corresponding ballot measure, 2014.

Fortunately, there exists an alternative method of approaching this question. In chapter 9, aggregated experimental data from 2010 to 2014 showed how reading Citizens' Statements could change voting choices, but those same results have a hidden finding: The CIR not only changed the balance of "Yes" versus "No" votes on ballot measures; it also decreased the *likelihood* that a respondent would abstain altogether from taking a position on an issue. The overall effect amounted to an eminently plausible and modest 3 percent increase in willingness to vote. With a large sample spread across eight different CIR issues studied in this way, the result was statistically significant.

More interesting was how that result varied depending on a respondent's general level of political engagement. Those who said they followed politics "some of the time" or even "most of the time" demonstrated the same drop in abstentions as seen in the overall population. The smaller subset of people who paid attention to politics "only now and then" (14 percent of our sample) showed a larger change. That group's abstention rate started much higher (18 percent) and dropped much further, down to 11 percent. Put another way, less politically engaged citizens who read the Citizens' Statement become about as likely to abstain as more active voters who didn't read a statement.

And what of the 4 percent of survey respondents who said they were "hardly at all" attuned to politics or public affairs? That group included just ninety-nine people in our combined 2010 to 2014 dataset, but their response to the CIR was starkly different. For that group, reading the Citizens' Statement *increased* abstentions. The percent declining to vote on the ballot measure addressed by the CIR rose from 18 percent for non-readers to 24 percent for readers.

At junctures such as this, two sometimes-rival theories of democracy have common purpose. Theorists who stress the importance of high public participation rates have worried that deliberative institutions can dampen turnout by bewildering voters into inaction. Watching PBS and showing up for a National Issues Forum can paralyze a person who might have been fired up by watching a more partisan news outlet or going into an online chat group with like-minded citizens. Our finding for the 4-percent sliver of respondents disengaged from politics appears to fit that pattern.

To see the larger picture, notice how this reduction of undervoting works in tandem with other democratic institutions. Participating in one deliberative process, such as a criminal jury, can inspire unsteady voters to participate more regularly. Those new voters, however, may be among those most likely to suffer "choice fatigue" in an election, but the CIR can provide them with a boost, which can encourage them to read on through a crowded voting guide and keep making decisions as they move down a long ballot.

The net effect of getting more people involved and encouraging them to return complete ballots could be considerable. Voter turnout studies have found that socioeconomic class consistently differentiates the frequent voter from the infrequent one. As more voters fill out more ballots, the electorate includes an ever-larger share of working-class and poor voters. In the aggregate, richer and poorer voters make very different choices in elections, whether selecting among candidates or judging proposed laws.

Discoveries such as these should give hope to those who wish to see stronger democratic institutions. That aspiration is shared among the individuals whose personal stories we've been following in this book. In our concluding chapter, we consider how Marion, Tyrone, Ned, and others like them from all across the globe have tried to make their society more participatory and deliberative through advancing the CIR and many other innovations that share a family resemblance.

Conclusion

What's Possible?

In the end, the story of democratic experimentation and political change is not the story of any one person, nor is it any one person's story. At any moment, the spotlight might fall on someone extraordinary—someone who has the right skills, know-how, and frame of mind to take a small opportunity for change and make an indelible mark on history. More often, though, such small acts of civic faith receive no special notice.

Thus, we began with the story of Marion Sharp, who stumbled her way toward a convention hotel in Salem, Oregon, in 2010. There, she made common purpose with other Oregon citizens, each of whom might take up the torch and carry it forward another short distance. One of those fellow panelists was Ann Bakkensen, the conservative voter who worked with Marion and twenty-two other Oregonians to deconstruct a poorly written sentencing law.

A retired librarian with a passion for information, Ann moved easily among both panelists and the staff. She'd put her easy smile and cheerful disposition to good work in her career, and she saw the CIR as a new opportunity for public service. Her passion for this democratic innovation grew so strong that, five years later, she found herself in another state capitol, this time seated before the House Committee on State Government in Olympia, Washington. Members of the Washington state legislature wanted a firsthand account of her novel experience as they considered bringing the CIR to their own state.

Sitting at the back of the long room, Ann chatted with university professors who would also be testifying. They had at their disposal Power Point slides and reams of statistical evidence. All she had were a few notes and a disarming smile. Though nervous, Ann wasn't disconcerted. Having spent years now speaking on behalf of and representing the CIR, Ann was confident that she had something to offer the committee members that the others couldn't—her personal experience as an everyday citizen who'd been empowered by participating in this democratic experiment.

Hope for Democracy. John Gastil and Katherine R. Knobloch, Oxford University Press (2020).
© John Gastil and Katherine R. Knobloch
DOI: 10.1093/acprof:oso/9780190084523.001.0001

After taking a swig of water and clearing her throat, she greeted the committee and introduced herself as "a retired elementary school librarian from Portland." She reminded the committee that a CIR panel is meant to include not only librarians but also people from any walk of life. She noted that her panel included a diesel mechanic, a coach, a baggage handler, a United Farm Workers activist, a small-business owner, a naturalized citizen from Canada, and a young man from eastern Oregon looking for work. These differences were interesting, but what they had in common was more important:

> When we came together the one big thing we had in common was that we were there to work together to provide a service for the voters of Oregon. . . . We were there to put our own opinions aside, analyze the information.

As much as Ann had reminded herself to keep to the script, she realized that she'd forgotten to breathe.

"I'm kind of nervous now," she said to the committee chair. "Sorry."

After a quick pause, Ann found her rhythm. She explained the purpose of the CIRs and tried to describe the visceral experience of doing important but difficult work alongside fellow Oregonians. "It felt really good," she said, "to unite with other Oregonians and feel like there was something greater than our own opinion. It was respecting each other, valuing each other, listening to each other, and coming up with some conclusions that were going to serve *all* Oregonians."

That didn't quite capture it. The words were still too abstract. Ann tried thinking of something personal, which might tie back to the committee members' own lives. "I'm a Republican in Portland," she said. Living in such a liberal bastion, she explained, "I don't even *admit* that I'm a Republican because it brings automatic judgment. When I say I'm a Republican most people say, 'You? You're a Republican?' I guess because they think I'm a nice person."

That worked. The committee chuckled, along with the small audience sitting behind her. Ann laughed with them, then drove home her point. It was a freeing experience to be among citizens serving on a deliberative body in which nobody asked if she was a Republican or dismissed her for being one. "On the panel," she explained "none of that is important. What's important is respect, listening, working together."

Having found a way to relate to the committee, Ann said more about the process and why she thought Washington voters would appreciate having it. Her personal reflections, though, were what resonated. Representative Sherry Appleton, who serves in a liberal district one short ferry ride west of Seattle, said to Ann, "I know how you feel about not saying you're a Republican. I happen to spend some time in Florida. I never tell anybody I'm a Democrat. So, it works both ways." The committee and audience laughed again.

The jokes were a bit stiff, but Ann had made a connection. Legislators know firsthand what it's like to be dismissed based on their party affiliation, as though there is nothing more to them than party politics and the allegiance to their caucuses. Such rigidity isn't inevitable in state legislatures, as was evidenced by the bi-partisan support the CIR won in Oregon in 2009 and has maintained ever since.

In Washington, however, there was no such luck. Representative Jeff Holy might have thought Ann was "very nice and wonderful," but he and his Republican colleagues on the committee recommended against passing the bill. They did so without registering an objection against it, and this pattern repeated when the bill went to the House Committee on Appropriations. Though the bill had narrowly advanced, thanks to Democratic majorities on both committees, the Speaker of the House did not bring it to a floor vote. It was fitting that a bill calling for more citizen deliberation died not by the force of the stronger argument against it but for reasons that have never been articulated, let alone placed in the public record.

The likely culprit in this unsolved case is anxiety on the part of the liberal policy advocates who have successfully run initiative campaigns in Washington. The Our Oregon leadership that opposed tinkering with the initiative process in their state might have conferred with their counterparts in Washington. They could have warned their northern neighbors of the independent and unpredictable voices of citizens like Ann. As she told the legislators, she viewed her job as listening to all witnesses and fellow panelists before writing a statement that should help all Oregonians vote wisely.

On the other hand, Healthy Democracy's experience with Our Oregon in recent years suggests that even some of the CIR's critics may have come to accept it. In a 2016 interview, Our Oregon Deputy Political Director Courtney Graham acknowledged that her organization still has no official position on the CIR. As she put it, the process has become "a small part of the many other activities and opportunities" for her organization in the course of statewide elections. Though her comments downplay the overall significance of the CIR, she made it clear that her organization would prefer citizens hear simply from pro and con advocates.

"The idea of 'independent experts,'" Graham explained, "is flawed and should be reconsidered. . . . No one is independent, no fact is unbiased, and by presenting some people as independent and some as advocates or biased, it creates a tension that the facts and reporting coming from campaigns is somehow less trustworthy." As public anxiety grows about "fake news" and "alternative facts," one might dismiss this concern as self-serving, but Graham points out that the

CIR Commission could play a stronger role in managing the tension between expert and advocate testimony.

As an advocacy group, Our Oregon wants to maximize its advantage in the process, but Graham's desire for "more transparency" in how the commission and Healthy Democracy staff manage the process resonates with broader concerns about public consultation processes. Even scholars sympathetic to the aims of deliberative democracy have found problematic the methods by which events are designed and executed. From Deliberative Polls to the America*Speaks* forums Marion attended before she joined a CIR panel, the integrity of any deliberative process requires that its inner workings remain visible to disinterested observers and policy advocates alike.

Expansion of the CIR

Washington House Bill 1364 may yet resurface, as such laws usually take time to germinate in a busy legislature that has at the front of its agenda more familiar and far-reaching legislation. Meanwhile, the staff of Healthy Democracy continue to look for other states in which the CIR could take root. Having run pilot projects in Arizona and Colorado in 2014, both remain potential candidates for adoption, but another possibility emerged in the spring of 2015 at the opposite end of the country.

Harvard's John F. Kennedy School of Government invited Tyrone Reitman to a day-long workshop and public event focused on the CIR on April 21, 2015. The most important part of the day was the gathering in the foyer of the Ash Center for Democratic Governance and Innovation for a panel discussion cheekily titled, "Getting to Yes (or No): Making Ballot Initiatives More Voter-Friendly and Deliberative." The faculty assembled at the end of the day to discuss the CIR included luminaries in democratic theory, community organizing, and public policy, some of whom had served the White House at one time or another—one had recently presided over the American Political Science Association.

After brief introductions, Ty opened his remarks by acknowledging the work of others. When he described the CIR process, he reminded the audience that it was "an adaptation of the Citizens' Jury method of public deliberation, which has been around for a long time, pioneered by Ned Crosby . . . about thirty years ago at this point." Not for the first time that day, Ty acknowledged a debt to the man who'd helped Ty blaze the CIR's trail through Oregon and Washington.

In his comments, Ty offered an explanation for why the CIR's trail had gone cold in Washington just a month earlier.

I've had conversations with a wide array of interesting people who work in direct democracy, some of which I would categorize as my heroes for sure, some of which I would say are borderline crooks, one of which actually landed in jail. I had a conversation with a very prominent campaign consultant in the state of Washington a few years ago that I think sums this up best. I kind of went through my usual spiel on the potential benefits of the CIR and talked about the inner workings and wanted to elicit her thoughts on this. And I asked her point blank, "What would you have to tell your clients about this particular idea?"

She said, "90 percent of the time I would tell them that deliberation, transparency, and sunlight are good things when it comes to direct democracy. But then there's 10 percent of the time where, frankly, my job is to pull the wool over the public's eyes to get the result that I know my clients want."

Such is the job of a campaign professional, as we discussed in chapter 2. Some might be more callous, and simply seek the election result that the client prefers, but the one Ty alluded to is a more common breed—one that has a passion for a particular policy outcome and believes some degree of trickery is necessary to get the result that's in the public's best interests, even if the public doesn't know it.

However common that viewpoint might be in politics, Ty remained undaunted. He concluded his opening remarks at the Ash Center by confessing to getting a "thrill" from the experience of discussing the CIR with those in attendance. He explained that he'd "started out as a concerned Oregonian wanting to see a direct democracy work" and never expected he'd be spreading an idea that could transform politics not only in Oregon but across the country.

Though Ty was the featured guest of the event, to his left sat a man in a dark blue suit who was on the panel despite confessing that he'd "never heard of [the CIR] until three or four months ago." Massachusetts state representative Jon Hecht (D-Middlesex) admitted that participating in the panel was, for him, principally "a great opportunity for me to learn and get the benefit of your thoughts on this as we move forward with the bill that I have filed, which . . . is now House 561." Again, sheepishly, he added, "To be honest with you, we cribbed the whole thing from Oregon."

Representative Hecht explained that Massachusetts needs to reform its initiative process because of the changes that have come to it in recent years. "For the first sixty-five years" of initiative elections in the state, he explained, "there were only twenty-eight initiative petitions put forward. In the thirty years since, we've had forty-seven." Recent years have seen a steady stream of three or four issues per election cycle, including "one on medication to end life, what the proponents called the Death with Dignity initiative. Pretty tough one." Issues such as these "brought to the surface some of the problems associated with initiative petitions . . . The complexity of the issues and the way in which the initiatives are written generates a lot of confusion among voters."

The representative recognized, however, that larger issues were at stake. He noted the alienation that voters can experience when initiative elections go sour.

> I'm also concerned about an existential problem, as it were, in our political system. The initiative petitions are contributing to that sense of a loss of control, sort of the voter's sense of a loss of control over politics and over our political system as they see all this money flowing into these battles. All of this media. All of this sort of extreme partisanship around the issues. [Campaigns say,] "If you support this, you'll be with all of the angels, and if you oppose it, you'll be with all of the devils."

That sentiment is the converse of the nonpartisan spirit Ann felt at the 2010 CIR. As she later conveyed to the Washington legislature, the CIR was a refuge from partisan bickering and divisive rhetoric—a place where people who are different can still respect and listen to one another. Many across the country share Ann's exasperation with conventional politics and desire for something better, but what led Representative Hecht to discover the Oregon CIR and advocate its adoption in Massachusetts?

The answer provides one more reason to be optimistic about the potential diffusion of democratic reform. Representative Hecht acknowledged that he'd learned of the CIR from one of his own staff. "I've been thinking about this and looking for ways to, in my small way, make a difference," he told the Harvard audience, "and fortunately I had a new legislative aid come to work with me."

That's right. It was an aide, fresh out of college, who made the connection. Sam Feigenbaum had been interested in better governance since taking a gap year between high school and college. Like Ty before him, Sam journeyed to distant parts of the globe with an eye toward understanding a life different than his own. Whereas Ty wanted to understand the world's religions, Sam hoped to become a poet. Studying abroad granted Sam a new imperative.

> I traveled fairly extensively in the developing world and become fascinated by the choices that governments in those countries had made and the impacts it had on people's lives there. When you travel in the developing world, you quickly realize the advantages [you have], and I felt like my government and my community was a big part of

that, and I felt some sort of need to give back. I think the place that I traveled where lack of governance and the deleterious effects of that was most prevalent was in Malawi, where I volunteered at an orphanage. I guess this explains my interest in state and local politics. There were a lot of young idealists in Malawi who were going to change the world, but they hadn't realized the extraordinary cultural barriers— the difficulty in making change in a community you're not part of. That experience planted a desire to get involved with the community that I had grown up in.

Sam took this experience with him as he began college, majoring in political science. For his senior thesis, Sam called on a long history of scholarship arguing for the need to better tether government decisions to considered public judgements. Political theorist Robert Dahl, said that democracy requires providing equal and adequate opportunities to formulate and express informed points of views on political issues. Most contemporary political systems can't meet that standard. Instead, everyday citizens watch politics from the sidelines, and levels of participation are often lowest among the least powerful. Sam agreed with those who believed deliberative political institutions could transform modern politics and move us closer to the democratic ideal.

Shortly after graduation, Representative Hecht hired Sam as a legislative aid. The two began talking about the potential for deliberation in Massachusetts. Hecht encouraged Sam to find out what other states were doing. Sam found his way to the same theories, research, and case studies described in this book. He read about Deliberative Polling. He learned about Citizens' Juries. The BC Citizens' Assembly crossed his radar. It all sounded exciting, but those processes hadn't been formally institutionalized in the United States. Hoping to find an example of a government-sanctioned deliberative endeavor, Sam went to the Internet. Google led him to the CIR.

Representative Hecht liked what he saw and thought it could be a model for Massachusetts. Without even contacting Healthy Democracy, Hecht filed a bill nearly identical to the one used to permanently institute the CIR in Oregon. What he now had before his colleagues in Massachusetts was, he admitted, "a very, very new" bill, only filed for the first time in 2016. "It's a new idea in Massachusetts, so we have a lot of work to do just to educate people as to what the concept is." Hecht noted that earlier that same day, Sam took Ty "to meet with the staff of our election law committee, which will presumably have jurisdiction over the bill and gradually, hopefully not too gradually, do our work of education among our colleagues." But that education had already begun. As Hecht noted, one of his legislative colleagues was in the Ash Center foyer, learning about the CIR for the first time.

Deliberation across the Globe

That is precisely the story of democratic innovation described in this book. Greek city-states experimented with new systems of government and learned by trial and error. Fellow Massachusetts politician John Adams and his contemporaries drew inspiration from the ancients when they dared to imagine the design of the emergent American republic. Now, as the CIR comes up before legislatures across the United States, so are a full range of ideas about deliberation and democracy spreading across not only North America but also Australia, Africa, Asia—anywhere there are officials like Representative Hecht who are listening to new voices, like that of his legislative aide, who in turn drew inspiration from the efforts of Ty and Ned to create the CIR.

Even in the details, there are striking parallels between the emergence of the CIR and another case of democratic progress five thousand miles south of the United States in Buenos Aires, Argentina.

Many features distinguish Argentina from other South American countries. It is the largest Spanish-speaking country on its continent and has the eighth-largest land mass for a single country in the world. Though it has struggled to maintain political stability and secure human rights for all its citizens, it has entered a period of relatively robust economic prosperity and political development. It is in this modern context that a handful of Argentinians have managed to build a deliberative institution more than a century overdue.

During a string of civil wars, a coalition of Argentine provinces established a constitution in 1853. By the end of the century, most of its provisions had gone into effect, but Section 24 had not. Listed among the "Declarations, Rights and Guarantees" was a passage that read, "Congress shall promote the reform of the present legislation in all its branches, and the establishment of trial by jury." That final phrase dangled precariously at the end of the sentence, and its grammatical insecurity proved prophetic. No regular jury system emerged in Argentina in the Nineteenth Century.

It was not until recently that Argentina finally saw a jury system established in any of its provinces. In 2015, the first jury trial occurred in Buenos Aires, and as goes the nation's principal region, so likely goes the rest of the nation. Within ten years, it is likely that Argentine citizens in every province will have the right to be called to serve on juries and to become as powerful in their own judicial system as those in the United States. Giving citizens that extra ounce of political control can nurture a more expansive sense of political capability and spur increased civic engagement, as discussed in the previous chapter.

Among the first Argentinians to serve as a juror was a fifty-five-year-old woman in the province of Neuquén. This woman, who we shall call Carla, lived in Piedra del Aguila, or "Eagle's Stone," a town name that accurately signals the remoteness of its location, along the Limay River below the Andes Mountains. Living closer to Chile's border than her own nation's provincial capital, Carla had little contact with her government prior to being called to serve. When the summons arrived, she asked her sister to open it because Carla couldn't read. When she arrived at the courthouse, she asked to be excused.

Like so many jurors before her, however, Carla had a transformative experience. Though she hadn't completed primary school, she was able to understand the essential details of the case, which involved a murder that carried a minimum sentence of fifteen years. The trial lasted several days, all of which Carla spent in Neuquén, at the expense of the court. The jury system in Carla's province didn't require unanimity, but she ended up in the majority, which reached a guilty verdict.

Afterward, Carla didn't understand why her period of service had come to a close, and she asked court officials if she could serve again. Once she returned home, Carla made herself a vow, which she has now fulfilled. She would return to school and complete the equivalent of at least a sixth-grade education in reading and writing.

Her story was tracked by news media in Argentina, then was spread wider by a small cadre of legal reformers. These individuals all belonged to the Asociación Argentina de Juicio por Jurados (Trial by Jury), which has a simple name that sounds like any other political or legal non-governmental organization—a formal body that advocates on behalf of one reform or another. As the example of Healthy Democracy shows, there are often more personal stories underlying the impersonal exterior of such groups.

Though various Argentinians have advocated for juries over the years, the current move toward a national jury system owes considerable credit to an individual law professor and a team of students he organized. Andrés Harfuch taught a seminar on trial by jury at the Universidad de Buenos Aires in 2012. But he recognized that his cause needed more than the new scholarly articles and books that he wrote and edited. It needed new faces, which he saw on his students.

Harfuch would walk anyone who cares to listen through the story of "a true feat of cultural resistance" by Argentina's jury advocates against "a retrograde and patriarchal legal tradition." He characterized his nation's legal establishment as "antediluvian," which technically means pre-dating Noah's voyage across the Good Lord's floodwaters. Skeptics argued that the "Argentine people lacked education and preparation for judgment." Critics told Harfuch that "jurors would be easily manipulated by eloquent lawyers or media. Judges, ultimately, were the only ones who could administer the law with rationality, correctness, sanity and common sense."

His refutations of such arguments inspired a handful of his students to join the cause for jury reform. Now, looking at the roster of the aforementioned Asociación, its senior officers are outnumbered by this team of young lawyers. Almost all of these woman began this work in their twenties, and they dubbed themselves "Las Chicas," meaning "The Girls." This group quickly gained a national—and international—reputation for effective advocacy. As fashionable as Eva Perón, minus the vague ideology, Las Chicas have worked alongside influential politicians and judges while traveling across Argentina to advocate for juries, present research on legal and political implications of the jury, and discuss the complexities of setting up a new jury system. The net result is unprecedented momentum toward fulfilling their nation's forgotten promise for jury deliberation.

The Pace of Political Change

"Momentum" is the right word. That is what Ty and his collaborators brought to the model of deliberation Ned Crosby invented in the 1970s. In chapter 1, we noted that momentum propelled the adoption of the initiative itself. After South Dakota led the way in 1892 and Oregon followed suit four years later, a wave of initiative adoptions broke across the nation, with seventeen more states—from California to Massachusetts—implementing one form or another of the initiative process.

Historians credit the spirit of the Progressive Era with causing this rapid spread, with citizens in various states seeking more influence over state laws so as to wrest control from lobbyists and a wealthy elite. Those same forces may be aligning at the present time. In 2014, the most frequent concern named by Americans was the "government" itself rather than, say, the economy or crime. That same year, nearly every major media outlet was discussing a study published in an academic journal with the droll title, "Testing Theories of American Politics: Elites, Interest Groups, and Average Citizens." Its authors used a newly created database that linked public opinion and policymaking data to show that "economic elites and organized groups representing business interests have substantial independent impacts on US government policy, while average citizens and mass-based interest groups have little or no independent influence." Among its findings: the net influence of citizens in the top 10 percent of income distribution was fifteen times greater than the rest combined.

Cultural divides notwithstanding, roughly nine in ten Americans agree with the assessment that elected officials in Washington, DC, are "heavily influenced by special interests." Surveys suggest that citizens' views of local and state government are more favorable, but the vast majority of voters who have an initiative process want to keep it in place for the power it affords them, even though—like Representative Hecht—they want to reform initiative elections.

How quickly could such changes arrive? Recent reform movements have benefitted from the accelerated pace of information diffusion and attitude change in the Internet age. In the United States, one way to look at the acceleration of change is to array the rate at which states join other states in removing bans on issues ranging from interracial marriage to recreational marijuana. *Bloomberg Businessweek* compiled the data and found a pattern. "A few pioneer states get out front before the others," their report found. "Then a key event—often a court decision or a grassroots campaign reaching maturity—triggers a rush of state activity that ultimately leads to a change in federal law."

It may seem curious to associate rapid change with deliberation, a form of talk designed to slow us down. For example, the movement for legalizing same-sex marriage in the United States, which culminated in the historic 2015 Supreme Court ruling *Obergefell v. Hodges,* has relied more on advocacy campaigns, protests, and legal challenges—all of which forcefully advance a point of view, rather than sitting down with opponents to have a discussion. That more visible strategy, however, obscures the real role that quieter conversations played in changing public attitudes.

A wave of reversals swelled within the Republican party and among cultural conservatives, such as Senator Rob Portman from Ohio. In 2013, Portman reversed course after his son came out as gay during his freshman year at Yale. Portman told a reporter that "it allowed me to think of this issue from a new perspective, and that's of a dad who loves his son a lot and wants him to have the same opportunities that his brother and sister would have, to have a relationship like Jane and I have had for over twenty-six years."

In a guest column for the *Yale Daily News,* Portman's son expressed pride in his father's reversal, "not necessarily because of where he is now on marriage equality (although I'm pretty psyched about that), but because he's been thoughtful and open-minded in how he's approached the issue . . . He's shown that he's willing to take a political risk in order to take a principled stand."

Today, same-sex marriage is the law of the land in the United States. Opposition is rapidly declining even as advocates continue to work towards full legal equality and fend off attempts to roll back progress But forerunners to Portman knew the stakes when they changed course. One of the most vivid examples was New York State Senator Roy McDonald, who in the summer of 2011 was the penultimate vote that tipped the scales to legalize same-sex marriage in his state. Hailing from an upstate district, which skirts the eastern edge of Albany, McDonald knew his constituents would balk at his change of heart, but he grew to resent the pressure exerted on him by party leaders and religious groups. He reflected on the issue and experienced a genuine change of heart.

"You get to the point," he explained in a press conference, "where you evolve in your life where everything isn't black and white, good and bad."

McDonald took pride in his reputation as a tough Irish-American, and he almost welcomed the scorn he knew would come from critics. For them, he had these words:

> Fuck it, I don't care what you think. I'm trying to do the right thing. . . . I'm tired of Republican-Democrat politics. They can take the job and shove it. I come from a blue-collar background. I'm trying to do the right thing, and that's where I'm going with this.

The next year, they *did* take his job and gave his seat to another Republican. In a three-way general election, only one in six voters marked McDonald's name, which appeared alongside the Independence Party after he lost his own party's primary.

Outside the United States, deliberation has played a more public role in advancing the cause of same-sex marriage equality. In particular, deliberative innovations enabled citizens to break through the same kinds of political logjams common in US politics. To see how, we turn to David Van Reybrouck, whose vision of democratic reform parallels his career in writing, appropriately enough, historical fiction. His book *Against Elections* hasn't reached many US readers because, alas, it is written in Dutch. The basic idea takes us back once more to Athens and resonates with our central theme. Western democracy is "fatigued" and requires the movement of citizens from the periphery to the center of political life. The ancient idea of selecting legislators by lot, also known as "sortition," holds particular appeal for him, and he points out that Venice and Florence continued this practice long after ancient Athens had collapsed.

Just as smaller western states like Oregon took the lead with the CIR and with the initiative process itself a century earlier, Van Reybrouck believes that "Ireland and the Netherlands are the real forerunners of democratic innovation in Europe. Small countries will play a major role in experimenting with new models, so that the big, really problematic democracies like the French can learn from them." In France, he reports that he sees "so much hatred vis-a-vis the elected that it sometimes feels like 1788."

Similar sentiments could be heard in the most recent US presidential election. Journalists and politicos repeatedly attribute the rise of Donald Trump, as well as Bernie Sanders, to a backlash against a political establishment that seems to ignore the will of the public. Some voters have begun to feel so disenfranchised that they see any defeat at the polls as proof of a rigged electoral system designed to protect elites.

Are these, in fact, revolutionary times? Are conventional politics so broken that the idea of randomly selecting citizens to do legislative work might hold a broader appeal? Van Reybrouck thinks so. One of his favorite examples reprises the issue of same-sex marriage in the "democratic laboratory" of Ireland, which held a constitutional convention using everyday citizens. In the wake of an economic recession, a group of academics persuaded the Irish government to experiment with a more deliberative approach to policy innovation. After piloting a citizens' assembly in 2011, modeled loosely on its British Columbian forerunner, Ireland established a Constitutional Convention that ran from 2012 to 2014. Like the one held in John Adams's day, the convention delegates featured prominent political leaders, including twenty-nine members of the Oireachtas, which is loosely analogous to the US Congress. But two-thirds of the ninety-nine delegates were selected at random from among the citizenry.

Of the eight issues placed on the convention's agenda in its charter, attention focused on number five: "provision for same-sex marriage." On July 2, 2013, the convention submitted to the government its report on this issue, a statement as brief as one from a CIR but more directive in its advice. The Convention on the Constitution called for "amending the Constitution to provide for same-sex marriage." That decision resulted from "over one thousand submissions lodged by citizens, advocacy groups and representative organizations," along with presentations from "legal and academic experts" and "advocacy groups," "round-table discussions," and "question and answer sessions." More than three-quarters of the convention delegates voted for "mandatory wording in the event of such an amendment going ahead, meaning that the State should be obliged to enact laws providing for same sex marriage," along with laws addressing "the parentage, guardianship and upbringing of children."

What followed two years later was unprecedented in two respects. Ireland became the first nation to legalize same-sex marriage through a national referendum. Perhaps more importantly, Ireland became the first nation to alter its constitution at the behest of a largely randomly selected advisory body. As an essay in the *Washington Post* explained after that historic vote, many came forward to claim credit for the victory. Gay-rights activists could rightly take credit for tilling the soil of a country that was 84 percent Roman Catholic, through years of protests and personal conversations. The political campaign for the referendum itself was crucial in winning 62 percent of ballots cast. The authors of the *Post* essay, however, were among those academics who brought the convention into being, and they offered this perspective:

> Arguably, the question would not have been put to the Irish people during this government's tenure if not for the Irish Constitutional Convention (ICC). Including representatives of all the parties in the

> ICC's deliberations . . . ensured a high degree of cross-party consensus
> in favor of marriage equality—both in favor of putting it on the ballot,
> and in favor of its success.

The point is not that the ICC single-handedly swayed Irish public opinion. In fact, polls suggested that a majority of Irish citizens already supported marriage equality when the convention was authorized in 2012. The key was putting behind the elected members of the convention the force of a deliberative public will, as manifested in the two-thirds of delegates who took part as everyday citizens:

> The reason for selecting citizens at random was to ensure that they were
> there in their own right as ordinary citizens; they didn't feel mandated
> as a result of fighting for office, nor did they feel duty bound to repre-
> sent vested interests. Rather than the norms of parliamentary grand-
> standing and debating from fixed positions that so often governs bodies
> of this type, the norm was deliberation, with detailed discussion after
> becoming informed on all sides of the issue, respecting differing views
> and being prepared to change one's mind.

For those citizens, party leadership wouldn't punish their vote by taking away committee assignments. There wouldn't be any primary challenger for them in the next election. In this sense, the citizens in the ICC couldn't be held politically accountable for their support of same-sex marriage in the way their distant Irish cousin Roy McDonald had been. Instead, they were held accountable to each other, to their consciences, and to the norms of public deliberation itself.

This was no surprise to those who have watched citizens deliberate in similar settings. In all the examples discussed in this book, democratic innovators are trying to render democratic decision making more inclusive and better informed. From constitutional conventions to jury systems, new deliberative ventures aim to diminish the power gap between elites and the most marginalized. They seek new ways to encourage people to make decisions together across differences and amid disagreements over both values and facts. Though no single process will revolutionize governance, and some may inadvertently worsen problems they hope to address, each success brings us closer to realizing democracy's potential.

Even modern Athenians don't need to look back centuries to see the power of deliberation. One of the Greek political parties used a Deliberative Poll in 2006 to select their candidate for a mayoral election. Multiple initiatives have also aimed to take deliberative civic engagement online in Greece. The digital platform vouliwatch has aimed to crowd-source the challenge of tracking a parliament, whereas the Greek Open Government Initiative works to promote forums by which citizens may comment directly on legislation. Efforts such as these are circulating around the world, and it's only a matter of time until a more robust online infrastructure provides citizens with the right mix of civic opportunities and incentives to tether their deliberative inputs to government policy-making processes large and small.

Toward the Far Horizon

Whether drawing inspiration from the democratic laboratories of modern Ireland or ancient Athens, political reformers have taken up the cause of democracy for centuries. Many of these activists aimed to cultivate a community committed not to political warfare but to the spirit of deliberation. A more reflective and respectful politics cannot resolve every cultural conflict, nor does it inexorably lead to optimal solutions to complex problems. Even so, a more deliberative system *does* increase the odds that we face up to the most serious challenges and make smarter decisions within the time constraints we place on ourselves.

A campaign for empathy and rationality, unfortunately, would have little sex appeal. The actual placards that citizens have carried for this cause have an intentional, or accidental, irony to them. The Tea Party began as a Tax Day protest, and seen among the placards was, "No taxation without deliberation." It's doubtful that this call inspired anyone to dump tea into Boston Harbor—not that doing so would make sense anyway. More suitable to any protest was a sign printed in all-caps Arial font at a 2010 rally sponsored by Jon Stewart and Steven Colbert: "My political views are too mature and sophisticated to be summarized on one poster." Or, if you prefer, "I'm reasonable as hell, and I'm not gonna take it anymore, unless you convince me otherwise with a rational argument." Closer to despair was the citizen who carried this sign: "I prefer facts, nuance, and intellectual debate, so I'm probably not a real American."

Satire, however, can only get us so far. The aforementioned 2010 protest, dubbed the Rally to Restore Sanity and/or Fear, foregrounded Stewart and Colbert's roles as hosts of their popular television shows on Comedy Central. All the guest stars, skits, and spoofs the crowds and viewers enjoyed or endured set the stage for the rally's most poignant sequence, when Stewart's closing monologues squeezed these observations between apologetic jokes and asides:

> And now I thought we might have a moment, however brief, for some sincerity, if that's okay. . . . I can't control what people think this [event] was, I can only tell you my intentions. This was not a rally to ridicule people of faith, or people of activism, or to look down our noses at the heartland, or passionate argument, or to suggest that times are not

difficult and that we have nothing to fear. They are and we do. But we live now in hard times, not end times. . . . The country's 24-hour, politico, pundit, perpetual panic conflictanator did not cause our problems, but its existence makes solving them that much harder. . . . We hear every damn day about how fragile our country is, on the brink of catastrophe torn by polarizing hate and how it's a shame that we can't work together to get things done. But the truth is, we do. We work together to get things done every damn day.

To illustrate Americans' capacity for harmony, he showed a video of traffic merging as it entered the Holland Tunnel that goes under the Hudson River to link Manhattan to Jersey City. Whatever beliefs might be emblazoned on the bumpers of their cars, more than thirty million drivers each year make way for each other as they squeeze into one of the tunnel's two-lane tubes. "At some point," Stewart admits, "there will be a selfish jerk who zips up the shoulder and cuts in at the last minute. But that individual is rare, and he is scorned."

For years, Stewart has performed his role as a critic of the media to make the case for public deliberation and reasoned compromise. He could not—and did not—offer a clear plan for what others can do to secure their democracy. Instead, Stewart counseled pragmatism and reason in both our personal lives and our politics.

To show what more one can do, we wrote this book. We introduced five different archetypes for engaged citizenship. Most of us can relate to at least one of these.

Marion and Ann come first, as they stand for the everyday citizen. Neither are policy experts, and before the CIR they had only passing experiences with politics. They got their inspiration from being drawn at random from their state's registered voter list to play a special role. Like the sixty-six citizens in the Irish Constitutional Convention, they won the civic lottery, and their experiences with the CIR spurred them to become vanguards in securing that process.

Since their time in Salem, Marion and Ann have traveled with members of Healthy Democracy to advocate for the adoption of the CIR in other states, with Ann even going to Washington to testify before the legislature. They've worked on the CIR Commission to ensure that the Oregon process maintains its integrity as it adapts to new challenges in every election cycle. Both continue to find ways, big and small, to make a difference in their community. As Ann said in her last interview for this book, "democracy can't be taken for granted."

For those who don't fall into a body such as a CIR, there exist ample opportunities to step into other public arenas and ask legislators and community leaders to practice a different kind of politics. Speaking at a school board meeting, community forum, or any other event requires a measure of courage, but those who engage leaders in a civil but firm manner may be surprised at how receptive officials are to such an uncommon approach. There is a place for righteous testimony, and sometimes only timely anger can break through an impasse. After the shouting and chants grab the community's attention, however, something else has to happen. In that moment, any Marion or any Ann in any town has a chance to take action in a deliberative spirit.

Such special occasions aside, each of us can do more every day than simply merge in traffic. We can reach out to those closest to us and have a conversation—the kind that helps legislators like Roy McDonald reconsider positions on even the most controversial and culturally charged issues. We hope this book has provided a better rationale and a clearer language for such activities.

These types of conversations are happening formally and informally all over the world. Your own community likely has a group that's trying to foster collaboration across the differences that can separate us. Local efforts feed back into larger strategies and networks, such as the National Coalition for Dialogue and Deliberation, and contribute to a growing culture of citizens working together in big and small ways to improve their communities Even one conversation that tries to uphold the ideals of learning and mutual respect can forge new connections in a divided society.

Other readers may have experience on the front line of political battles but know that something must change about the very nature of politics itself. This was Ty's journey. As he explained to the Harvard audience in 2015, his early experiences as a campaign worker left him frustrated. By seeing "the inner workings" of the electoral process up close, he came to understand "how poorly voters are treated in terms of the information they are provided." The problem wasn't that he was bad at his jobs. "I was a hell of a good signature gatherer," he said, "but working in the field" showed him how easy it was "to manipulate voters to get signatures on a piece of paper." As on the street corner, so in the voting booth.

Ty was not the first activist who sought more fundamental change and shifted tactics. The problem is how to advance the deliberative cause without drawing fire from peers who continue to practice a more conventional form of politics. "The pushback" against the CIR, he told us, comes from "a small community of political professionals that run campaigns for initiatives." The CIR has been criticized openly in the press and quietly within legislative offices by "those groups that feel that the CIR takes away their ability to control their campaign message. It's a pretty understandable point of view." After all, each year the CIR "engenders, to a degree, a sense of winners and losers."

How does one convince today's losers that their defeat is, in the long run, in their own best interests? One doesn't. Instead, one needs to mobilize sufficient support for deliberative politics to overcome the opposition on any given issue, some of which will come from political professionals who sense a looming existential threat.

Ty has left Healthy Democracy, but he followed up a sabbatical of sorts by founding a new organization that aims to promote a range of deliberative processes that goes beyond the confines of the CIR. Meanwhile, a veteran from the nonprofit sector now acts as Healthy Democracy's executive director and oversees a capable staff. Though many names have changed since the days when Ty and Elliot ran the show, some of the CIR moderators continue to work with Healthy Democracy. They and the cohort of other moderators who have conducted the CIRs since 2010 continue to invite critical feedback as they refine the process.

The Healthy Democracy team now focuses their attention on expanding the CIR to more states and adapting it for different purposes. In 2016, they ran another CIR in Oregon and worked with Representative Hecht and Sam Feigenbaum to run a pilot CIR in Massachusetts. That same year, Healthy Democracy continued a partnership with the Morrison Institute at Arizona State University to implement a statewide CIR there.

Despite being in the midst of a hyperbolic election, everyday citizens in all three states had civil conversations about the contentious ballot questions put before them. As one participant from Massachusetts noted when that CIR came to a close, "People here had a difference of opinion, but the respectful and honorable way that everybody behaved really touched me. . . . Right now in our country, there is a lot of hostility and anger. We can do with a lot more cooperation and peace."

Work has continued in Arizona and Massachusetts to adopt their own variations of the Oregon CIR, and future iterations might come with more changes. For instance, persons recruited at random for the CIRs who can't attend might still want to play a role. The CIR could pull in this much larger number of citizens as co-participants online; they could discuss the same issues before the small group of citizen panelists and, using online decision tools, even pass along a manageable number of concrete suggestions or edits for draft Citizens' Statements. Media partners could also be cultivated to better publicize and leverage the statements so that an ever-wider number of voters could use them.

As the process grows and innovates, however, old obstacles remain. In 2018, Oregon didn't host a statewide CIR. As noted in chapter 7, the state legislature never allocated funding for the CIR, which relied on the generosity of private donors to ensure its implementation. That optimism seems to have been misplaced. As the CIR ages, its appeal to nonprofit entities wanes. Looking for the next exciting experiment, funders are less eager to pour their limited dollars into an established governing institution. Instead, Healthy Democracy hosted a CIR in the Portland area on a regional ballot. Local processes are cheaper to run and have the potential to have a bigger impact on a smaller population, but this meant that Oregon's electorate didn't have the benefit of a Citizens' Statement when filling out their statewide ballots. Stories like this are abundant in the world of democratic innovation and speak to the difficulty of institutional change.

The Experiment Continues

For democratic reforms like the CIR, triumphs and setbacks are the norm, not the exception. Experimenting with new institutions is endemic to democracy itself, and the challenge is to find what part of the system one can change *now*. For many, the obvious need for systemic intervention concerns campaign finance reform. For others, it's about ensuring that the largest number of eligible voters can participate, without impediments, in elections. Organizations like Common Cause and the League of Women Voters have worked for decades on such causes. The best place to embark on a journey of deliberative reform often begins by building connections with such entities, as Ty did in Oregon.

Ned Crosby also worked with such groups when he pioneered the Citizens' Jury system and adapted it into the CIR. His archetype is that of the veteran visionary, who tries to keep a wide-angle focus on at all times. As his wife Pat described him once in an interview, "Ned never thinks small. He always thinks about grandiose ideas."

The day that the CIR became law in Oregon in 2009, he called the first author of this book and was greeted by an answering machine. In an ebullient four-minute message, he began by sharing the big news but quickly moved past it to pitch a new idea. What the country really needed, he explained, was a network of deliberative panels that could scrutinize the biggest federal issues, such as the war in Afghanistan. Such behavior was quintessential Ned. Like so many other entrepreneurs, he stays focused on the next great challenge ahead even when a victory was at hand.

Ned had hoped to see more citizen panels that evaluate candidates, rather than only ballot measures. This had been his original aspiration since the successful deployment of the Citizens' Jury method in the 1992 Pennsylvania senate race brought the IRS to his door. One recent venture was a chain of deliberative panels that the Jefferson Center convened in Ohio's sixteenth congressional district, partly chosen because it featured a competitive race between two incumbents, whom redistricting had made into rivals. The *Washington Post* ranked that contest as among the ten toughest congressional battles that year.

A series of three Citizens' Election Forums identified priority issues, studied those issues carefully, then evaluated the candidates' positions, as well as their "campaign conduct," and drafted a thirty-two-page *Voter's Guide* that included these ratings, along with detailed analysis. The forums gave a clear nod to Republican Jim Renacci, and publicity of that result may have contributed to a close win for the GOP congressman.

It remains to be seen whether this particular political invention will take hold. After the 2016 US presidential election, it is easy to doubt the viability of a more rational political process at any level of government.

Lest such despair draw one back into that familiar sense of political alienation, it may help to recognize that our current mood has ample precedent. Two centuries ago, John Adams had lost much of his faith in Congress, as it savaged the sixth president of the United States, his son John Quincy. "Our American chivalry is the worst in all the world," he wrote to Thomas Jefferson in 1826. "It has no laws, no bounds, no definitions; it seems to be a caprice."

Successful inventors often have experiences like that of Adams. At times, Ned has had to watch helplessly as critics deride his creations. The CIR has more than survived, and many other variations on the Citizens' Jury have married with other ideas and moved out of the house.

One such cousin ended up dropping the family name to become a "People's Panel," put on weight as it swelled to a size of forty-three members, and shacked up with Participatory Budgeting for six weekends to develop a financial plan for the city of Melbourne, Australia. The process had tremendous publicity, and the end result was the Melbourne City Council adopting a five-billion-dollar financial plan. This put in motion a ten-year plan that will raise developer fees, sell off assets, maintain public services, and do much more—all on the advice of a randomly assembled body of citizens. Not too shabby.

For the young and old who share Ned's disposition, the good news is that democracy will always need new ideas such as these. Civic innovations have more value now than ever because of the rapid diffusion and adaptation that our online age makes possible. Melbourne's success with the People's Panel has had parallels across the globe, so democratic reformers in any part of the world will often find like-minded citizens receptive to whatever civic inventions they might devise.

Two other archetypes in this book have been introduced in less personal terms. Throughout these pages, academics and public officials have played pivotal but distinct roles. One reason Ned and Ty have had success in their efforts is that they have cultivated partnerships with academic institutions. Academics who have tenure can afford to invest in long-term research projects that sort out the strong from the weak ideas for democratic reform. The spirit of experimentation becomes a formal method of inquiry in the hands of social scientists, and though reformers on tight budget cycles often lose patience with ponderous academics, there can be a symbiosis.

Careful readers have likely discovered that the authors of this book have been present since the inception of the CIR itself. Though often working at a distance, we have kept a careful eye on the CIR and assessed it every election cycle to discern the quality of its deliberation and the extent of its impact. Those broad purposes, formulated as precise hypotheses, have secured funding from the National Science Foundation and various universities, as well as research contracts with civic organizations, including the Kettering Foundation and the Democracy Fund. Though our findings are not always good news for Ned, Ty, Marion, Ann, and the others who continue to nurture the CIR, the legitimacy they gain from our independent evaluations make us worth the trouble.

That was apparent from the first time we testified before a legislature, after the 2010 cycle of CIRs. One Oregon legislator looked to his colleagues during our evaluative remarks and asked why lawmakers don't get to hear social scientific research on *all* the bills they pass. That was a good day in public relations for the National Science Foundation's Directorate for Social, Behavioral, and Economic Sciences.

That interaction offers one more glimpse into the life of the legislator. The success of the CIR depended—and still depends—on the far-sightedness of the Oregon legislature, as well as that state's governor and secretary of state. However maddening politics may feel, the fact remains that many elected officials get up each morning hoping to make their city, state, or nation a better place. The most memorable cinematic and literary portraits of politicians may be power-hungry manipulators, but in the state houses and local governments, the norm is less intriguing but more human characters, like the state senators and representatives described earlier in this chapter.

Those who work in government as elected officials, appointees, or staff, along with those who serve as informal advisors to such individuals, have a special role to play in democratic reform. A sturdy and mature democratic government has never fallen to revolutionaries, but every mature democracy has improved or worsened over time as the result of a series of small institutional adjustments. Even modest electoral reforms like the CIR, however, require a measure of political courage, because no such change occurs without opposition.

Take the example of Representative Hecht in Massachusetts. Toward the end of the Harvard panel discussion, Hecht offered these final thoughts about the prospect of institutional change:

> I am interested in terms of where [this reform] fits in the political process as a whole.... We have a certain type of legislature in Massachusetts that operates in a certain fashion, has a certain set of power dynamics, interacts with interest groups in a certain way.... Many of the issues that now go to the ballot in Massachusetts I would prefer to see handled

through the sausage making process in the legislature. I have a hunch that part of what is going on now is we have a legislative gridlock that is the result of powerful interests that would prefer to see the issue go to the ballot because they feel they can win, again because of the campaign finance and media and other contexts that operate. I think it's interesting also to think about where the CIR might fit into our sort of broader agenda of political reform.

Hecht envisioned the CIR not as an alternative to politics but as a way of improving the existing system, in both direct and indirect ways. The obvious benefit of the CIR as a means of improving voters' judgments brings with it a more indirect power—the ability to push away misguided solutions to the state's most vexing problems. Hecht hoped that by blocking bad choices from succeeding directly via the ballot box, the CIR might force the legislature to act.

In the end, the success of any democratic experiment relies on a convergence of roles. We will never know the names or faces of the multitudes who gave Cleisthenes the power to secure ancient Athenian democracy. Each advance in the US experiment likewise credits unheralded efforts, which provided inspiration and support to the likes of John and Abigail Adams. Thus, Tocqueville's

Participants in the 2018 Massachusetts CIR pilot project with Representative Jon Hecht and Sam Feigenbaum (top row left). *Source:* Healthy Democracy.

account of early American democracy attributed much of its success to the experiences of everyday people governing themselves through juries, town meetings, and civil associations.

Today is no different. The grand visions and small triumphs that show the way forward have come from political leaders, activists, scholars, community leaders, and—most of all—everyday citizens. After all, deliberative theory trusts in the untapped capabilities of the wider electorate. People already know how to merge in traffic. They know how to have difficult conversations, even across partisan lines.

What has yet to happen is for a public to *demand* such behavior of its leaders. It is one thing to decry political manipulation, posturing, and oversimplification. It is another to enforce it on candidates in a way that has real consequences, one election after another. The CIR and processes like it have the potential to habituate the public to this entirely different orientation to politics and public life. As much as the jury teaches citizens what it takes to make good decisions in the legal branch, so too could the CIR, Participatory Budgeting, citizen conferences and conventions, and other such processes cultivate our collective appetite for deliberation in the legislative and executive branches.

If that comes to pass, the way forward becomes clearer. Strong candidates would have solid deliberative credentials by having shown the capacity not for single-mindedness but for openness. Effective leaders would model cross-cultural empathy, rather than hyper-partisan intolerance. Such leaders, inside and outside of government, would retain their good standing by delivering not on specific policy proposals but on the promise to listen carefully, and act accordingly.

So goes one vision for a different kind of politics, a more deliberative democracy. History is littered with such ideas. Most get discarded as utopian, with the rest tested and found unworkable. By degrees, however, institutions and cultures can change. Marion felt that shift happen under her feet because of a dream Ned related to Ty, who crafted it into a process that researchers tested and legislators adopted. What more might come to pass as this century unfolds? Working together, or fighting against one another, we will answer that question.

DETAILS AND DIGRESSIONS

These brief essays provide references for readers curious to learn more about the subjects in each chapter. This section also permits us to pull back the curtain on our own role, as researchers, in the evolution of the CIR. We kept ourselves out of the main narrative because the characters we describe in this book lead more interesting lives than we do. Those seeking methodological details about our research can find them online at the Citizens' Initiative Review Research Project archive.

Introduction

Seattle activist Dick Falkenbury provides a colorful account of the Seattle Monorail Project in his 2013 self-published work, *Rise Above It All*. The independent film *Grassroots* captures the atmosphere of the time. Project cost estimates and election details come from accounts in the *Seattle Post-Intelligencer* and *Seattle Times*. Traffic statistics come from the INRIX Traffic Scorecard. Details on the existing Seattle Monorail come from its official website. The *Simpsons* reference comes from "Marge vs. the Monorail" (episode 9F10, first aired January 14, 1993).

. On the ubiquity of initiatives, see the USC Initiative and Referendum Institute. Its executive director, John Matsusaka, defends the virtue of direct democracy in *For the Many or the Few*. The *Daily Mail* reported the post-election poll on Britain leaving the European Union; second thoughts about that vote often appear with the lovable hashtag #Regrexit. The Ken Burns and Lynn Novick film series *Prohibition* chronicles the unintended consequences of the Eighteenth Amendment to the US Constitution.

The reference to Robert Dahl comes from *On Democracy* (pp. 187–88). The more proximate inspiration for John's work on citizen panels is Ned Crosby,

Hope for Democracy. John Gastil and Katherine R. Knobloch, Oxford University Press (2020).
© John Gastil and Katherine R. Knobloch
DOI: 10.1093/acprof:oso/9780190084523.001.0001

who wrote a book on the subject during the Seattle monorail debate (*Healthy Democracy: Bringing Trustworthy Information to the Voters of America*). Other key works include Benjamin Barber's *Strong Democracy*, Jane Mansbridge's *Beyond Adversary Democracy*, and James Fishkin's *Democracy and Deliberation*. The critique of *By Popular Demand* by Christopher Wlezien appears in the *American Political Science Review*.

For an overview of the prospects for deliberative democratic reform, see Matt Leighninger's book, *The Next Form of Democracy*, and the volume he co-edited with John, Michael Weiksner, and project leader Tina Nabatchi, *Democracy in Motion*. Australian National University professor John Dryzek provides a more theoretical account in *Foundations and Frontiers of Deliberative Governance*. Those who wish to read more about public deliberation but lack access to a university library can find excellent work in the open-access *Journal of Public Deliberation*.

Lest we sound too triumphant, we should stress that forward progress toward the democratic ideal is not inevitable. The deliberative impulses in the present day are a resurgence of ideas that have come (and gone) before, as John shows with William Keith in their chapter of *The Deliberative Democracy Handbook*, "A Nation That (Sometimes) Likes to Talk: A Brief History of Public Deliberation in the United States."

To take just one example, the Republican Party in the United States recently rolled back the Voting Rights Act and enacted state-level reforms designed to suppress voter turnout, as detailed in Ari Berman's *New York Times* essay, "Voting Rights in the Age of Trump." On the April 2017 marches, see Laura Smith-Spark and Jason Hanna, "March for Science: Protesters Gather Worldwide to Support 'Evidence'" at CNN.

Chapter 1

Details about Marion Sharp's experience with the CIR stem from extensive interviews as well as informal discussions and survey responses. Later chapters use these same methods to convey Ann Bakkensen's story.

Considerable evidence supports the contention that US citizens have lost faith in their government. Robert Putnam's *Bowling Alone* popularized this insight and stirred up a debate about why public trust was falling and what might replace it. Useful reference points include Lance Bennett's "The Uncivic Culture" in *PS: Political Science and Politics*, Timothy Cook and Paul Gronke's "The Skeptical American" in the *Journal of Politics*, and the Russell Sage Foundation volume, *Trust and Governance*, edited by Valerie Braithwaite and Margaret Levi. Even more has been said about money and politics. We draw directly on Jacob Hacker and Paul Pierson's *Politics & Society* essay, "Winner-Take-All Politics."

A few years after Marion participated in the America*Speaks*' forum on the economy, that organization closed its doors. Details of its programs remain online, such as at the Participedia archive, which has a complete entry on the "Our Budget, Our Economy" project Marion attended. The *Oregonian* column supporting the process, "The Federal Deficit: Your Chance to Change the Future," was from June 21, 2010. Critiques included the CEPR's "America Speaks: What Is Not on the Program," and the Oregon Center for Public Policy's June 26, 2010, note, "America*Speaks* Town Hall Meeting."

In *Do-it-yourself Democracy*, Caroline Lee critiques the America*Speaks* forums Marion attended and other processes like it. Lee worries that this civic reform movement could become another bureaucratic obstacle to genuine citizen empowerment. "It appears ironic," she writes, "that the solution to increasing professionalization in activism would be a new wave of experts in lay participation" (p. 45). A good companion to Lee's work is Christopher Karpowitz and Chad Raphael's *Deliberation, Democracy, and Civic Forums.* They urge nonprofits to be more transparent about how they design and execute events that claim to record the public's "authentic" voice.

We recognize that some scholars have tried making even Congressional "town hall" meetings more deliberative. In *Politics with the People: Building a Directly Representative Democracy*, Michael Neblo, Kevin Sterling, and David Lazer show how electronic town halls can be redesigned to generate more honest exchanges between members of Congress and their constituents. In his doctoral dissertation, "Congressional Town Hall Meetings: Rhetoric, Inclusion, and Deliberative Democracy," John Rountree argues that these meetings often contain a deliberative impulse but are hampered by poor design choices and deep political distrust.

For background on initiatives and their contemporary significance, see Shaun Bowler and Todd Donovan's *Demanding Choices,* Joseph Zimmerman's *The Initiative,* and John Matsusaka's *For the Many or the Few,* as well as his essay with Arthur Lupia, "Direct Democracy," in the *Annual Review of Political Science.* On the problems posed by initiative elections, see Elisabeth Gerber's book *The Populist Paradox* and her chapter with (who else?) Arthur Lupia, "Voter Competence in Direct Legislation Elections," in *Citizen Competence and Democratic Institutions.* For a more comparative perspective on the subject, see David Altman's *Citizenship and Contemporary Direct Democracy,* which discusses a variety of reforms including the CIR.

Our claim that many Oregon voters believe the initiative process needs repair is supported by surveys conducted before and after the creation of the Oregon CIR, which we discuss in more detail later in the book. Most recently, our 2016 evaluation report on it found a connection between the perceived utility of the Oregon CIR and the desire for reform. Among those survey respondents who found the 2016 CIR to be a "very helpful" voting aide, a plurality favored changes to the initiative process, with 40 percent wanting "minor changes" and 34 percent preferring "major changes."

The organization that ran the CIR in Oregon was originally named Healthy Democracy Oregon. It dropped the state from its name when it sought a more national profile. For simplicity, we refer to this entity throughout the book as Healthy Democracy.

To taste direct democracy's flavor a century ago, see George Guthrie's 1912 essay, "The Initiative, Referendum and Recall," which appeared in *Annals of the American Academy of Political and Social Science*. On the process in Oregon, see "Initiative, Referendum and Recall Introduction" in *The Oregon Bluebook*. Useful summaries of these rules, such as those regarding signature requirements, appear at ballotopedia.org. The fiscal cost estimate of Oregon's initiatives and many other useful insights appear in Laura Keown's University of Oregon thesis, "Making Policy Deliberative."

If one wishes to heed the call for less idealism in democratic theory, make a stop at John Mueller's essay, "Democracy and Ralph's Pretty Good Grocery," in the *American Journal of Political Science*. As David Held argues in *Models of Democracy*, the realist conception of democracy (known as "competitive elitism") sounded cynical to many but was not intended as such by its architects, such as Joseph Schumpeter. The most skeptical accounts of democracy that have found an audience among serious scholars argue that ostensibly democratic institutions do little but obstruct healthy revolutionary impulses. Thus, Slavoj Žižek can quip that "Democracy Is the Enemy" in a blog post during Occupy Wall Street. Such arguments, however, often depend more than anything on clever definition of one's terms.

Deliberative democratic theory has its origins in a mix of political theories that lie at various points along the ideological spectrum. Many credit Jürgen Habermas and John Rawls as the earliest modern theorists who tried to glimpse a way for public reason to address political and moral disputes. A common portrait of deliberative democracy, such as the one painted by David Held in *Models of Democracy*, pits a picture of an impartial, consensus-oriented public up against the realities of a pluralist society. Joshua Cohen's vision of deliberation reconciles the two by acknowledging the need for majority rule in his much-reprinted essay, "Deliberation and Democratic Legitimacy." Likewise, Jane Mansbridge's co-authored essay "Norms of Deliberation" argues that the actual practice of deliberation involves emotion, narrative, and flowing exchanges of ideas more than merely the rational exchange of evidence and logic. An interview with Habermas in the *Oxford Handbook of Deliberative Democracy* shows that he, too, embraces this expansive view.

We refer to a textbook by Joseph Bessette and John Pitney, *American Government and Politics: Deliberation, Democracy and Citizenship*. Another recent example of such texts is Tina Nabatchi and Matt Leighninger's *Public Participation for 21st Century Democracy*, which has special relevance to students of public administration. Before these came John's *Political Communication and Deliberation*, which reframed existing theory and research in political communication.

On the idea of democracy as a civic renewal movement, see Peter Levine's *We Are the Ones We Have Been Waiting For* and Susan Clark and Woden Teachout's *Slow Democracy*. Participatory Budgeting appears frequently in such works as a successful civic innovation, and a recent study of its impact and pitfalls appears in Hollie Rossum Gilman's *Democracy Reinvented*. To our chagrin, as our book bided its time at our publisher, Nelson Dias titled his new book on the subject *Hope for Democracy*. Here's hoping Google's algorithms can sort out the resulting confusion.

The overview of deliberative practices we provide comes from an entry we wrote with Jason Gilmore, "The Internal Dynamics and Sociopolitical Power of Public Deliberation in Groups," in the *Oxford Handbook of Political Communication*. For more on the National Issues Forums, see the corresponding chapter in the *Deliberative Democracy Handbook* and David Mathews' essay, "A 35-Year Experiment in Public Deliberation," in the *Journal of Public Deliberation*. These forums were the focus of John's doctoral dissertation, which grew into two articles with Jim Dillard in *Political Communication* and *Communication Education*, plus one that required bringing Patricia Moy on board as first author before it appeared in *Political Communication*.

Chapter 2

The Massachusetts Historical Society has made the Adams family's letters and papers available online. Lively correspondence between Abigail and John, along with David McCullough's *John Adams*, were some of the inspiration for the 2008 HBO miniseries of the same title. The long quote from John Adams combines different passages from his letter "Ancient Democratical Republics," in *Defence of the Constitutions of the United States*. Any reader who winces at the spellings and extra syllables in eighteenth-century English fails to appreciate the folly of language, though we join those who gently edit some spellings for readability.

To discern the classical influences on the Founders, we drew on the writings of Carl Richard's *The Founders and the Classics*, Bernard Bailyn's *The Ideological Origins of the American Revolution*, and the edited volume *Athenian Political Thought and the Reconstruction of American Democracy*. The Josiah Ober quote comes from his eminently readable *Boston Review* essay, "Learning from Athens." That short piece draws on his numerous scholarly works, such as "What the

Ancient Greeks Can Tell Us About Democracy" in the *Annual Review of Political Science*.

We also gained insight from Arlene Saxonhouse's *Free Speech and Democracy in Ancient Athens*, in which we found the "deliberative circle" and Odysseus's harsh rebuke. For more on that ancient rap battle, see Marc Hooghe's essay in *Acta Politica*, "The Rebuke of Thersites."

Some of the best recent work on town meetings comes from University of Vermont emeritus professor Frank Bryan, who co-authored *Real Democracy* with John McClaughry. In *The Vermont Papers*, Bryan advocates restructuring US government on the town-meeting model. Jane Mansbridge put the New England Town Meeting into a larger theoretical context in her landmark work, *Beyond Adversary Democracy*. A 2010 *Boston Globe* article by Rich Fahey, "Look Who's Not Here," provides a worrisome portrait of this institution. The portion of the Massachusetts constitution we reference comes from Article LXXXIX: II, Section 2. (Athens shaped their government, but Rome gave them numerals.) Henry David Thoreau's praise for town meetings comes from his crowd-pleasing speech, "Slavery in Massachusetts," given on July 4, 1854. Democratic theorist Benjamin Barber describes the Swiss forerunner of modern town meetings in *The Death of Communal Liberty*.

To this day, the deliberative promise of the town meeting animates many who live under that system. A web search led us to the Dartmouth Hitching Post, where a resident blogger decried an effort to weaken town meetings as "yet ANOTHER attempt to take power from the 'people.' Why not just have a King of Dartmouth if we are taking control out of OUR hands!!! Representative town meeting is what our founding fathers wanted for us and what has worked for Dartmouth for hundreds of years. I will never vote for this!" So there.

As for the US jury system, much of the best writing has come from collaborations with Valerie Hans, who co-authored *Judging the Jury* with Neil Vidmar and *The American Jury* with Harry Kalven. Dennis Hale traces the haphazard evolution of US juries in *The Jury in America: Triumph and Decline*. On jury deliberation and reforms, we also recommend the works of Shari Diamond, who wrote "The Modern American Jury: A One Hundred Year Journey" with Andrea Ryken for *Judicature*. Diamond's work shows that Arizona, of all states, has hosted some of the most innovative experiments designed to improve jury deliberation.

Tocqueville quotations on juries and town meetings appear in *Democracy in America* Book I (chapters 5 and 16) and Book II (chapter 7). The Supreme Court case quoting Tocqueville is Powers v. Ohio (1991). Powers was an unlikeable fellow who, after an aborted career as a self-employed hit man, lucked into meeting an ambitious defense attorney. His lawyer successfully argued that excluding African-American jurors from an Anglo defendant's trial was unconstitutional because it violated the prospective jurors' right to serve. For more on this case,

Tocqueville, and empirical evidence of the jury's civic impact, see the book John co-authored with Perry Deess, Phil Weiser, and Cindy Simmons, *The Jury and Democracy*, along with Albert Dzur's *Punishment, Participatory Democracy, and the Jury*.

Many scholars have documented the decline of deliberative rhetoric in government. The quote on this from Robert Kraig appears in *Woodrow Wilson and the Lost World of the Oratorical Statesman* (p. 6). Joseph Bessette's *The Mild Voice of Reason* provides a relatively optimistic account of Congressional deliberation. A less sanguine view comes in Stephanie Burkhalter's 2007 doctoral dissertation, "Talking Points: Message Strategies and Deliberation in the US Congress." The legislative karaoke metaphor first appeared in John's *Political Communication and Deliberation*.

In arguing for the influential nature of US politics, we quote Gordon Wood in *The Radicalism of the American Revolution* (pp. 5–6), but most of our sources in the final section of chapter 2 concern modern US politics. Data on the cost of elections comes from the Center for Responsive Politics website. Data on spending appeared in a 2012 *Washington Post* story, "How the Presidential Campaigns Are Spending Money, in One Chart." Romney's dismal Gallup poll numbers appeared at Gallup on April 11, 2012.

Robert Dahl explains the concept of polyarchy in *Democracy and Its Critics*. Data on democracy come from the Polity IV metric, as collected by the Center for Systemic Peace. For more on the distinctions among democratic and non-democratic systems, see "Autocracy and Anocracy" by Norman Schofield and Maria Gallego in *Institutions, Economic Governance and Public Policies*. Also see William Robinson's *International Relations* retrospective, "Promoting Polyarchy: 20 Years Later."

Of the numerous volumes chronicling the rise of professional political consultants, David Dulio's *For Better Or Worse? How Political Consultants Are Changing Elections in the United States* is especially good. For an account of early twentieth-century consultants, see Jill Lepore's *New Yorker* essay, "On the Campaign Trail," or dive into Mary Stuckey's account of early polling in *Voting Deliberatively: FDR and the 1936 Presidential Campaign*.

We drew on several sources for our assessment of contemporary US politics, with elections and voter turnout data coming from the US Elections Project. Those seeking comparative data should peruse reports from the Electoral Integrity Project. The *PolitiFact* website provided comparative data on candidates, and it bears noting that John McCain in 2008 and Mitt Romney in 2012 also scored noticeably worse on the Truth-o-Meter than their Democratic Party counterparts. Throughout the election, the quantitative news site FiveThirtyEight provided data on how voters assessed Trump's presidential debate performances. Campaign spending data comes from the Center for Responsive Politics' portal,

OpenSecrets, "Total Cost of 2016 Election Could Reach $6.6 Billion." On the rise of fraudulent reporting in 2016, see the *New York Times* article, "From Headline to Photograph, a Fake News Masterpiece." The estimated value of Trump's free media during the 2016 election cycle comes from Emily Stewart's reporting at TheStreet, "Donald Trump Rode $5 Billion in Free Media to the White House."

To track the US presidential approval rating or similar statistics, we relied on Gallup, which devotes one of its daily portals to "Trump Job Approval." The idea that many US citizens may turn away from politics comes from essayist Garrison Keillor. The morning after the 2016 election, the *Washington Post* ran "Trump Voters Won't Like What Happens Next," in which Keillor joked, "We liberal elitists are now completely in the clear. The government is in Republican hands. Let them deal with him."

Chapter 3

Evidence of the public's disengagement and passivity comes from Nina Eliasoph's *Avoiding Politics*. Some data suggest that the public would like to hand the keys of governance over to public officials and be done with it, as argued in John R. Hibbing and Elizabeth Theiss-Morse's *Stealth Democracy: Americans' Beliefs About How Government Should Work*.

One underlying problem is the decline in efforts to organize "on-the-ground actions." Historically, the social movements, unions, and other mass associations that generated such actions sparked policy change. Switching from mass publics to political professionals has the effect of "domesticating" public opinion, as Benjamin Ginsberg argues in *The Captive Public: How Mass Opinion Promotes State Power*. Such efforts give political elites, rather than the public, power in shaping and expressing public opinion.

By contrast, social movements and the civic associations they spawn can provide opportunities for citizens to participate in and learn about civic life. This can forge new relationships and attitudes that strengthen the public and its power, at least when their internal operations model the principles of deliberative democracy. On this, see Francesca Polletta's *Freedom Is an Endless Meeting* and Sara Evans and Harry Boyte's *Free Spaces*.

Many studies have shown that the political elites are more sharply divided than the public at large. So argues Kent Jennings in "Ideological Thinking among Mass Publics and Political Elites" in *Public Opinion Quarterly*. While Congress has become more polarized, the public has not split as deeply as it might seem, according to Morris Fiorina, Samuel Abrams, and Jeremy Pope in *Culture War? The Myth of a Polarized America*. On the corrosive effect of the partisan divide, see David King, "The Polarization of American Parties and Mistrust of Government" in *Why People Don't Trust Government*. The corresponding result shown in Figure 3.1 comes from data compiled by the Pew Research Center, "Public Trust in Government: 1958–2019." Unfortunately, the public's growing awareness of the partisan divide also exacerbates it, as Jacob Westfall and colleagues argue in their *Perspectives on Psychological Science* essay, "Perceiving Political Polarization in the United States."

When elites shift to ever-greater extremes, it can spur party realignment, as Geoffrey Layman and Thomas Carsey show in their *Political Behavior* article, "Party Polarization and Party Structuring of Policy Attitudes." Hence, the rise in independent voters, as shown in Figure 3.2, which combines data compiled by Gallup and Pew. For a skeptical view of supposedly nonpartisan voters, see Bruce Keith, David Magleby, and Candice Nelson's *The Myth of the Independent Voter*.

Earlier versions of ideas in this chapter appear in John's *By Popular Demand: Revitalizing Representative Democracy through Deliberative Elections*. That work, in turn, stands on a variety of polling data, voting studies, and more critical cultural works, such as Murray Edelman's *Constructing the Political Spectacle*.

A special tip of the hat goes to Benjamin Barber's oft-quoted scatological view of voting, from *Strong Democracy*: "Our primary electoral act, voting, is rather like using a public toilet: We wait in line with a crowd in order to close ourselves up in a small compartment where we can relieve ourselves in solitude and in privacy of our burden, pull a lever, and then, yielding to the next in line, go silently home" (p. 188).

The discussion of alienation draws on Katie's University of Washington doctoral dissertation, *Civic (Re)Socialization? Exploring Deliberation's Effects on Political Attitudes and Actions*. The discussion of alienation adapts dissertation material that also appeared in her *Javnost–The Public* essay, "Public Sphere Alienation: A Model for Analysis and Critique."

The idea of alienation has become so commonplace that the *Matrix* movies seem more of a cultural critique than a science fiction premise. Thus, we turned to classical works for our sources. These include István Mészáros's 1970 book, *Marx's Theory of Alienation*. We adapted our five-part definition from Melvin Seeman's 1975 "Alienation Studies" article in the *Annual Review of Sociology* and his 1959 essay in the *American Sociological Review*, "On the Meaning of Alienation."

Jurgen Habermas' *The Structural Transformation of the Public Sphere* shows the essential role of the public sphere in a democratic society. Numerous authors have elaborated on this idea. On the role of elites, see Seraina Pedrini's "Deliberative Capacity in the Political and Civic Sphere" in the *Swiss Political Science Review*. On the role of civic groups, see Carolyn Hendriks, "Integrated

Deliberation: Reconciling Civil Society's Dual Role in Deliberative Democracy," in *Political Studies*. On how the Internet could link elites, civil society, and the public, see Antje Gimmler, "Deliberative Democracy, the Public Sphere and the Internet," in *Philosophy and Social Criticism*.

Chapter 3 also drew on diverse democratic theories, such as Robert Dahl and Edward Tufte's *Size and Democracy*. That concise book shows the relationship between the scale of a democracy and the power each citizen holds. The references to John Parkinson and Jane Mansbridge's *Deliberative Systems* come from their introduction to that volume (pp. 5, 11).

We rely extensively on Richard Lau and David Redlawsk's book *How Voters Decide*, with a quote from p. 258. The reference to poor candidate selection in the 2008 primaries comes from Lau's *Political Behavior* article, "Correct Voting in the 2008 US Presidential Nominating Elections." The idea that even biased voters can reach a tipping point beyond which they change their stubborn minds comes from Redlawsk's co-authored *Political Psychology* article, "The Affective Tipping Point: Do Motivated Reasoners Ever 'Get It'?" Those interested in following this concept farther should read "Correct Voting Across Thirty-Three Democracies" in the *British Journal of Political Science*. In that article, Lau and his colleagues show that election systems with more distinct political parties and stronger independent media induce more correct voting.

Writings by Dan Kahan and his many collaborators, including this book's authors, can be found online at the Cultural Cognition Project. The blog on that website includes links to Kahan's recent work on biasing across the political spectrum, such as "Ideology, Motivated Reasoning, and Cognitive Reflection" in *Judgment and Decision Making*. Other works cited in this chapter, from various journals, include "'They Saw a Protest': Cognitive Illiberalism and the Speech-Conduct Distinction," "The Polarizing Impact of Science Literacy and Numeracy on Perceived Climate Change Risks," "Who Fears the HPV Vaccine, Who Doesn't, and Why? An Experimental Study of the Mechanisms of Cultural Cognition," and "The Cultural Orientation of Mass Political Opinion."

For a good example of recent research showing motivated reasoning among partisans, see Michael Bang Petersen's co-authored essay in *Political Behavior*, "Motivated Reasoning and Political Parties." As Michael Hameleers and Toni van der Meer show in the *Communication Research* study "Misinformation and Polarization in a High-Choice Media Environment," even though fact checking can reduce one's biases, people tend to avoid reading fact checks that might threaten prior beliefs.

Finally, on the shifting media landscape in Europe, see Raymond Kuhn's co-authored volume, *Political Journalism in Transition*. The idea that public opinion slowly shifts toward more sensible positions comes from Benjamin Page and Robert Shapiro's classic, *The Rational Public*. The model of voters' brains as buckets of information comes from John Zaller's *The Nature and Origins of Mass Opinion*, a book notable for both the elegance of its analysis and its author's unwavering confidence in the curative powers of biased filtering.

Chapter 4

The biographical details on Tyrone Reitman, Elliot Shuford, Ned Crosby, and Pat Benn come from extensive interviews, as well as firsthand experience with each of these individuals over several years. John met Ned in the mid-1990s and Pat shortly thereafter. Both of us have known Ty and Elliot since the inception of the CIR. For readability, we have edited quotes and details from these interviews. For example, Ty *thinks* that he "drank a Pabst Blue Ribbon" that fateful night at Taylor's Bar & Grill. Brazenly, we assert that he simply *did* drink one. Each interviewee has had the opportunity to review what we wrote about them in this and other chapters. Though we welcomed their feedback, we only made corrections for accuracy. As best we can tell, all our interviewees have thick skins.

Both of us shared Tyrone's desire to effect social change through graduate studies. John helped design the graduate program that Katie completed in the Department of Communication at the University of Washington. That unique curriculum emphasized "public scholarship"—the idea that an academic should be engaged with public concerns while retaining the intellectual independence and objectivity required for professional social science research. That program had once had a required semester-long seminar on public scholarship, which was cancelled years ago. Faculty worried that too many new students became enamored of the idea of public engagement to the detriment of their methodological training. John was the lone dissent when the question came to a final vote after a year of debate. A commitment to deliberation sometimes means accepting defeat when one's arguments fail to persuade.

The Wisdom Councils referenced in the book were conceived by Jim Rough, who trained Elliot Shuford in the "dynamic facilitation" method. Perhaps not coincidentally, Jim lives in the same town in Washington where Ned and Pat set up their second residence—Port Townsend, a colorful community that attracts hippies, ex-hippies, and people who love boats.

Tom Atlee's work is detailed at Co-intelligence.org, where one can find his books, including *Empowering Public Wisdom* and *The Tao of Democracy*. Both are designed to bring abstract ideas about democracy and public wisdom to a general audience.

In addition to the aforementioned book *Healthy Democracy*, Ned Crosby penned op-eds with John that suggested adopting prototypes of the CIR in

Washington: "Voters Need More Reliable Information" in the November 6, 2003, *Seattle Post-Intelligencer;* "Taking the Initiative" in the November 26, 2006, *Seattle Times;* and "Hey Washingtonians! Show Some Initiative," a cheeky essay in *Washington Law and Politics* in 2005.

Back in the late 1970s, Ned drafted a book laying out a strategy for reforming democracy with a prominent role for "Citizens Juries." (He chose to leave off the apostrophe when he coined the term, though the unwelcome punctuation mark became the convention, which we follow.) The unpublished volume showed a long road ahead, but also a need to move forward quickly.

"Sometime in the next fifty years," Ned wrote, "the future path of American democracy will be clarified. . . . If we do not plan ahead for major changes in our governmental institutions, we are quite likely to slide into an authoritarian regime. Some major crisis or series of crises will be handled so ineptly by our current form of government that the citizens will demand that the President be given emergency powers. . . . The pressures of events and the relative success of the Presidency as compared to Congress will lead to a Presidential supremacy which will slip into dictatorship."

Whereas Ned Crosby had to endure the behaviorist orthodoxies of the day, by the time John entered college, psychology professor Barry Schwartz had published his anti-behaviorist manifesto, *The Battle for Human Nature.* John read it while taking a course from him at Swarthmore College, though Schwartz was too humble to put it on the syllabus.

Ned's ideas about ethics, deliberation, and attitude change pre-date the more widely read work of James Fishkin, who moved from moral philosophy to democratic theory with works such as the 1991 book, *Democracy and Deliberation,* which introduced his Deliberative Poll. That same year, public opinion scholar Daniel Yankelovich published *Coming to Public Judgment.* Many works would follow in this vein, such as *Democracy and Disagreement* by Amy Gutmann and Dennis Thompson.

A branch of modern "epistemic" democratic theorists have taken this view so far as to claim that deliberation can resolve political disputes most effectively, at least to the best of the public's knowledge at any given time. David Estlund in *Democratic Authority* and Hélène Landemore in *Democratic Reason* advance this view, though skeptics point out the impossibility of independent judgment in a pluralist society (see Sean Ingham's 2013 essay in *Politics, Philosophy and Economics*). On criticisms of deliberative democracy more generally, see Loren Collingwood and Justin Reedy's chapter, "Listening and Responding to Criticisms of Deliberative Civic Engagement," in the edited volume *Democracy in Motion.*

For more on the British Columbia and Ontario Citizens' Assemblies, see Patrick Fournier and colleagues' book, *When Citizens Decide: Lessons from*

Citizen Assemblies on Electoral Reform, the volume edited by Mark Warren and Hillary Pearse, *Designing Deliberative Democracy,* and Lawrence LeDuc's *West European Politics* essay, "Electoral Reform and Direct Democracy in Canada." The Participedia archive has brief descriptions of both events, along with hundreds of other examples of participatory and deliberative democratic experiments.

The assembly's organizers learned of the Deliberative Poll through University of British Columbia political science professor Richard Johnson, who attended a Deliberative Poll in 1996. Johnson and his colleagues had already developed a critique of conventional referendum politics in their 1996 book, *The Challenge of Direct Democracy: The 1992 Canadian Referendum.*

The vernacular description of ballot measures provided by the CIR complements the more legalistic sections of conventional voter guides. Robert Richards addresses this issue in his 2016 doctoral dissertation, *Intersubjectively Relevant Information: An Account of Citizen-Centered Information and Communication in Democratic Deliberation about Ballot Initiatives.* Richards argues that the goal of neutrality unintentionally limits the descriptive quality of legal information that officials provide to voters or, for that matter, legislators.

Chapter 5

The letter inviting Oregon voters to participate in the CIR included a brief demographic survey in which prospective panelists provided information about themselves, such as their ethnicity, education, and party identification. Healthy Democracy used that data to create balanced panels. The selection process was constructed in consultation with the Portland survey research firm Davis, Hibbitts, and Midghall and was overseen by the League of Women Voters of Oregon. This practice of partnering with polling firms and other good-government organizations has continued to be the norm for choosing CIR participants, with selection often done publicly to ensure transparency. The modest honorarium provided to participants was pegged at the median hourly wage in Oregon. To ensure that participants didn't incur any unintended costs, Healthy Democracy provided reimbursement for individual needs such as childcare.

To get a feel for what it's like to receive an invitation (from 2014), picture letterhead with the Oregon state seal. The letter addresses you by name and begins with these words: "The Citizens' Initiative Review Commission invites you to respond to this mailing for an opportunity to serve your fellow voters by participating in a public evaluation of a ballot measure. If you choose to accept this invitation, you may be selected as one of forty-eight Oregon voters to participate in an official review of a statewide ballot measure. This unique opportunity will allow you to serve the people of Oregon for three and a half days, learning and talking with other voters about an important issue that will be on your November ballot. You will be compensated $350 for your participation." The rest, as they say, is details.

The demographics we cite on representation in US government come from the Pew Research Center's various reports on the 116th Congress. Drawing on findings such as these, some argue for replacing part or all of a legislature with randomly selected citizens—a process dubbed "sortition." The Sortition Foundation keeps tabs on the use of this process across the globe, and John teamed up with Erik Olin Wright present this idea, along with critiques thereof, in *Legislature by Lot: Transformative Designs for Deliberative Governance*.

We have recorded—and used a professional service to transcribe—every CIR from 2010–2014, and we sent an observation team of three or more researchers to every CIR from 2010–2016. The quotes of panelists and witnesses come from these transcripts, with ellipses often removed for clarity of presentation. We use pseudonyms for two witnesses whose stories we convey in this chapter. Though they used their real names at the CIR, we choose to protect their privacy when sharing their narratives with a larger audience. We use the same discretion when referring to participants at the 2010 CIR who we quote but who have not been interviewed for this book, namely "Alex" and "Mark." Unedited transcripts are available through the CIR Research Project archive.

When discussing the panelists' response to advocates' emotional appeals, we rely on research Katie conducted with Genevieve Fuji Johnson and Laura Black, "Citizens' Initiative Review Process: Mediating Emotions, Promoting Productive Deliberation" in *Politics & Society*. Findings suggest that the CIR's structure helped subvert the strategic use of emotion. Advocates relied on emotion to highlight the importance of their case, and CIR participants could use those appeals to better understand the lived impact of decisions. Ultimately, however, CIR participants continually returned to questions of facts to determine the best information they could pass along to voters. Also see Johnson's co-authored follow-up in *Social Science Quarterly*, "Emotions and Deliberation in the Citizens' Initiative Review."

The text of the 2010 Citizens' Statement on Measure 73 provides a good example of how citizen panelists write about ballot measures. Laid out on a single page in a two-column format, the body of the statement was as follows. First came the "Citizen Statement of a Majority of the Panel," which included these Key Findings:

- M73 shifts the balance of power in court proceedings, giving the prosecution additional leverage in plea bargaining and limiting the judge's discretion in sentencing individual cases. (21 out of 24 agree)

- Passed in 1994, Measure 11 (ORS 137.700) provides mandatory minimum sentencing of 70–300 months for the major felony sex crimes defined in Measure 73. (24 out of 24 agree)
- Mandatory minimum sentencing has not proven a significant deterrent to future DUII or sex crimes. (21 out of 24 agree)
- An unintended consequence of M73 is that juveniles aged 15 to 17 are subject to 25-year mandatory minimum sentences. (20 out of 24 agree)
- Oregon spends over 10.9 percent of its general funds on corrections—a greater percentage than any other state. (19 out of 24 agree)

The con arguments appeared under the header, "Citizen Statement Opposed to the Measure POSITION TAKEN BY <u>21 OF 24</u> PANELISTS." These panelists opposed the measure for five reasons:

- Longer mandatory sentencing has little or no effect as a deterrent and has not been proven to increase public safety. Furthermore, mandatory sentences are already in effect under Measure 11.
- Measure 73 takes discretion and power away from judges giving leverage to the prosecution. People charged under this measure may be forced to plea bargain whether they are guilty or not, depriving them of their right to trial by jury.
- Measure 73 requires projected expenditures of $238 million over the next 10 years which must come from cuts in other programs or new taxes.
- This initiative leads to unintended consequences.
- Sexting falls under the definition of explicit material. No one convicted for felony sex offenses would receive the opportunity for treatment.

Finally, the three citizens who wrote the "Citizen Statement in Favor of the Measure POSITION TAKEN BY <u>3 OF 24</u> PANELISTS gave the following rationale:

- This is a public safety measure.
- This measure will take minimum mandatory sentences (70–100 months) on four major sex crimes to mandatory 300 months (25 years).
- This measure changes a third conviction DUII from a misdemeanor to a Class C felony.
- Measure 73 specifically targets only repeat serious sex offenders and repeat (third conviction) intoxicated drivers.
- Statistics support that mandatory sentencing is effective on reduction of violent crime rate.
- Measure 73 will cost only 1/5 of 1 percent of the General Fund.

- Summary: Measure 73 is carefully targeted at repeat violent sex offenders and third time DUII convictions. If passed it would make all Oregonians safer.

Chapter 6

Our discussion of small-group behavior refers to a broad range of research, some of which can be found in John's *The Group in Society*. To get a feel for how researchers commonly aggregate individual preferences into predictions about groups, read John Levine's essay in *Organizational Behavior and Human Decision Processes*, "Transforming Individuals into Groups." Dean Hewes has long argued that too little evidence shows meaningful influence in groups, as in his *Human Communication Research* essay, "The Influence of Communication Processes on Group Outcomes." Charles Derber provides a very readable account self-obsessed conversational behavior in *The Pursuit of Attention*. Fortunately, there exists solid evidence of people actually listening to and influencing one another. The best example is the structurational research effort led by Marshall Scott Poole, including the landmark *Communication Monographs* study, "A Comparison of Normative and Interactional Explanations of Group Decision-Making."

Neuro-cognitive studies of ideology, partisanship, and biased information processing have begun appearing frequently not only in political science journals but also in psychology and neuroscience journals. John Jost is among those encouraging such research, as seen in his co-authored *Political Psychology* essay, "Political Neuroscience: The Beginning of a Beautiful Friendship." These studies provide neurological evidence for phenomena already well understood in terms of self-reported and behavioral data. An example of such findings is Jost and David Amodio's *Motivation and Emotion* essay, "Political Ideology as Motivated Social Cognition." Christopher Beem's *Democratic Humility* argues that these studies address deeper questions about democracy.

To see the larger significance of the fourth-century Athenian decision, see Emily Wilson's *The Death of Socrates*. The quote from John Adams on the subject comes from his Letter XLI, "Ancient Democratic Republics."

On the mechanics of deliberative polling, see James Fishkin and Cynthia Farrar's chapter in *The Deliberative Democracy Handbook*. The Fishkin quotes come from *Democracy and Deliberation: New Directions for Democratic Reform* (p. 93), *The Voice of the People* (p. 43), and *When the People Speak* (p. 124). "Deliberative Polling" is a trademark used by the Stanford University Center for Deliberative Democracy. We also recommend Ethan Leib and Baogang He, *The Search for Deliberative Democracy in China*. We quote He from a ChinaFile interview, "China's Experiment with Democracy."

The Ireland case insights come from Tom Arnold, who chaired the convention, and the event's two lead organizers, David Farrell and Jane Suiter. They have published numerous essays about this experience, but we drew these particular insights from their chapter, "Lessons from a Hybrid Sortition Chamber: The 2012–14 Irish Constitutional Convention," in *Legislature by Lot*.

Our discussion of culture and cognition draws on a range of sources, many of which are referenced in the notes for chapter 3. On cross-national differences, see Geert Hofstede's *Culture's Consequences* and Eunkook Suh's "The Shifting Basis of Life Satisfaction Judgments across Cultures" in the *Journal of Personality and Social Psychology*. George Lakoff has published widely on the themes in this chapter, and we recommend reading *Moral Politics: How Liberals and Conservatives Think*. On how cultural cognition relates to polarization, see the *Boston Review* essay John co-authored with Dan Kahan and Don Braman, "Ending Polarization: The Good News about the Culture Wars."

The aforementioned book by Morris Fiorina and colleagues, *Culture War? The Myth of a Polarized America*, puts polarization in context. Jonathan Haidt provides an alternative account in *The Righteous Mind: Why Good People Are Divided by Politics and Religion*. A greater plurality of perspectives comes through recent books, including *Political Polarization in American Politics* (edited by Daniel J. Hopkins and John Sides) and *American Gridlock* (edited by James A. Thurber and Antoine Yoshinaka). Observations we make about voter polarization in the 2016 election come from Milo Beckman's "Religion and Education Explain the White Vote" at FiveThirtyEight, as well as from exit poll data provided by the *New York Times*. The 2014 Pew Research Center study we cite is *Political Polarization in the American Public*. Their 2017 report that we reference, *The Partisan Divide on Political Values Grows Even Wider*, paints an even bleaker picture.

National survey data on public attitudes comes from the same National Science Foundation funded research that appears in the *Journal of Empirical Legal Studies* article, "Culture and Identity-Protective Cognition: Explaining the White-Male Effect in Risk Perception," by Dan Kahan and colleagues. The particular analyses presented herein are described in more methodological detail in the *Public Administration* article, "Participatory Policymaking across Cultural Cognitive Divides," which we co-authored with Dan Kahan and Don Braman.

One tricky methodological detail about measuring culture merits mention. We draw on multiple surveys that use the same survey items to measure cultural differences for different populations. When represented graphically, the middle of the cultural grid is simply the midpoint of the response scales we provided survey respondents. There is no objective basis for defining the true middle of a cultural continuum. Our interpretation aligns with other measures of ideology in the United States, but one can't estimate the proportion of people who are, say, hierarchical versus egalitarian, without making a judgment call about where to draw the line between such categories.

For those who enjoy perusing the details, we provide here representative survey items used to measure the two cultural dimensions. Respondents stated their level of agreement/disagreement with these items: "The government interferes far too much in our everyday lives" (individualism); "Sometimes government needs to make laws that keep people from hurting themselves" (collectivism); "We have gone too far in pushing equal rights in this country" (hierarchism); and "Our society would be better off if the distribution of wealth was more equal" (egalitarianism).

The discussion of the conflict between self-interest and preference consensus leans heavily on the work of Jane Mansbridge, particularly her chapter "Conflict and Self-Interest in Deliberation," which appears in *Deliberative Democracy and Its Discontents*, edited by Samantha Besson and José Luis Martí. Mansbridge highlights the inherent self-interest and conflict present in any deliberative discussion and warns against ignoring self-interest to arrive at a false consensus. Simon Niemeyer and John Dryzek provide a detailed discussion of the types of "meta-consensus" that could be sought in discussion—namely consensus on facts, the relevant values, and the validity of competing solutions or preferences. In their article, "The Ends of Deliberation: Meta-Consensus and Inter-Subjective Rationality as Ideal Outcomes," they argue that rather than trying to achieve preference consensus, participants should be able to reach agreement about the validity of the underlying arguments that support competing perspectives, even those with which they ultimately disagree.

Our analysis of the cultural locations of past Oregon ballot measures shown in Figure 6.2 was completed with the assistance of Mark Henkels at Western Oregon University and a team of University of Washington undergraduates: Sara Farinelli, Brianne Ibanes, Brian McCoy, and Ann Young. As for the cultural distribution of yes and no votes in Figures 6.3 and 6.4, a careful reader will notice that some of the "Yes" and "No" preference icons are lighter than others. Those cultural locations were estimated using imputation, as detailed in our *Public Administration* article co-authored with Dan Kahan and Don Braman, "Participatory policymaking across cultural cognitive divides: Two tests of cultural biasing in public forum design and deliberation."

Polling data on the 2010 ballot measures studied by the CIR was conducted for us by the University of Washington Survey Research Center, as a pilot for the main surveys we discussed in our 2010 report to the Oregon legislature. (Additional private polling is archived online at Ballotpedia.) To take an example from our data, excluding undecided voters, 70.5 percent of Oregon voters who we identified as egalitarian said that they intended to support the medical marijuana initiative (Measure 74), whereas 71.5 percent of voters who we identified as hierarchical pledged to oppose it. This issue gets a more detailed treatment in the *International Journal of Public Opinion Research* article John co-authored with Justin Reedy and Chris Wells, "Knowledge Distortion in Direct Democracy: A Longitudinal Study of Biased Empirical Beliefs on Statewide Ballot Measures."

Our claim that it's hard to predict which issues will lead to opinion change is based on research we've conducted on the effects of context on deliberative outcomes. That article is tentatively titled "How Deliberative Experiences Shape Subjective Outcomes: A Study of Twelve Minipublics from 2010–2016." Though we can't yet tell you where that research will appear, we're always happy to share as-yet-unpublished papers on request, along with the data underpinning them.

The Ohio experiment presented at the end of this chapter references Nathan Larkin's 2017 undergraduate honors thesis, "Of Marijuana and Monopolies: Increasing Correct Voting in U.S. Ballot Measure Elections with the Citizens' Initiative Review." The careful reader will notice that Larkin links his study back to Lau and Redlawsk's "correct voting" paradigm.

Chapter 7

Our account of the lobbying effort and challenge to the CIR by Our Oregon relies on interviews with the principal actors described in the chapter, plus our direct observations. From 2010 to 2012, we spent considerable time in Oregon and had the opportunity to meet with legislators. Accounts of the events would likely differ if more critics of the CIR made themselves available for interviews, but we have had limited success eliciting direct criticism of the process, except in informal conversations with those who testified before CIR panels. Speaking of which, Doug Harcleroad, the advocate in favor of mandatory minimum sentencing from the 2010 CIR, did appear at the legislative hearing where Marion testified. She noticed him, but she didn't say hello.

Our Oregon quotes come from a December 6, 2016, interview with their Deputy Political Director, Courtney Graham. We had requested an open-ended exchange, which would have permitted more probing questions. Graham was able to provide only written answers via e-mail, with no opportunity for follow-up. Despite these limitations, we were grateful for the opportunity to hear an official account of the decisions made by that organization's leadership.

The quotes from activists critiquing deliberative processes comes from Peter Levine and Rose Marie Nierras' essay, "Activists' Views of Deliberation," in the *Journal of Public Deliberation*. Some of these worries have been borne out in practice, as noted in Carolyn Hendriks's "When the Forum Meets Interest Politics" in *Politics & Society*.

Derek Willis at the *New York Times* has been following the work of Lawrence Lessig. Though Willis remains a skeptic, he gives props to the innovative approaches Lessig takes, as evidenced in "Campaign Finance Reform Turns to Reward and Punishment" and "Mayday, a Super PAC to Fight Super PACs, Stumbles in Its First Outing." For a full-throated version of his views from 2011, see Lessig's *Republic, Lost: How Money Corrupts Congress—and a Plan to Stop It*. A more recent example of his views, and his battle against cynics, appears in his *Atlantic* essay, "Campaign Finance and the Nihilist Politics of Resignation."

Background on the corporate tax reform proposed in Measure 85 comes from a variety of Oregon media sources, many of which are archived at Ballotpedia. The Wayback Machine Internet archive proved essential in finding campaign materials from 2012, such as on the Defend Oregon website. Later, that organization appeared revise its site in response to the CIR, at one point using the headline, "Simple and clear information on the seven statewide ballot measures appearing on Oregon's November 2014 ballot and recommendations from many of Oregon's most trusted organizations." The bottom of the page read, "The following groups present the Defend Oregon Ballot Measure Guide as a service to Oregon voters."

Possible spending totals on Measure 85 could be over $2.7 million for and $500,000 against, but both spending figures are likely gross overestimates. Six of the seven registered organizations reporting expenditures campaigned on multiple measures in 2012, and Oregon's campaign finance data do not separate out expenditures for each measure. One exception is the single-issue advocacy group Corporate Kicker for K1, which spent nearly $650,000 supporting Measure 85.

We have co-led the research team studying the CIR since 2010. Each of our reports have suggested revisions to the process to make it more deliberative, democratic, and useful to voters. Enumerated lists that go on for many pages (at times, to the annoyance of Healthy Democracy) appear toward the back end of our reports in 2010, 2012, 2015, and 2016–2017, which are all available on the CIR Research Project website.

Chapter 8

Prior to writing *Democratic Illusion*, Genevieve Fuji Johnson had warned about deliberation's shortcomings in a 2009 article in the *Canadian Journal of Political Science* and *Deliberative Democracy for the Future*, published the previous year (and quoted in this chapter, from p. 106). A 2005 chapter, "Future Directions for Public Deliberation," in *The Deliberative Democracy Handbook* warned that deliberative experiments hadn't yet been tested by the external interest group pressures they would soon come to face.

The figures on initiative campaign spending come from research by the Center for Public Integrity. Their October 2014 study estimated $119 million spent on political television ads, but when they revisited the issue in February 2015, the final totals were closer to $266 million. The top fifty donors accounted for three-quarters of that spending, most of which was spent on (successfully) opposing proposed laws. The top five represented health insurance and gambling interests, including the Native American casino Table Mountain Rancheria, near Fresno, California.

Considerable research has investigated the efficacy of initiative campaigns. The balance of evidence suggests that they matter a great deal. Broader accounts include Shaun Bowler and Todd Donovan's *Demanding Choices* and Joseph Zimmerman's *The Initiative*. A precinct-level analysis happens to come from data collected in Oregon from the 2008 elections. In their *Political Behavior* study, Todd Rogers and Joel Middleton conclude that advocacy campaigns defeated two ballot initiatives that would have passed in that year's election.

As for the casino debate at the CIR, the development plan details come from Associated Press reporting in August 2012, with the bulk of coverage on the casino campaign appearing in the *Oregonian* and its companion website, OregonLive. Particularly amusing is the article, "Political Consultant Fires Facebook Shots Over Demise of Pro-Casino Campaign." Among the choicest quotes are this one from Josh Kardon, who was chief of staff for a US Senator: "Crooked and ethically challenged campaign consultants all across the country have no problem telling clients what they want to hear in order to set the consultants up for giant paydays. Landing a well-funded client in a media-intensive campaign brings in millions in revenues and hundreds of thousands in pure profits to political consultants." The full exchange makes for good reading.

The digression about debates references the October 17, 2012, *New York Times* article, "Would You Please Let Me Finish . . . " Through the lens of deliberative democratic theory, debate itself comes in for harsh criticism, as with David Mathews's *Politics for People*. The problem is the actual practice of contemporary candidate debates, rather than the kind of substantive clash that could help the public understand issues and tradeoffs. On the evolution of presidential debates, and how candidates have taken control of them, see Sidney Kraus's *Televised Presidential Debates and Public Policy*, updated in 2011. Articles published in *Communication Monographs* in 2002 and 2003 showed that, whatever their flaws, candidate debates have a variety of effects on the voters who watch them; see "Meta-Analysis of the Effects of Viewing US Presidential Debates" and "The Role of Communication in the Formation of an Issue-Based Citizenry."

Our assessments of the CIR draw on reports we presented to the state legislature (2010), to the CIR Commission (2012), and to that same commission and the Democracy Fund (2015–2017)—all available through the online CIR

Research Project archive. The note about the preferred reading level in Oregon comes from the Oregon Department of Administrative Services 2015 document, "Department of Administrative Services: Readability—Frequently Asked Questions." The vote tallies in Table 8.1 from the pilot tests of the CIR come from research surveys of panelists; by design, no official vote was taken at those events. For more detail on the effect of the CIR on voter knowledge, see the report we co-authored with Robert Richards, "Empowering Voters through Better Information: Analysis of the Citizens' Initiative Review, 2010–2014."

James Fishkin speaks of the "recommending force" that deliberative public opinion should have on policymakers and the public generally. That phrase appears often in his book, *When the People Speak*. Therein, he explains that most Deliberative Polls have been advisory, but many were "advisory in circumstances that endowed them with recommending force" (p. 156). In a sense, this is the opposite of the circumstances that occur in cases like those detailed by Johnson, in which the conclusions of a deliberative body get ignored, dismissed, or rejected without justification.

Chapter 9

For more background on the Citizens' Juries, see the Jefferson Center website, which includes the Clinton healthcare jury described in this chapter. The first detailed write-up of this method either of us saw was Ned Crosby's 1995 chapter in *Fairness and Competence in Citizen Participation*. That book was among the first earnest efforts to translate Jürgen Habermas's abstract conception of deliberation into practical guidelines for public forums.

The controversy over the CIR with Our Oregon was well covered by Oregon newspapers. The most important exchanges appeared in the *Oregonian*, such as the July 30, 2012, article, "Sponsors of Oregon Tax Measure Won't Participate in Citizen Review Panel." Toward the end of the chapter, the quote from the CIR Commission comes from its official website.

On Deliberative Polls, visit the website for Stanford University's Center for Deliberative Democracy. The description of the Deliberative Poll on Iraq came from a 2003 Brookings report by Henry Brady, James Fishkin, and Robert Luskin. The results of the California poll (referenced at the end of the chapter) can be seen at the website What's Next California? One can read related material at the Ballotpedia webpage for California Proposition 31 (2012).

The idea of a Deliberative Poll first appeared in print when Fishkin penned the August 1988 *Atlantic* essay, "The Case for a National Caucus: Taking Democracy Seriously." He got his wish when the Deliberative Poll appeared on US soil as the 1996 National Issues Convention in Austin, Texas. John got the chance to see this event firsthand, which is the source of the vignette about a welfare recipient's experience of deliberation. For making that field trip possible, thanks go to the Kettering Foundation and the University of New Mexico Institute for Public Policy.

The CIR research project we oversee uses a diverse team of scholars and remains open to anyone interested in studying the process. This book includes only some of the findings accumulated so far. The evidence makes a strong case for the CIR as a deliberative panel and as a mechanism for improving large-scale deliberation during elections, but each new article we publish also shows its limitations. The plurality of voices on our research team helps ensure new insights will continue to arise about the CIR and related processes for years to come.

A research method used extensively in this chapter is the survey experiment, which treats respondents taking a survey as though they were in a laboratory. Each respondent is randomly assigned to conditions that expose them to different experimental stimuli. Jason Barabas and Jennifer Jerit caution against over-interpreting such experiments. The principal worry in their *American Political Science Review* essay ("Are Survey Experiments Externally Valid?") is that researchers generalize too quickly from experiments on government notices and media coverage to real-world encounters with such phenomena. We believe that survey experiments on the CIR have more ecological validity. In our studies, voters encounter the Citizens' Statements in a context where they are actively seeking information and taking the time to read and consider it carefully while perusing the *Voters' Pamphlet*.

Another example of a compelling experiment on public deliberation is the series of studies led by Michael Neblo, which includes "Who Wants to Deliberate—and Why?" in the *American Political Science Review*. Neblo demonstrates that US voters—particularly those alienated by the major political parties—are keen for opportunities to take part in issues forums and honest conversations with their elected officials. He folds these findings into a larger theory in *Deliberative Democracy between Theory and Practice*. For an overview of experiments like these, along with their closest cousins, see John's "The Lessons and Limitations of Experiments in Democratic Deliberation" in the *Annual Review of Law and Social Science*.

Full details on the CIR surveys used in this and other chapters can be found in the methodological appendices of our CIR reports published from 2010 to 2017. (We collected survey data in 2018, but it did not include a statewide survey of Oregon.) Though many people have abandoned their landline phones, the phone survey method remains one of the most effective ways of learning the experiences of a large population, and we have used it to compare Oregon voters' general awareness of the CIR since 2010. Those surveys had low response rates typical of the modern phone survey, with roughly one in ten households called providing a completed survey. Nonetheless, our survey respondents' voting choices aligned well with the election results, and the survey sample matched the political profile of the Oregon electorate.

In the final weeks of our 2010 survey, for example, 59 percent of respondents said they would vote for the mandatory sentencing ballot measure, which was close to the 57 percent of actual ballots favoring the initiative. Republicans comprised 36 percent of the phone survey sample, which matched their percentage of actual ballots completed in 2010. Democrats were 41 percent of respondents, compared to 44 percent of actual ballots.

Online surveys are a different kind of beast. Our 2012 survey was a solicitation sent to tens of thousands of Oregon voters who, thanks to a commercial data warehouse, had e-mail addresses associated with their voter registration records. That survey had a very low response rate (less than 2 percent of those emailed returned complete surveys), but as with the phone survey, the sample was broadly representative of the general Oregon electorate both demographically and in terms of its voting preferences. The other online surveys have used panels managed by YouGov/Polimetrix (2010) and Qualtrics (2014–2018). When reporting population frequencies, we attach weightings to those data so they better match the general population, but no such weighting is necessary for comparisons of experimental groups.

The earliest one-on-one interviews our research team conducted with voters were by Katie, Justin Reedy, and research assistants. Some of those appear in this chapter, but the larger sample of interviews were conducted in research facilities in Portland and Denver by the Bentley University User Experience Center. In the Portland laboratory, twenty voters read the Citizens' Statement on Measure 90 (open primaries), and an equal number read the statement for Measure 92 (labeling of food containing genetically modified organisms). Half of those participants were chosen because they had used Citizens' Statements in the past, and the other half were novices. To compare the Oregon experience with a state considering adopting the CIR, another sample of twenty voters were interviewed in Denver as they read the pilot CIR's statement on Colorado Proposition 105 (another labeling measure regarding genetically modified organisms). All of these individual voters are represented by pseudonyms when a name is given.

If 50 percent of Oregonians being aware of the CIR seems like a low number, let us suggest some titles that show the dim prospects of capturing the mass public's attention. Begin with the classics, such as Samuel Popkin's *The Reasoning Voter* and John Zaller's *The Nature and Origins of Mass Opinion*. Those books manage to sound an optimistic note about democracy by accepting the limited rationality of the electorate as somewhere between inevitable and desirable. Then turn to Benjamin Page's *Who Deliberates?* to hold out the hope that citizens may learn by watching elites argue. Two decades of research have followed to show what the public is—and is not—capable of doing in the midst of an election. In the context of such research, our findings about the Oregon CIR signal that this unique process has managed to capture *and hold* the public's attention in a way that any modern campaign or media outlet would envy.

The figures on voting and issue knowledge compare survey respondents exposed to the CIR against all other experimental conditions combined. Comparisons against just the control group produce similar results. In the archetypal laboratory, participants are seated and exposed to some stimuli for a fixed period of time. In typical web-based survey experiments, there is no guarantee that a respondent pays any attention to the web page or other content to which the experimenter assigns them at random. One can, however, track how long a person spends on a page. Starting in 2012, we set a threshold of one minute for exposure to any experimental treatments. Another important methodological note concerns the Phoenix CIR experiment, which was testing selective exposure. In this instance, reading the Citizens' Statement (and other material) was an option presented to participants, rather than a random assignment. We considered leaving that particular case out of the dataset, but in spite of its distinct method, it fits within the larger pattern.

It is with a mix of pride and embarrassment that we confess that the bit about Ted Cruz came from an article in *USA Today*. Pure serendipity inspired the purchase of that paper from a local gas station on the day the story ran. The article in question was, "Cruz Outburst Reflects Rise of Political Fact-Checking." Related coverage can be found at *PolitiFact*.

One can't help but speculate that some of Cruz's casual use of evidence comes from learning precisely the wrong lessons as a member of the parliamentary debate circuit in college, during the heyday of that process when improvisational comedy was as important as a firm grasp of the facts. John capitalized on this fact during his contemporaneous debate career. See the April 22, 2015, *New York Times* article "Ted Cruz Showed Eloquence, and Limits, as Debater at Princeton."

Chapter 10

This chapter uses notes from conversations and interviews with Marion, Ned, Ty, and others. We also reference interviews with a juror who participated in the Jury and Democracy Project and a voter interviewed by the Bentley University Design and Usability Center.

The full CIR Commission on which Marion and Ann served consists of four former panelists, two former CIR facilitators, a member selected by the state senate's Republican leadership, and one recommended by the senate Democrats.

Ned Crosby, Pat Benn, and Larry Pennings devised that panelist-heavy configuration when they first designed the CIR for the State of Washington, which has yet to adopt it. We share their view that a citizen-centered board remains one of the surest ways to ensure long-term process integrity. Limited terms of service keep infusing new, randomly elected citizens into the mix while maintaining a supermajority of commissioners with CIR experience.

The aforementioned Jury and Democracy Project is an ongoing collaboration among John and colleagues scattered across multiple universities. The key publication is a 2010 book titled, naturally, *The Jury and Democracy*, but numerous articles and essays before and after flesh out the details of how participation in juries influences citizens. A more recent analysis of civil trials conducted with Valerie Hans in the *Journal of Empirical Legal Studies* suggests that key features of the jury experience include serving on a twelve-person jury tasked with reaching a unanimous verdict. The maximum civic benefit of jury service comes from deliberating in a diverse group of peers who must all work together to reach a decision.

In addition to the national archival study referenced in the text, the Jury and Democracy Project surveyed thousands of prospective jurors in and near Seattle, Washington, before, just after, and several months after they served on juries. Consistent with our findings about the impact of CIR participation, these surveys showed that many jurors refined their civic attitudes and increased their political engagement as a result of participating in the jury system. Key features of jury trials explained the jury's civic impact, and the CIR shares many of those. For instance, jurors experienced the most powerful changes when they felt that judges and attorneys respected their service. Jurors who found their trials more interesting and emotionally engaging also experienced relatively profound changes. When jurors were satisfied with their deliberation and verdict, they were more likely to become engaged in public life after leaving the courthouse.

The central work of Albert Bandura that shapes our thinking on civic education comes from *Social Foundations of Thought and Action*. We quote that book (p. 27) and his *American Psychologist* article, "Human Agency in Social Cognitive Theory" (p. 1182). With special relevance to our discussion of emanating effects is his *Media Psychology* essay, "Social Cognitive Theory of Mass Communication."

On the educative effect of deliberation, we draw on a wider body of literature. Heather Pincock provides a good summary of this work in her *Democracy in Motion* chapter, "Does Deliberation Make Better Citizens?" We talk about deliberation and political socialization in our *Politics* article, "Civic (Re)socialisation: The Educative Effects of Deliberative Participation."

That essay details the subjective impact of the CIR and Australian Citizens' Parliament, and its ideas and title come from Katie's doctoral dissertation.

Katherine's work went far beyond John's own dissertation, the most relevant portion of which appears in the *Adult Education Quarterly* article, "Adult Civic Education through the National Issues Forums: Developing Democratic Habits and Dispositions through Public Deliberation." Katie's dissertation is also the source for our discussion of "emanating effects." A more complete version of that research appears in a *Political Studies* article Katie and John co-authored with Michael Barthel, "Emanating Effects: The Impact of the Oregon Citizens' Initiative Review on Voters' Political Efficacy."

Our follow-up surveys with both CIR and Australian Citizens' Parliament participants had outstanding response rates—a common feature of studies on minipublics, owing to the good will generated among participants toward the organizers and affiliated researchers. For instance, the year-later Australian survey had an 87 percent response rate. (All rates use AAPOR's RR2 metric.) The year-later follow up with CIR participants in 2011 had a 77 percent response rate. Even the two-year follow-up survey had a response rate of 58 percent, and this figure was lower partly owing to dated contact information. Regarding the two-year follow up survey, see Katie's March 2015 Kettering Foundation report, "Assessing Participant Change Two Years Later."

We talk about the CIR building confidence in the responsiveness of government, but too much faith in government can undermine civic engagement. Writing with Michael Xenos, John showed this in a *Journal of Communication* essay, "Of Attitudes and Engagement." More unambiguous benefit comes from building up one's "internal efficacy," or political self-confidence. Michael Morrell demonstrates this in his 2005 *Political Behavior* essay, "Deliberation, Democratic Decision Making and Internal Political Efficacy."

On minipublics, we recommend three edited volumes: *The Deliberative Democracy Handbook, Democracy in Motion,* and *Deliberative Mini-Publics.* Useful articles include Robert Goodin and John Dryzek's *Politics & Society* essay, "Deliberative Impacts: The Macro-Political Uptake of Mini-Publics," Archon Fung's *Journal of Political Philosophy* essay, "Recipes for Public Spheres," and the *Journal of Public Deliberation* essay that Carolina Johnson's co-authored with John, "Variations of Institutional Design for Empowered Deliberation."

The study on undervoting appears in a March 16, 2015, University of California, Berkeley working paper by Ned Augenblick and Scott Nicholson, "Ballot Position, Choice Fatigue, and Voter Behavior." An early study on the concept of voter fatigue appears in Shaun Bowler and Todd Donovan's 1992 essay, "Ballot Propositions and Information Cost," in *Western Political Quarterly.*

The undervoting data from survey experiments uses the same data we discuss in detail in our chapter 9 notes. As for the concern of self-conscious respondents wanting to please interviewers, a good review of the literature and a comparable web experiment appears in the *International Journal of Public Opinion Research* article, "Measuring Political Participation: Testing Social Desirability Bias in a Web-Survey Experiment," by Mikael Persson and Maria Solevid.

One irony about undervoting is that ballot propositions far down the ballot can increase overall voter turnout. It's not the presence of the initiative or referendum, per se, but the campaigns associated with them that spur higher voting rates, as shown by Matt Childers and Mike Binder in their *Political Research Quarterly* essay, "Engaged by the Initiative."

Though jury service has a larger and more lasting effect on voter turnout than conventional "get out the vote" efforts, the opportunities to serve as jurors are rare, whereas campaigns reach out to voters regularly. For more on this, see the second edition of Don Green and Alan Gerber's *Get Out the Vote!*

Contrasts between participatory and deliberative democracy have been drawn by many scholars, including Diana Mutz in *Hearing the Other Side*, which inspired a series of essays in a 2013 issue of *Critical Review*, notably including Simone Chambers's "The Many Faces of Good Citizenship." Peter Levine argues for a synergy between deliberative and participatory models of democracy in *We Are the Ones We Have Been Waiting For.* Magdalena Wojcieszak and her co-authors show that deliberation may do more good for ideological moderates than for others in their *International Journal of Public Opinion Research* study, "Deliberative and Participatory Democracy?"

Conclusion

It speaks to the authenticity of Ann's testimony that it was based on written notes, which were marked up heavily before she spoke. Complete audio of her testimony, along with that of other advocates for the bill, can be found through Washington State's bill tracker at leg.wa.gov (House Bill 1364 in 2015). Unfortunately, the committee's camera focused on the legislators themselves, with Ann completely off screen. Worse still, the video features the John's balding scalp, which shines through the entire session.

We regularly provided legislative testimony on the CIR process and confined our remarks to describing research findings. John also helped organize the Harvard panel at which Tyrone Reitman and Representative Hecht appeared. That panel's short title—"Getting to Yes (or No)"—is a cheeky riff on another Harvard product, the bestselling negotiation primer *Getting to Yes*, by Roger Fisher and William Ury. The inspiration for the panel came from Finnish doctoral candidate Maija Karjalainen, who was a Visiting Fellow at Harvard's Ash Center of Democratic Governance and Innovation studying under the direction of Dr. Maija Setälä (no first-name relation, if that's a thing). Karjalainen's studies led her to the CIR and other processes described in this book. She and

Representative Hecht's legislative aide belong to a new generation of young scholars and citizens who have become intrigued by the potential for building deliberative democratic institutions.

Looking to an older generation of scholars, Robert Dahl describes the five criteria for democracy in the previously mentioned 1989 book, *Democracy and its Critics*. We are not the first to note that deliberation can move us toward better realizing democracy by enacting Dahl's criteria. For that, see the long list of political theorists and social scientists who contributed to the newly published *Oxford Handbook of Deliberative Democracy*.

The Argentina case came to John's attention when he joined a few other US scholars who went to that country together in 2015 to exchange ideas about jury systems with Argentinian academics, officials, and activists. Much credit goes to Cornell University professor Valerie Hans, who had visited previously and first introduced Andrés Harfuch to John over dinner at her home. Her husband cooked the main course that night, but still, much credit goes to Valerie. The quotes from Andrés are translated from his prologue in the edited book *Juicio por Jurados en la Provincia de Buenos Aires*. The Asociación Argentina de Juicio por Jurados tracks the progress of reform in Argentina.

Returning to politics in the United States, information on the spread of initiatives comes from the Initiative and Referendum Institute. For background on the initiative's history, a great place to start is Thomas Cronin's classic 1989 book, *Direct Democracy*.

Polling data from Gallop comes from an article posted online by the Independent Voter Project on January 5, 2015, "Poll: Government Now Biggest Concern for Americans." Public perceptions of special interests' influence come from the Major Institutions subsection of PollingReport. Polling results regarding public attitudes toward initiatives come from surveys compiled by the Public Policy Institute of California and the University of Washington Survey Research Center. Private polling sponsored by Ned Crosby in anticipation of advocating the CIR has produced similar results.

Insights on who influences public policy comes from Larry Bartels' April, 2014, *Washington Post* essay, "Rich People Rule!" It appeared in the Monkey Cage blog, which provides original reporting on political research, often written by political scientists themselves. The blog's title is a reference to notoriously cynical H. L. Mencken's assertion, "Democracy is the art of running the circus from the monkey cage." It's not clear how that metaphor works out, exactly.

The full article on public influence by Martin Gilens and Benjamin Page appeared in *Perspectives on Politics* in September 2014 as "Testing Theories of American Politics: Elites, Interest Groups, and Average Citizens." When the lead author presented their findings at the invitation of Pennsylvania State University's McCourtney Institute for Democracy, he emphasized the growing concentration of campaign finance as a culprit in explaining why public opinion has such a limited influence. By his own admission, however, the data don't fit that pattern. In their data, public influence was nil from the outset, so the changes in campaign finance since (and before) *Citizens United v. FEC* could not have reduced an influence level already at zero. One could argue that the public's "zero influence" has become stickier, but the appeal of processes like the CIR is that they provide a direct conduit to fellow citizens that circumvents the media system and paid advertising more generally.

On the changing pace of social change, see Allison Fine's *Momentum: Igniting Social Change in the Connected Age*. Accelerating adoption rates for new legislation appear in Alex Tribou and Keith Collins's April 2015 *Bloomberg* infographic essay, "This is How Fast America Changes Its Mind."

Public officials' shifting views on social issues became a news theme from 2011 to 2015. The reporting we cite comes from ABC News ("High-Profile Politicians Who Changed Their Positions on Gay Marriage" and "Republican Rob Portman Supports Gay Marriage") as well as Will Portman's "Coming out" essay in the *Yale Daily News* (March 25, 2013). The Pew Research Center's "Changing Attitudes on Gay Marriage" shows that opposition to same sex marriage dropped from 57 percent in 2001 to 32 percent in 2017. Coverage of the New York state senate debate and subsequent election comes from the *New York Daily News* (January 15, 2011) and the *Saratogian News* (November 6, 2012).

Moving across the pond to Europe, the David Van Reybrouck quote comes from e-mail correspondence with him on June 8, 2015. A summary of his argument appears at the Equality by Lot blog, which also provides considerable context on Ireland's Constitutional Convention. One can also return to the Monkey Cage (June 5, 2015) to read more about how that convention led to the Irish vote on same-sex marriage. The official report on the convention, meeting records, and submissions received are archived at constitution.ie. One of the first academic sources on that event is the *International Political Science Review* essay, "When Do Deliberative Citizens Change Their Opinions? Evidence from the Irish Citizens' Assembly." Background information about Ireland comes from that country's Central Statistics Office, a November 2012 *Irish Times* poll, and a survey published the previous month by the *Sunday Times*. Broader context comes courtesy a May 19, 2015, *New York Times* article by Douglas Dalby, "Gay Marriage on Ballot Shows Shift in Irish Attitudes."

Back in the United States, we were unable to trace all the political protest signs cited in this chapter back to their original sources. Most connect to the Rally to Restore Sanity and/or Fear, and many more have been collected by Máirín Knox Veith on Pinterest under the label "My Favourite Protest Signs." That spelling suggests a British influence, though the collector claims to have been born and raised in Endicott, New York ("Go Union-Endicott Tigers!"). If these protests resonate with the reader, we point you to the web portals for fellow deliberationistas at the National Coalition for Dialogue and Deliberation and the Deliberative Dialogue Consortium.

For those who wince at the idea that heated protest has no place in deliberation, fear not. We recognize that forceful protest can put important issues on the agenda for future deliberation, as argued in an essay co-authored with Mark West, "Deliberation at the Margins." In "Against Deliberation," Lynn Sanders suggests that strident testimony may be warranted to give voice to the voiceless. One's dissent may be "reasoned" even when aggressive, as argued in Karen Tracy's *Challenges of Ordinary Democracy*.

If one is more comfortable in a committee room than at a public protest, a useful reading between bill hearings is Joseph Bessette's *The Mild Voice of Reason*. Bessette sees the best hope for legislative deliberation in the committee sessions held by the US Senate. Even in 1997, however, Bessette could see the prospects for reasoned talk diminishing. Stephanie Burkhalter showed this a decade later in her doctoral dissertation, "Talking Points: Message Strategies and Deliberation in the US Congress." A more recent account of deliberation in the nooks and crannies of state government comes from Dede Feldman's 2014 book, *Inside the New Mexico Senate*. Feldman enjoyed a long career as a state senator in spite of hiring John as her initial campaign manager.

There are many promising variants to the CIR model for influencing elections and policymaking. For theoretical approaches to deliberative citizen panels, see James Fishkin's *Election Law Journal* essay, "Deliberation by the People Themselves: Entry Points for the Public Voice," and the article John wrote with Robert Richards for *Politics & Society*, "Making Direct Democracy Deliberative through Random Assemblies." A broader range of such processes appear in the edited volume, *Deliberative Mini-Publics*.

One minipublic that didn't appear in our main text but warrants honorable mention is the California Redistricting Commission. This process was established by initiative and first put into practice in 2010. The fourteen-member commission exercises redistricting authority in a large and powerful state, and its judgments have real consequences for the shape of state legislative and congressional districts. Its selection process is unusual and interesting: the state auditor reviews volunteer applications, then random selection determines the sixty finalists from which new commissioners are chosen. Former commissioner Angelo Ancheta provides a firsthand account of this process in his *Harvard Law and Policy Review* essay, "Redistricting Reform and the California Citizens Redistricting Commission." In 2018, Colorado and Michigan voters approved similar commissions to redraw their district lines after the 2020 US Census.

One problem commissions like this could address is the sense that elections are "rigged." On the reality of such a problem, we draw on annual reports from the Electoral Integrity Project. As for the perception problem, an October 13–15, 2016, Politico poll found that 44 percent of Clinton supporters were "very confident" that votes would be counted fairly, compared to only 15 percent of Trump supporters ("Poll: 41 Percent of Voters Say Election Could Be 'Stolen' from Trump"). When Clinton lost despite carrying the popular vote (and her party lost congressional seats partly owing to gerrymandering), the electoral frustration script flipped.

Given the importance of redistricting in the United States and countries with similar systems, the notion of using randomized commissions has appeal. This prospect has sparked work toward that end by Arizona State University political science professor Amit Ron and his collaborators, including Tyrone Reitman. A loose network of "sortitionists" have begun championing the idea of using random samples to replace anything from student government to legislative chambers, as detailed at the Equality by Lot blog and in John and Erik Olin Wright's *Legislature by Lot*.

Another practical approach to deliberative reform goes online, as referenced in the Greek examples gleaned from the Participedia archive. One promising experiment is "Common Ground for Action," an adaptation of the National Issues Forums that was developed by Amy Lee, Luke Hohmann, and their collaborators. This and other examples fold into a vision for bringing citizens and government closer together in the *PS: Political Science and Politics* essay, "Embracing Digital Democracy: A Call for Building an Online Civic Commons." An array of successful tools appear in Eric Gordon's edited volume, *Civic Media*.

The Ohio project that Ned Crosby helped steer has been evaluated by public administration scholar Tina Nabatchi, and a published account by her and Greg Munno appears in the *Journal of Public Deliberation* article, "Public Deliberation and Co-Production in the Political and Electoral Arena: A Citizens' Jury Approach." One of the first stories about the district where these Citizen Election Forums took place appeared in a July 8, 2011, *Washington Post* story, "The Top 10 Battles Between Members of Congress in 2012." Updates near election day saw the race as close. RealClearPolitics rated the race as a "toss up," and OpenSecrets posted the note, "Hot Race in Ohio's 16th."

A large-scale variant on these ideas, with less emphasis on small-group deliberation, appeared in Bruce Ackerman and James Fishkin's *Deliberation Day*. Though it seems doubtful that elected officials would enact such deliberative panels to evaluate themselves, such reforms might come through an initiative process. Moreover, incumbent candidates have often benefitted from the evaluations given them by newspapers, civic clubs, and other ostensibly nonpartisan organizations. It would be something else, however, if those ratings appeared in official candidate guides mailed to every registered voter.

A scholarly treatment of the Melbourne People's Panel has not yet appeared, but much can be read about its design and results. (Currency traders reading this book might note that five billion Australian dollars would convert, at the time of the panel's report, to just under four billion US dollars.) One simple overview by Melbourne University's Nicholas Reece appears in *The Sydney Morning Herald*, "Experiment Pays Off: Melbourne People's Panel Produces Quality Policy." Reece recognizes that the People's Panel fits into the wider constellation of deliberative practices, such as Oregon's CIR. He argues that the "Melbourne City Council is to be congratulated for opening the door to major democratic innovation in Australia. We, the people, must now push it open."

ACKNOWLEDGMENTS

We owe our biggest debt of gratitude, and our most sincere apologies, to those whose stories we tell in this book. Transforming real people into nonfiction characters presents hazards. We cannot illustrate the full complexity of these individuals, but we hope our depictions are honest and reflect the respect we have for each of them.

Marion Sharp and Ann Bakkensen have been particularly generous in allowing us to tell the stories of their political transformations. In an age where political discussion feels perilous, these two women have shared their experiences with us. We hope their stories inspire you as much as they inspire us.

Ned Crosby and Pat Benn have been equally magnanimous in their support of the CIR and their feedback on every aspect of this research project. Both of them asked the big questions while worrying over the smallest details. At different times, they have influenced our research strategies, challenged our interpretations, and given us the encouragement to complete our work. This book would not exist without its central subject, and the CIR might never have come into existence were it not for the efforts of Ned and Pat.

Finally, we cannot overstate Tyrone Reitman's contribution. He granted us entry into both his professional and personal life, which was necessary to understand his role in this story. We are thankful for the hours he spent on the phone and his indulgence of any question we asked. As directors of Healthy Democracy, he and Elliot Shuford found a way to do what more experienced civic reformers couldn't: they institutionalized a deliberative process into their state's electoral system. Although Ty and Elliot might have had second thoughts about the level of access they granted us, they did the CIR a service by letting us see every detail of their organization and their management of the process. Even "closed" sessions, with CIR staff or citizen panelists, remained open to our research team. The precision of our evaluation and the breadth of our analysis owe much to their cooperation. Even when we gave Ty and Elliot headaches, they were stead-fast in their support for our research. (Did we leave out of the book the time we drew the ire of a ranking member of the Oregon legislature? Well, we'll leave that for a conversation over drinks someday.) We hope other nongovernmental organizations—and government agencies—recognize the value of the feedback and perspective Ty and Elliot received by welcoming curious researchers into their world.

Many others at Healthy Democracy and its partner organizations also made our research possible. Claire Adamsick, J. P. Bombardier, Tony Iaccarino, and Lucy Palmersheim Greenfield deserve special recognition for politely respond-ing to our requests even when they had more pressing business. The CIR panel moderators also helped our credibility with citizen participants, even though we spent significant time at the end of each CIR session telling the moderators everything the participants thought they were doing wrong. Special apprecia-tion goes to Larry Pennings, Molly Keating, and Robin Beam for their insights along the way. We also appreciate that Robin Teater, Jessie Conover, and Linn Davis kept the CIR running smoothly even after both Ty and Elliot had left Healthy Democracy. They—and their successors—can look forward to research requests for many years to come.

As the CIR moved outside of Oregon, the number of people who had to approve our access similarly grew. Each organization and individual has con-tinued the generous spirit of Healthy Democracy, including Erica McFadden, Andrea Whitsett, Joseph Garcia, and David Daughtery at the Morrison Institute for Public Policy at Arizona State University; Brenda Morrison (no rela-tion) and Maureen Wolsborn at Engaged Public; Bill Fulton at Civic Canopy; Representative Jonathan Hecht of Massachusetts and his legislative aide Sam Feigenbaum; and Peter Levine's team at the Tisch College of Civic Life at Tufts University. A full list would be even longer, and we apologize to any whose names we omitted here.

Many other people contributed smaller stories that appear in this book. Most of all, the CIR panelists were ideal research participants. At the end of eight-hour days, these citizens were willing to fill out surveys, without fail. From 2010 to 2016, we put over three thousand pages of survey questions in front of the CIR panelists, and fewer than twenty came back blank or spoiled. The follow-up response rates for surveys sent out months or years after the CIR remained strong, but the near-perfect completion of the daily CIR surveys was beyond our wildest hopes. These citizens permitted us to record countless hours of their conversations and deliberations and were endlessly patient when members of the research team pulled up a chair to hover even more closely over their shoul-ders. Though many of the pro and con advocates who testified were not as open, we can still appreciate their willingness to participate in the CIR itself. Justin

Martin was the exception, in that he volunteered candid recollections to provide insight we otherwise would have missed.

The number of individuals who helped us collect and analyze data but who are not included as coauthors on this book is nearly a scandal. Our CIR Research Project site lists our principal collaborators, many of whom have published articles separately or in partnership with us. Two individuals stand out for their contributions. From attending CIRs to offering their methodological expertise, each has played a critical role in the development of our larger research program. David Brinker's meticulous data management has been a tremendous help. In addition to providing original insights to our analysis, he developed ingenious methods for streamlining our data collection and integrating data. He is truly an enemy of entropy.

Robert Richards's conscientiousness and thoughtful analysis also has no parallel. We discuss in this book his insight into the content of the CIR Citizens' Statements, as well as how voters make sense of these documents. Robert's thoroughness in copyediting and critiquing our work cannot be overstated. He has likely saved us from any number of embarrassments, be they methodological or grammatical.

Now, on to our woefully incomplete listing of other collaborators. Individuals who have contributed significantly to research design, data collection, or analysis include Justin Reedy, Kathy Cramer, Mark Henkels, and Michael L. Barthel. Each has been a coauthor on the central studies discussed in this book, and their intellectual contributions have been considerable. As the CIR expanded, we had to expand our research team to observe and evaluate each individual CIR. Chris Anderson, Laura W. Black, Stephaie Bor, Kacey Bull, Stephanie Burkhalter, Traci Feller, Genevieve Fuji Johnson, Soo-Hye Han, A. Lee Hannah, Jessica Kropczynski, Ekaterina Lukianova, Cheryl Maiorca, Michael E. Morrell, John Rountree, and Leah Sprain each observed at least one CIR. This required them to sacrifice their time and intellectual energy in exchange for mediocre hotel accommodations and per diems that may or may not have covered their actual expenses. Without this team we would not have been able to collect the data we rely on in this book. We hope that access to our datasets provides some modicum of recompense for their work. Hopefully, they don't yet realize we grant that same access to anyone who asks.

The panel management staff at Qualtrics, led by Dustin Simmons, aided in the implementation of multiple online surveys over the past several years and has helped us work through our most tedious survey design decisions. Matt Barreto and his staff at the University of Washington Survey Research Center obtained our 2010 phone data, while Polimetrix (now YouGov) managed our online surveys. In 2012, Brian Sonak and Eric Plutzer assisted with our online survey implementation, while Stuart Elway (Elway Polling Inc.) conducted the phone survey. Elizabeth Rosenzweig and Lena Dmitrieva at the User Experience Center at Bentley University conducted the 2014 study that asked voters to think out loud about their experience with the Citizens' Statement. Alice Blackwell at MDC Research and Ari Wubbold at DHM Research helped us conduct the 2014 mail and phone surveys, respectively, while DHM's John Horvick implemented our 2016 Oregon phone survey. Ernest Paicopolos and Jennifer Watters from the Opinion Dynamics Corporation conducted the focus groups of Massachusetts voters in 2016. Jim Golightly and Paul M. Garten supervised transcription of all of the reviews conducted between 2010 and 2014, a task we would not wish upon our worst enemies.

Finally, graduate and undergraduate research assistants are the unsung heroes of large research teams. In addition to listening patiently to their rambling advisors get lost in their own heads, these intrepid assistants offered all manner of support, such as cold calling CIR participants, building surveys using tricky software, managing massive datasets, and editing an ungodly number of CIR recordings. Kalie McMonagle, Krystina O'Neal, and Cramer McGinty served as graduate research assistants, while Jed Chalupa, Dayna Jones, Nathan Larkin, Katie Lee, Brendan Lounsbury, Jacqueline Mount, Victoria Pontrantolfi, Vera Potapenko, Rory Raabe, and Caroline Schmitz have acted as (generally unpaid) undergraduate research assistants.

Many of those already listed—along with Lauren Archer, Jennifer N. Ervin, Mark Hlavacik, Jeremy David Johnson, Mark Major, Lilach Nir, Amanda Parks, Jane M. Prescott-Smith, and Robyn Stryker—attended a multiday workshop on CIR research in 2013. They provided their thoughts on past and future research plans and feedback on our ongoing analysis, which helped us refine our largest successful grant proposal. Along the way, other colleagues have offered their expertise on methodological questions, interpretation, or grant development, including many of those named already, plus Chris Beem, Joe Bonito, Paul Becker, Lyn Carson, John Crowley, Jim Dillard, James Fishkin, Hollie Russon Gilman, Janette Hartz-Karp, Sean Ingham, Maija Karjalainen, Rachel Garshick Kleit, Jane Mansbridge, Carmen Sirianni, Graham Smith, Mark Smith, and Chris Zorn. Lance Bennett, Leah Ceccarelli, Christine DiStefano, and Walter Parker all joined John on Katie's dissertation committee, and they provided what Katie considers an exceptional (maddening) level of advice and support. Conference audiences and attendees have also provided feedback on drafts of our ideas. We benefitted from comments on earlier versions of this research presented at the state legislature in Oregon, Massachusetts, and Washington, at the Ash Center for Democratic Governance and Innovation, Arizona State University, University of Arizona, University of Alberta, University of Oklahoma, University of Washington, Pennsylvania State University, University of Illinois-Chicago, University of Southern California, University of Utah, Institute of

Rural Management-Anand (India), King County Bar Association, and conferences convened by the National Communication Association, International Communication Association, National Coalition on Dialogue and Deliberation, and National Institute for Civil Discourse.

A whole host of individuals have provided editorial feedback, including Pennsylvania State University graduate students Michael Broghammer and John Rountree, whose dissertation we reference. Most notably, Stuart Horowitz helped us think through the narrative arc of this book and shepherded us through the task of writing for a nonacademic audience. Mark Gottlieb at Trident Media Group served as our agent and helped us find our publisher, with thanks to the always abiding David McBride at Oxford University Press. Some of the research presented here has also benefitted from blind peer review and editorial guidance on work previously published in *Deliberation: Values, Process, Institutions* (A. Przybylska, S. Coleman, and Y. Sintomer, editors), *American Politics Research, Communication and the Public, Field Action Science Reports, The Good Society, International Journal of Communication, Journal of Applied Communication Research, Journal of Politics, Policy and Politics Journal, Participations* (France), *Political Studies, Politics & Society,* and *Public Administration.* We also got feedback from journals that chose not to publish our work, but we won't mention those by name.

We'd like to acknowledge the many organizations that provided funding for this research over the past several years. Though any opinions, findings, conclusions, or recommendations expressed in this material are those of the authors and do not necessarily reflect the views of the funders, their support has been incalculable. (Actually, you probably could put a number on it, at least in dollars.) Funding from these entities allowed us to produce the research provided herein, while simultaneously providing funding for several undergraduate and graduate students at the University of Washington, Pennsylvania State University, and Colorado State University. This holds special significance for Katie, who began her work on the CIR as a beneficiary of such grant-based graduate assistance.

Most of all, the National Science Foundation served as one of the principal funders for this research. The scale and depth of the findings discussed here would not be possible without this federal funding, and we hope that our work speaks to the need to continue to fund and study political innovations and the social sciences more generally. The Directorate for Social, Behavioral and Economic Sciences' Political Science Program (Award #0961774) recognized the importance and timeliness of evaluating the implementation of the initial Oregon CIRs in 2010 and the Decision, Risk and Management Sciences Program (Awards #1357276 and 1357444) allowed us to continue our research as the CIR expanded to other states and locations in 2014 and 2016. The Democracy Fund supplemented our NSF funding in 2014 and 2016 and allowed for comparisons across states and over time. Additionally, we partnered with the Kettering Foundation on a learning agreement that supported our 2012 research. Kettering program officers Alice Diebel and John Dedrick contributed to the design of that study.

University support has also been essential. Our earliest funding was provided by the University of Washington Royalty Research Fund and the Department of Communication, and our current universities have continued to provide support. Both the Pennsylvania State University's Department of Communication Arts and Sciences and Colorado State University's Department of Communication Studies have provided supplemental funding, especially for undergraduate and graduate research assistants. The McCourtney Institute for Democracy and the Social Science Research Institute at the Pennsylvania State University made possible a summer workshop on the CIR. Colorado State University's Center for Public Deliberation, helmed by Martin Carcasson, continues to provide all manner of support, from undergraduate and graduate research assistance to funding for recording equipment.

We would be remiss if we did not thank faculty—and especially staff—at each of our home institutions over the life of this project. We surely became nuisances to those responsible for administering our grants. How many times do we need to be reminded about competitive bidding, the gathering of receipts, or optimal data archiving methods? Special thanks to Winnie Cao and Nika Pelc at the University of Washington, Carol Mellot, Sandi Rockwell, Sonia Stover, and Rocco Zinoble at the Pennsylvania State University, and Sue Pendell, Greg Dickinson, Gloria Blumanhourst, Dawn McConkey, and Catherine Kane at Colorado State University.

Lastly, we would like to thank our families. Both of Katie's children, Colette and Gibson, have had to share their babyhood with this book. Thankfully, they are unlikely to remember that. Toby the poodle enjoyed sleeping to the clacking of John's keyboard, but months of writing also necessitated regular walks, which were even better. Cindy Simmons and Aaron Knobloch have solidified their designations as our betters and ensured our survival throughout this project. We appreciate both their emotional and culinary support. Perhaps the best way to show our appreciation would be to stop writing. Now.

INDEX

For the benefit of digital users, indexed terms that span two pages (e.g., 52–53) may, on occasion, appear on only one of those pages.

Tables, figures, and photos are indicated by *t, f,* and *p* following the page number